HOW ACCOMPLISHED PEOPLE RETIRE SUCCESSFULLY

BEYOND WORK

BILL ROITER

WILEY

John Wiley & Sons Canada, Ltd.

Library and Archives Canada Cataloguing in Publication Data

Roiter, Bill

    Beyond work : how accomplished people retire successfully/Bill Roiter.

Includes index.

ISBN 978-0-470-84094-8

    1. Retirement—Planning.   2. Retirement income—Planning.

3. Finance, Personal. I.   Title.

HQ1062.R64 2008   332.024'014   C2008-901367-0

Production Credits
Cover design: Jason Vandenberg
Interior text design: Jason Vandenberg
Typesetting: Thomson Digital
Cover photography: Igor Terekhov/iStockphoto, Stacey Newman/iStockphoto, Willie B.Thomas/iStockphoto, Photodisc
Author photo: Patrick O'Connor Photography, Inc.
Printer: Tri-Graphic Printing

John Wiley & Sons Canada, Ltd.
6045 Freemont Blvd.
Mississauga, Ontario
L5R 4J3

This book is printed with biodegradable vegetable-based inks on 60lb. white paper, 100% post-consumer waste.

Printed in Canada

1 2 3 4 5 TRI 12 11 10 09 08

To Pearl Shectman Roiter and Ann Robinson Hardy,
who taught me how to enjoy the life I have

CONTENTS

PREFACE

I entered the workforce as a jerk, a soda jerk to be more specific. That was 45 years ago and I was 13 years old. Working three hours every Saturday morning at a local pharmacy for one dollar an hour changed my life. I was still a kid, but I was no longer a child. I had responsibilities, I met new friends, I was a member of the community and some girls thought it was cool. Most importantly, I could make my own decisions. After work I was paid my three dollars (cash, no taxes) and then I strode down the street to spend it all on racing slot cars. After two weeks of this extravagant freedom, my mom stepped in and took a 50 percent savings tax before I could spend it all. I was now truly learning what it was like to be an adult.

Our entry into adulthood is usually initiated by our entry into the adult world of work. We are less the child of our parents and more the person with a job. Our individual experiences may foster feelings of responsibility and effectiveness or discomfort and concern. Whatever the result, it is usually work that propels us into our adult lives.

Work, whether focused on a job or raising a family, also defines a good part of our adult lives by setting schedules and providing the basics of safety and shelter. It also impacts our relationships with family and friends, and our status in our world. If, like me, you are older than 55, work has probably been a major component of your life. You can then understand why moving beyond work, as in retiring, is a big deal. It's worth taking some time to learn about this major transition in life and to learn from some people who are doing it and from experts who are studying it. This book will add to your knowledge about life beyond work, and, as we know, knowledge is power.

There is a part of the book that looks at the benefit of realistic thinking and the role of healthy skepticism. The idea is not to believe everything you read, while also questioning both your new ideas *and* your long-held beliefs. As an example, I would suggest that you pass a skeptical thought my way: "Who is this author and why should I consider his ideas?"

Good question; thank you for asking. I did enter the world of work as a jerk but quickly grew past that to flunk out of college in my freshman year. I had a shaky entry into adulthood. This early crisis actually served me well, and after a year working as an architect's assistant, I went back to college and did very well. I graduated and was quickly hired as a sixth-grade teacher. Let me say that this was not a good fit for me, although it helped me learn that I was interested in psychology. I returned to college and earned my doctorate in educational psychology and I have been a psychologist ever since.

I worked as a clinical psychologist for a time and then in 1980 began working as a business psychologist. As time progressed I found myself working with business people similar to me in age, helping them reach for and fulfill their goals. This group and I aged together, grew families and increased our experience and knowledge. I have happily spent the past 30 years understanding the realities of work for people of my age and sharing my perspective with my clients. Since 1996 I have worked as an executive coach with clients who are transitioning to a new role and want to be thoughtful about this transition. I had the enjoyable opportunity to co-author a book, *Corporate MVPs* (Wiley, 2004), with Margaret Butteriss. Margaret and I looked at what makes the most valuable people in business so valuable. We looked across businesses, for-profit and not-for-profit, large multi-national businesses and small local ones. We found that no matter the size of the business, nor their roles within it, MVPs shared common traits that made them exceptional people with whom to work.

At about that time I began receiving requests from business people I had known and worked with for years for advice on how to think about and plan their retirement. I must say that this came as a shock, as my coaching and consulting business has relied on the ongoing relationships with people who had grown into the business's leaders and decision-makers. The people taking their place were 45 to 50 years old and had their own favored group of consultants with whom they had worked for 10 years or more. My business model was changing, and I had to either change with it or be left behind.

And then my wife retired from her corporate job and the siren song of slowing down and possibly retiring myself filled my ears and my thoughts. "But I am not ready to retire," "Can we afford it?" and "What would I do with my time?" became concerns.

In the fall of 2006 I was asked by two colleagues, Scott Randall and Frank Aubuchon, to work with them on a program they had devised for senior tenured faculty who were considering retirement. It would be sponsored by the faculty's college or institution, 13 in all from the Boston area. Because this program was conducted outside of their institution, and it included about 10 other professors with similar thoughts, the participants were free to explore, question and dream about retirement without making any commitment to actually retire. As you may know, tenured professors do not have to retire and many do not. Their institutions find that this makes it difficult to build staffing plans and to offer tenure to younger professors.

The groups of professors were curious, energized and very creative. While our purpose was to stimulate their thinking about retirement, their institutions hoped that they would make actual plans to retire—which they did. Once they began thinking about it in real terms and with good information, their concerns diminished and their excitement grew. As an added benefit for me, I learned a great deal from these accomplished people about their thoughts on retirement and what helped them and what got in their way. One evening I was listening to the group's discussion about an issue, and I realized that this was the next book I wanted to write. How do accomplished people retire? The answer to this question is the book that follows.

I have been working on this book project since 2006, and I have had great help along the way. My greatest collaborator and love continues to be my wife Jane. There are not enough words to describe what she means to me except to say "I love you." My son Brian is a great discussant who is always presenting me with new ideas to consider, which is a proven way to stay young. Brian, whom I love and respect, is a Buddhist monk living in India. His Buddhist name is Tenzin Gache.

I also want to thank my editor, Karen Milner, and her team at John Wiley & Sons Canada, for her sponsorship of this book project and their guidance throughout. They all helped improve this book and helped me make it relevant to readers in both the United States and Canada. Michael Erkelenz of Nine Design and Brenda Missen of MIA Communications provided great editorial support as I wrote each chapter, frequently confirming my sanity. It was comforting to talk with thoughtful people who understood. Tom Webber, Allyn St. Lifer, Steve and Martha Roiter, Bob Hardy, Paul and Ann Brown, Denise Barreira, Rick Thau and David Potel were very helpful as well.

Dr. Paul Barreira of Harvard University listened to my early, unformed ideas and was very helpful in confirming some ideas, challenging others and creating new ones. He also identified many of the people I eventually interviewed and experts that I read. Bill Hodgetts of Fidelity Investments was instrumental in introducing me to many of the financial people who are described in the book. Dr. Geoffrey Ginsburg of Duke University's Institute for Genome Sciences & Policy, Center for Genomic Medicine, guided me through many of the medical concepts you will find in the book. All three men were more helpful than they might know.

I interviewed many people for this book whom you will learn about as you read. They told me what to write. There were others whose names I had been given but whom I did not have the opportunity to contact and interview. I consider this my loss, as I enjoyed every interview and know that every person I have talked with has contributed to what you will read. Finally, there were additional people with whom I spoke, formally or informally, who sparked ideas—people such as Jimmy the cab driver and Bill the executive who is about to retire and move out of my building. These chance encounters added life to the book. It is quite possible that I have not acknowledged all the people who contributed, but please know that you added to this book as well.

Whatever you gain from this book is due to those who have assisted me with this project. I am responsible for the rest.

Bill Roiter
January 30, 2008

PART

1

LIFE BEYOND WORK

CHAPTER ONE

AS ACCOMPLISHED PEOPLE RETIRE

"The future ain't what it used to be."
—Yogi Berra

RETIREMENT IS A BIG DEAL

Most baby boomers will do retirement well; a few of us may struggle. Your future is in your hands in a way that you may not have had to face before. Retirement is the ultimate "it's up to you" challenge. It's on par with becoming an adult, beginning a career, getting married, and becoming a parent. So when you see the "happy" retirement books with their cute names and travel brochure language, be wary. It is not that easy and you are not being a wimp for worrying. I urge you to take yourself seriously, consider your concerns, and look for ways to ease them as you move into this new era of life.

For many of us, retirement seems like a withdrawal from life, a putting aside of ambition and curiosity. In fact, this stage of life is the diminishment of your career and the ascendancy of your self. As modern-day philosopher Bob Newhart once exclaimed, "All I can say about life is, oh God, enjoy it!"

To get you started thinking about what retirement will mean for you, consider the two scenarios below and see which reflects your view of what your retirement is—or will be.

Tim Moves Beyond Work

Looking back, it all seemed so easy, so right. At the time, however, it wasn't easy at all, far from it. Tim had a flourishing career as a director of operations for a business unit of a dynamic organization. His wife worked part-time in a small business, and their two children had grown up to be achievers in their own right. Life seemed perfect just as it was. Tim had acknowledged for more than ten years that retirement some day was a reality. Finally, one July a few years ago, he had become eligible for retirement. He recognized the irony of being at the top of his game while also being in a position to walk away from it. Could he really retire? Friends didn't think so: "You're too driven; you can't not work."

When the day finally came, Tim took on retirement as he had every other major decision in his life—head on. He and his wife had worked with a financial planner and they felt that they had a secure future. His wife believed that he could be happy in retirement and wanted him to make the change: "You've worked for more than 35 years; you've earned it." More importantly, Tim thought he had earned it too. He knew he could move beyond work and into the next phase of life. He responded to the challenge of retirement with thought, research, learning, talking with others, and self-exploration. Now three years later, retirement fits Tim just fine, and those who doubted he would enjoy retirement are envious of his post-work success. Tim and his wife are busy planning for the next three years beyond work.

Now let's look at how Margaret manages in a scenario that has the same basic elements as Tom's.

Margaret's Unhappy Move Beyond Work

Looking back, it all seemed so regrettable. That July when Margaret became eligible for retirement, she was more surprised than happy. She had put everything she had into her job as the director of operations for a business unit of a dynamic organization. Retirement was not part of her plan—she had too much work to do. Of course, she had known that she would reach the magic number made up of years at work plus her age to make retirement an option. There was only one problem: work was her life. Her husband always complained that her job meant more to her than her family did, and she knew he was right. But then a new boss arrived and began to make work a misery for her.

When she was offered an enhanced retirement package, she took it. While Margaret wasn't exactly forced out, her boss certainly made no effort to dissuade her. The move felt more like quitting than retiring.

Margaret hadn't really planned for retirement at all. She just left, knowing that her finances were probably in good shape. After the first week at home, she began calling friends at work to find out what was happening. It wasn't until a friend told her others were complaining about her frequent calls that she realized she was no longer part of the team. She never called again. Three years into retirement, Margaret was not doing well.

WILL MY RETIREMENT WORK?

There is a little of Tim and Margaret in most of us. Your own story will likely have some parallels with both of the stories above. Why does one person thrive beyond work while the other shrivels? Each of us sees and experiences the world in our own way. What we bring to retirement is as important as what retirement brings to us. Einstein's theory of relativity is applicable here. It demonstrates that everything, even time itself, is based on our perceptions. Einstein described his theory this way: "Put your hand on a hot stove for a minute, and it seems like an hour. Sit with a pretty girl for an hour, and it seems like a minute. That's relativity." Our experience of life beyond work is not fixed; it relates to how we see our world.

Much of this book will seek to answer these two questions:

- Why do some people thrive in retirement while others shrivel?
- What can you do to ensure you will thrive in retirement?

You are not the first baby boomer to retire and you surely will not be the last. You can learn a lot about retirement from those who have done it well and from the scientists, psychologists, physicians, financial experts, philosophers and clergy who use their talents to understand what works and what does not work as we retire. These are the people I interviewed for this book, asking the questions I think you would like to have answered:

- How do I know if I am financially secure?
- Can I trust my financial advisor?

- How do I know if I have a good doctor?
- What is my role in taking care of my health?
- What does it take to make friends outside of work?
- Will I be lonely?
- Are people really as happy/sad as they appear to be?
- Can I do this?
- I am not really sure what I want as I move beyond work. How can I find out?
- Is this really the beginning of the end?

These are some of the questions that I explored during my research with the experts. The results of this research are in this book. The focus is on what you want to know and what else you should know as you contemplate moving beyond work and living life as a new adult. Consider *Beyond Work* your guide into your new life.

WHAT IS IN THE BOOK

Beyond Work looks at how our shared cultural experiences from the mid-1940s to now have affected who we are today and who we will likely be tomorrow. This examination will help us to understand how we are transitioning from our career focus, including raising a family, to our life beyond work, our new adulthood. This next stage in life broadens our focus from career and family to four domains that provide structure and meaning during our new adulthood. These four domains are our financial, physical, social, and personal lives. When they are in balance, these life domains create a fulfilling life. When they are out of balance, we experience varying degrees of dissatisfaction and unhappiness. A successful retirement depends on your ability to balance these four domains. Later in the book I describe them in detail, along with ways to balance each domain.

The book is made up of two parts, beginning with what it means to be part of a generation experiencing retirement and still called "baby boomers." We are babies no more; we are a generation with shared experiences and individual thought. How do your views on being part of this big baby boom generation affect your specific ideas on retirement? Also, is there a word that better describes moving beyond work than the word *retire*? I believe there is.

The second part explores what it means to live life on your terms. What are your terms and what impact do they have on your life? For many pre-retirees and retirees the most obvious retirement challenge is securing their finances. How can you live life on your terms if you cannot support yourself? Your finances are one of the four challenges that you face as you build a successful retirement. The other three challenges are your physical, social, and personal well-being. I have separated out your financial well-being as the first challenge because without it your focus in retirement is usually on the money. It is hard to find time to consider your physical, social, and personal well-being when your decisions are always based on your financial state. In fact, financial security is often the first criterion people use to consider themselves to be accomplished. As you will see in the following pages, the perception of financial security is more important than the actual dollar amount when people think about their finances. When you do not feel that you have enough money you are likely to make most of your decisions based on money. When you do feel secure in your finances you can consider decisions based on what enhances your overall well-being. Knowing and managing all four life domains is key to a successful retirement.

WHAT IT MEANS TO BE ACCOMPLISHED

I want to be clear on what I consider an accomplished person. Money is important but it does not equal accomplishment. It is difficult to feel accomplished when you believe that you do not have enough money to live life as you want. On the other hand, financial security is not sufficient to feel accomplished.

I met a very accomplished person the other day. His name is Jimmy. Forty-five years ago, Jimmy started out his career as a baker. It did not last long. He told me, "The hours were killing me." He quit and began driving a cab while he figured out what to do next. He found that he liked the flexible hours and the people he met. He kept driving a cab, for the next forty years. I met Jimmy when I hopped into his cab. Jimmy is a very engaging guy. As it turns out, Jimmy is also a very accomplished guy. Soon after becoming a cabbie, Jimmy and his wife saved enough money for him to buy his own cab and taxi license. He soon owned 10 cabs and was running a business in addition to continuing driving.

About two years ago, Jimmy's wife died of cancer. I could hear the pain in his voice as he talked about her. Jimmy sold nine of his cabs, providing him with what he considered to be enough money to retire. As he drove me to my destination I asked him, "If you have retired, why am I riding in your cab, Jimmy?"

"I wake up at four in the morning anyway; what am I going to do, stare at the ceiling? I might as well drive. It gets me out of the house, I see friends, and I meet interesting people. By noon I get lunch and put the cab away."

I asked him if he is happy in retirement. He told me, "Yeah, I like the life. The only wish I have is that my wife was here with me." Jimmy is an accomplished person.

Throughout this book, I will introduce you to many accomplished people. I do not have a formula for deciding who is accomplished and who is not. What I do know is that many people feel they have been successful in their lives and they feel accomplished. All have had successes and failures. None has been free of struggle and uncertainty, and they expect more to come, but they have come to a point in their lives where they feel mostly pleased with how they have lived and will live. I have found that about a third of us consider ourselves to be accomplished, while another third consider ourselves to have done well enough to see that we have accomplished a good deal. The remaining third of us feel that accomplishment has evaded us. But it's not too late; now we have the opportunity to make peace with life and accomplish a successful retirement.

The book also looks at how you use your expanded knowledge and understanding of retirement to live the good life. Rollo May (1909–1994), a respected American psychologist and the author of *Love and Will*, believed that "the good life comes from what we care about." That's a good starting point for retirement: let's find out what you care about.

YOUR RETIREMENT IS YOUR CHOICE

Tim and Margaret are a composite of many people I have worked with over the years. If you read both stories closely, you can pick up some clues as to why some people are successful and others unsuccessful as they move beyond their work life. Tim loved challenge and success and knew that retirement was coming, and, most important, he approached the challenge head-on. Margaret viewed work as her life and she was surprised when she was eligible and encouraged to retire. She left work feeling as if she had quit and kept herself immersed in her work world until a former colleague and friend told her to stop. She sank into retirement while trying to hold on to the fraying lifeline of work. She didn't choose retirement, and three years into life beyond work she was still unhappy.

The good news is this: your retirement can be like Tim's, not Margaret's. Having a successful retirement is *your choice*. Whether you are considering retirement or are already retired, you have choices to make. Retirement is not a "thing" that is either good or bad. It is an on-going set of choices and decisions that determine how today will be and how the future can be. These are the choices that guide our lives when we are focused on building our career or raising a family and they are the choices that guide your life beyond work.

A Simpler Life?

Most of us consider retirement to be a simpler life than the one we lived during our hectic career and family years. Less hectic, yes; simpler, no. We may have felt burdened by the demands of work and family, but we also relied on them to structure and limit our life decisions. Retirement frees us from these structures and limits and then barrages us with competing choices and important decisions. How many times have you been roused by the alarm to get to work on time or get the kids off to school and wished that you could just shut it off and get up whenever you pleased? Retirement grants you this luxurious choice, day after day after day. Then you get up and what do you do? It is your choice. When to get up in the morning—or even whether to—is one decision among many that both frees and burdens us. Successful retirees stay active by actively making and renewing decisions about how to live their life. Ernest Hemingway, a very active guy, admonished us to "never confuse movement and action." You can move by falling off a log as you doze, but action requires a choice to sit on the log in the first place. Here is an example of someone who chose to help a friend's child and in the process helped herself to find a happy retirement.

A very accomplished person, Bobbi White Smith had a successful career in consulting and was highly respected and valued by her colleagues and friends. After 20 years, she left the business she had worked for when it was bought by a larger company. She was able to sell her stock in the company, which provided her with enough financial security to support her future. Bobbi's husband had already retired and they wanted to spend more time together.

Bobbi had many choices available to her; each could take her in a different direction. She turned down offers from people in her industry to take on interesting challenges, because she felt that this part of her life was complete. She did not know what she would do, but she believed that something interesting would surface. She had tried out some ideas that in the end just did not work for her, but she felt that they had been good choices, as they helped her to know what she did not want to pursue. Over coffee one day, she was talking to a friend about the friend's daughter, a fashion designer. The young designer had no idea how to run a business and Bobbi offered to help her make the business viable. Bobbi loves clothes and enjoys fashion, but aside from being a fashion fan, she had no fashion industry experience. However, she did know what it takes to run a business. She also felt good about helping a friend's daughter.

Bobbi became more familiar with the workings of the fashion industry and she began to meet people in the industry. One day she received a call from a designer who sold her designs through trunk shows. These are periodic private sales open to invited guests and often take place in a hotel meeting room. The designer asked to meet Bobbi to talk about running trunk shows in her area. It felt right, and Bobbi chose to try out this new venture. Four years later Bobbi is running three to four trunk shows a year and is truly enjoying herself. She now considers this her "retirement career." This all began when Bobbi chose to offer to help out a friend's child.

Bobbi, a naturally active person, also took up golf and tennis while continuing to run the household and working on volunteer projects with her husband. She never had time for any of this when she was pursuing her career.[1]

The most important choice in early retirement is to decide whether you will passively allow your past and your perceived future to dictate how

1 Personal interview, May 29, 2007.

your life will be or you will actively use your past experience and knowledge along with your hopes for the future to live your life as you want. I can guarantee that the choices you do not make will be made with or without your help. You just might not be very happy with the results.

Choose Wisely

You might think that the more choices people have, the happier they are likely to be. You would be wrong. We all want as many choices as possible, but being presented with too many choices often seems burdensome and worrisome. If you were a child in the 1950s you may recall the plate spinner on *The Ed Sullivan Show*. He would place a spinning plate on more and more vertical sticks embedded into a long table, running back periodically to re-spin the faltering plates. I watched this with great delight as a kid, not knowing that it would become a popular metaphor for adulthood. Choices are like the plates: the more plates you spin, the more work it takes to keep them spinning.

The key point is to narrow your choices and choose wisely:

A 60-year-old man had been married for 40 years to his wife, who was also 60. His entire adulthood has been marked by his chronic sense that he did not have enough. By all outside measures, he was accomplished and happy, but this dissatisfied corner of himself persisted.

One day while out walking through the woods, he tripped over a stone and hit his head on a fallen tree limb. Coming to a few minutes later, he found an imposing bright-green genie standing over him: "I am the genie of the log you bumped and you disturbed me. I came out to see what caused the noise just as you were awakening and you saw me. You cannot tell anyone that you saw me, so I will buy your silence by granting you one wish and one wish only. Quick, what is your wish?"

As the man groggily sat up, he said, "I love my wife but I have always wanted to be married to a woman 30 years younger than I am."

The genie raised his mighty green hand and said, "Your wish is granted, you are now 90 years old." Then he disappeared.

The magic and the curse of retirement is that it is the same as your earlier life; it is all up to you. You can pursue whatever you wish. Just be careful what you wish for.

DELUSIONS OF AGE

Philip Levendusky is associate professor of psychology at the Harvard Medical School and vice-president of McLean Hospital. Phil, whom I have known for many years, and talked with me about what he has observed among people who are moving beyond work.

I have seen very competent and accomplished people let go of their rational minds and be taken over by the delusions they create as they enter their 60s and 70s. These delusions are their false or mistaken beliefs about aging that cause them to behave in ways that are consistent with these false beliefs.

There is the delusion of poverty . . . a terror that they will run out of money because they may live too long.

It is a real dilemma; we obviously want to live as long as we can. But what if we do live too long and don't have deep enough pockets to support our growing needs? . . . Some of us may fantasize about what it will be like at 92 and broke, but the fear is that we will not have choices at that age if we do not have the money. Money is often equated with choices, and choices allow us to make decisions and making decisions provides a sense of control.

Also, many of us begin to feel we are reducing our choices as we continue to age. This creates a false belief that we will continually lose control as we age. So add to the delusion of poverty the delusion of loss of control.

What this illustrates is the circle of life. When we're born we're totally dependent, and if we get into our 80s or 90s, we're again very dependent. It feels like a shift back to infancy. The difference is that you can't control your birth dependency, but as an aging adult there's at least some opportunity to control some of the variables.

Many of my accomplished clients who are facing retirement come to me to learn how to battle the inevitable losses that will occur when they retire or feel now that they are retired. We end up talking about their fears of aging and the realties of what aging means today.

I ask them "What are you going to do for your quality of life?" I put the responsibility for their future right where it should be—on them. For folks who have lifelong hobbies or have been looking forward to rambling in the RV, hitting every state, having dinner in every state capital, they've got a fantasy that will work. But even these ideas will run out after a while. What will they do to fill their life in a way that makes them feel like they are not just getting up in the morning to have moss grow under their feet?

We spend so much of our adult years completing the next task, and now that task becomes creating a good quality of life. Many of us are unprepared and inexperienced to manage the details of our lives. It can feel like finding yourself in a new world where you do not speak the language and cannot read the signs. "Lost" is a pretty good description people use. "Lost" can motivate the person to orient themselves or it can expose paralyzing fears.

Delusions of youth can energize you but they may also injure or embarrass you. Approach the future with a realistic acceptance of your age and the limits of your physical abilities.

As we age, new worries and new opportunities appear. You will see later in the book how very ill people keep their sense of well-being and how perfectly healthy people are sick with worry and fear.

FIND WHAT WORKS FOR YOU

"A perpetual holiday is a good definition of hell."
—George Bernard Shaw

"Work is a necessary evil to be avoided."
—Mark Twain

You have the best odds of making good choices when you know what works for you and what does not. Consider the contrasting views of leisure and work expressed by the two intelligent and successful writers quoted above. How can they view work and leisure so differently? Neither is right or wrong. Similarly, there is no right or wrong approach to your retirement; it can be successful or unsuccessful. In retirement, Shaw would seek work and Twain would shun it. They each knew themselves well enough to know what work meant to them, so they could choose wisely. How well do you know yourself? As you continue through this book, you will learn about a framework for understanding choices and making each decision a wise one. The goal of this book is to clear the fog so that you do not fly blindly into your future but make wise, clear choices based on what's best for you. This is what accomplished people have done throughout their lives and continue to do today.

THE BOOMER GENERATION

You are a baby boomer if you were born between 1946 and 1964 in the United Kingdom, the United States, Canada, or Australia. Throughout World War II these allied countries worked together to defeat the axis countries led by Germany and Japan. No small feat. At war's end, exuberance broke out in the allied countries in a manner that the world had not seen before. It began the idea of global experience, a world-changing concept that continues today. In the 1950s and 60s, our parents' generation looked with hope to the future, rather than to the past, with its depression, war, and ultimate victory. Those born during this time were the tangible expression of our parents' post-war exuberance.

And here we are; 40 or 50 years later still thought of as the baby boomers. We have also been called the "me" generation in honor of our varying degrees of self-centeredness. I will stick with the "boomer" moniker until we create a better name.

One of our continuing, and often grating, attributes is to think of ourselves as unique and special. I do not see us as particularly special but I do see us as unique. The circumstances of the world we grew up in are unique in the world's history. We responded to our circumstance as has every other generation preceding us. We are products of unique times defined by the interaction of the increasing pace of innovation and the evolution of Western cultural norms and institutions such as democracy.

Accelerating Innovation × Western Culture = Mature Boomers

It is worth taking some time to understand our generation's remarkable circumstances by conducting a brief survey of the pace of innovation and of our shared cultural history.

THE PACE OF INVENTION AND CHANGE

"The greatest invention of the nineteenth century was
the invention of the method of invention."
—Alfred North Whitehead (1861–1947), mathematician and philosopher

The "Modern Age," a time of rapid change that continues to accelerate, began in the early 19th century. Two great cultural shifts joined to change the world. The first was the Industrial Revolution, when inventors such as James Watt, who patented a workable steam engine in 1769, and Robert Trevithick, who in 1802 created a functional steam locomotive, created technology that would change manufacturing forever. While transportation remained difficult by our standards, it was a huge technological leap from just 25 years before. Continuing improvements in transportation had the same effect on society as the Internet is having today. New ideas spread faster than they ever had before. By 1800, the Industrial Revolution was powered by a full head of steam and it just kept accelerating.

Canned food, the commercial railway, telegraph and Morse code, photography, ocean-going steamships, sewing machines, typewriters, high-volume steel mills, dynamite, telephones, phonographs, light bulbs, skyscrapers, machine guns, automobiles, movies, and aspirin: each invention created pressure on society to change.[2]

One example of continual progress can be seen in the speed of transatlantic crossings. The time for information to cross from Europe to the Americas shrunk dramatically. Here is how long it took a ship to bring a letter across the Atlantic in different ages:

Mid-1600s: 10 weeks
Mid-1770s: 6 weeks
Mid-1800s: 2 weeks
1900:   1 week

Of course, by 1900 information was crossing the Atlantic via the 1866 transatlantic cable in minutes, not weeks. Information and ideas were no longer tied to the speed of ships.

The second great shift involved the availability of education to more people than ever before. The effect was staggering. As literacy spread, the masses gained unprecedented access to information. Newspapers fed the new appetite. Living in a small town no longer meant that you had to rely on your "elders and betters" to explain the world to you. Questions developed, answers were demanded, and dreams seemed possible. Freud got people to think about what it means to be human. Darwin made, and still makes, people rethink their history and their relatives. Marx, yes

---

2 Mark Feeney, "Science Museum Honors a Natural Selection," *Boston Globe*, February 19, 2007.

Karl Marx, taught people to question the economic models that kept rich people so rich and the masses so poor. New ideas and inventions pushed our culture to adapt or break.

Then came the time, following the worldwide depression of the 1930s, that our parents faced World War II. It was surely filled with great pain but it also spawned rapid industrial development. Inventions that could not have been imagined ten years earlier took hold and gained strength. The war and the depression that preceded it left our parents with an enormous appetite for peace, a strong belief in the power of our allied countries, and a stockpile of new technology looking for, and finding, hungry markets.

Ideas spread by transportation, radio, and television. People around the world learned of the life our parents had built and they wanted it as well. The world had dramatically shrunk in less than 20 years, while our ideas kept expanding and inventing.

YOU AND THE PACE OF INVENTION AND CHANGE: 1945 TO THE PRESENT

North Americans were also as affected by the mobility of ideas and inventions as the rest of the world was. Television not only changed how we learned, it also changed what we learned. The evening news told us and showed us as many problems as solutions. It forced our growing minds to keep asking why.

The "Leading-Edge Boomers," those born between 1946 and 1955, were of an age to fully experience the 60s. I graduated from high school in 1967 and entered college. My brother, seven years older than I, had just left the army for a business career. Our worlds could not have been more different. His life was on track and working; my world was exploding.

If you lived through the 60s and early 70s, I do not need to remind you of the high and the low points of our formative years. Whether you actively took part in this history or not, we all lived through it together.

Here is a reminder of how one issue, sexism, looked in 1965. At that time, men were in business and women were tolerated there. The 11th edition of *Emily Post's Etiquette* (published in 1965) had separate index listings for men and for women in business. The section on business etiquette sets the stage:

Every executive knows how important etiquette is, both in managing his career and in dealing with other businessmen. No man can ever tell when knowledge of it will be to his advantage, or when the lack of it may suddenly turn the scale against him. The man who remains "planted" in his chair when a lady speaks to him... who does not take off his hat when talking to a lady or take his cigar out of his mouth when addressing her, impresses others not only by his lack of good manners, but by the business incompetence that this attitude suggests.

Further along, Post addresses women in business because "very few are the businesses that do not have women secretaries, bookkeepers, receptionists, operators, clerks and typists."

One last note on Emily Post's 1965 view of the problems of women in business:

At the very top of the list of women's business shortcomings is the inability of many of them to achieve impersonality. Mood, temper, jealousy, especially induced by a "crush on" her employer or fellow worker—these are the chief flaws of the woman in business and a constant source of annoyance in every office where she works.[3]

The 17th edition of *Emily Post's Etiquette*, published in 2004, makes no differentiation between women and men in business, but it does hold forth on the value of etiquette in the workplace. Both the 1965 and the 2004 editions of *Emily Post's Etiquette* accurately reflected the social norms of their times.

Aside from revealing unconscious sexist attitudes of the time, the 1965 edition also reminds us that men once smoked in the workplace. They smoked cigars, no less!

These are only some of the experiences and ideas that we grew up with. So yes, we are unique. We are as unique as is every other generation that is sculpted by the times in which they live. However we are not particularly special since each generation is a reflection of its times.

---

3 Elizabeth Post, *Emily Post's Etiquette*, 11th revised edition (New York: Funk & Wagnalls, 1965), pp. 537–39.

BOOMERS' FUTURE RETIREMENTS—THE IMPACT OF OUR GENERATION'S EXPERIENCE

"In January 2011 the leading-edge baby boomers will begin to turn 65. They will continue to turn 65 at a rate of 10,000 per day for the next 18 years, resulting in an increase in the number of people age 65+ from 40 million to 70 million in less than 20 years. Add to this the fact that the average life expectancy of a typical 65-year-old is now 82. Rather than just conjecture how boomers planned to spend those 18 years, we decided to actually ask them."
—Lori Bitter, JWT Retirement Revolution

JWT, a global communications company, is generously sharing its 2006 "Third Age" (ages 45 to 75) study prepared for its Mature Market Group (MMG). JWT's clients depend on the company to produce accurate, up-to-date descriptions of the people who make up their target markets.

What, if anything, differentiates the retiring boomers from the generations before? According to the JWT authors, the study "reveals an interesting contradiction. The new definition of retirement now means working. Boomers view retirement as a transition, not a single watershed event signaling the end of a lifetime of work." There is a clear expectation of continuing productivity, however that is defined by each individual. In support of this finding, my colleague, Scott Randall, compares retirement to marriage: "If a wedding is an event, while a marriage is a transition, then retiring is an event and retirement is a transition." And a lot of us are already transitioning.

Will this productive retirement be a blessing for us and our country or a burden? It is one of the questions that our generation will answer as we move forward. One thing is clear: for many, retirement does not mean what it used to mean. For instance, many of us are considering what used to be called early retirement (or moving beyond work)—leaving work before the age of 65. Early retirement not only increases the rapid growth of the number of retirees but also dramatically changes the definition of retirement. This new definition is discussed in Chapter 3.

FORMATIVE YEARS: GROUPS WITHIN THE BOOMER GENERATION

JWT produced a useful summary of the generational formative experiences in the United States from 1930 to 1983. These experiences help to form a person's view of the world.

My interest lies with the "Leading-Edge Boomers," whose formative years occurred during the 60s. Looking at their core traits, we see the fault line between the Ikes' status-quo, respect-authority orientation and the Leading-Edge boomers' idealistic, demanding, and personal gratification orientation. We could say that the difference in moving *beyond work* for these two cohorts can be summed up by two questions. While the Ikes tend to ask, "How should I retire?", the Leading Edgers ask, "How do I want to retire?"

Harry Hobson, Jr., the president and CEO of a non-profit community, Plymouth Harbor on Sarasota Bay, Florida, provided an interesting perspective on the issue of generational attitudes to retirement in an interview in May 2007. Hobson suggested that the really important fault line is one that exists between the WII-ers and the Ikes. There are many WWII-ers and Ikes within his continuing-care retirement community, which in fact feels more like a luxury resort than the term "continuing care" might conjure up. Many successful business people, academics, and professionals reside at Plymouth Harbor. Considering the WWII-ers who looked for a continuing-care community 20 years ago and the Ikes who are looking today, Hobson observed:

If I were to compare the 75-year-olds in 2007 with those from 1987, what we would have seen with the 75-year-old in 1987 was someone who really was looking forward to us saying, "We are going to take care of you." Today, we don't use that phrase with 75-year-olds. What they want to know is not whether we will take care of them but whether we will be there for them if they need us. The assumption of us taking responsibility for them is gone. They don't want to give over responsibility for their care to us; they want to be in partnership with us.

In 1987, the 75- to 80-year-olds contemplated a much shorter life horizon before them; they were really preparing more for death. The 75- to

Generational Cohort Influences: Formative Years					
	WWII	Ikes*	Leading-Edge Boomers	Middle Boomers	Trailing Boomers
Age (in 2005)	76+ years	59 to 75 years	52 to 58 years	46 to 51 years	40 to 45 years
Formative Years	1930 to 1945	1946 to 1963	1960 to 1970	1967 to 1977	1974 to 1983
Political/ Social	Prohibition, Social Security, FDR/New Deal, Bread Lines, WWII, Labor Movement	McCarthyism, Cold War, Brown vs. Board of Education, Suburbanization, Highways, Korea	JFK, LBJ, MLK, Civil Rights, Vietnam, Woodstock, Kent State, Draft Lottery	Vietnam, Watergate, ERA, Roe vs. Wade, No-Fault Divorce, Casual Sex	Hostage Crisis, Reagan, Terrorism, Middle East Conflict, Rise of Conservatism
Economic	Stock Market Crash, Great Depression, Keynesian Economics	G.I. Bills, Housing Act, Economic Prosperity	New Frontier, Medicare, Great Society	Price Controls, Nixonomics, Inflation	Oil Shocks, Reaganomics, Stagflation
Popular Culture	Chaplin, Babe Ruth, "Talkies," F. Scott Fitzgerald, Movies, Lindbergh, no TV	Sinatra, James Dean, Elvis, Marilyn Monroe, Disneyland, Hot Rods, Duck & Cover, Sputnik, Family TV	The Beatles, Dylan, *Rolling Stone Magazine*, Moon Walk, The Pill, Psychedelic Drugs, News TV	*Saturday Night Live*, *All in the Family*, *Mary Tyler Moore*, *Ms. Magazine*, Counterculture TV	*Star Wars*, Disco, Fitness Craze, Punk Rock, Space Shuttle, Crack and Drugs, Crime and Violence TV
Core Traits	Thrifty, Patriotic, Sacrificing, Defer Gratification	Status Quo, "Don't Rock the Boat," Respect Authority	Idealistic, Demanding, Nonconformist, Seek Immediate Gratification	Status Conscious, Individualistic, Seek Immediate Gratification	Pragmatic, Apolitical, More Conservative, Fade to GenX

*Ike is the nickname for General Eisenhower, the Supreme Commander of the Allied Expeditionary Force and the president of the United States for most of the 1950s.

Source: Segmentation: A Mature Market Perspective, Chuck Hurst, Director of Research and Database Marketing, JWT Mature Market Group, October 2005.

80-year-olds of today are thinking more about preparing for the cruise two years from now.

We are surrounded here with people that are 80 and over, but 80 is not looked at as being old. We would see people in 1987 leaning on us, meaning the community, to provide activities and programming for them. Now, we just facilitate that process. These people today, the 80-year-olds, are coming in computer literate. We just find them an extension cord. Once we give it to them, they take it from there. They are much more active. The 80-year-olds of 20 years ago, being really, truly part of that GI generation, were much more comfortable looking toward authority to set the direction of their lives.

Let us remember that the WWII-ers' and Ikes' experience was that the former allied countries' elected officials knew what they were doing and could be relied on. These were not naïve people who blindly gave over their allegiance to elected officials. They laughed along with Will Rogers, the great critic of politics, as he pointed out its shortcomings, "Be thankful we're not getting all the government we're paying for." This generation had experienced FDR and Churchill as they led us out of the Great Depression and then on to victory in the war. Prosperity touched most families. Government surely worked.

Harry Hobson went on to focus more specifically on the attitudes of today's 80-year-olds:

Saying the current generation will challenge authority may be an over-statement, but they do often challenge authority. The challenge is "We're not sure your way is the best way; explain it to me." [Here's] a quick example. I met with a couple yesterday that were ready to move in. I think he is somewhere around 83—you'd never know it. She is probably 79 and both were accomplished people. The level of questioning that they had for us was not something we would have ever heard 20 years ago. He asked, "When I live here, how do I get onto some sort of a committee, task force so I can get closer to understanding the decisions here?" This is an example of a very engaged people. This never would have happened in 1987.

I had a conference call a couple of days ago about this whole issue with a colleague in North Carolina who said, "The resident of today is saying we know we have a competent management team, we know we have a high-powered board of trustees made up of industry and community executives, etcetera, and that's fine, but we as the residents have skin in the game, so you will be seeing us as part of the decision-making process." Today's residents are coming in shoulder to shoulder as our strongest trustees. It's great.

I found Hobson's observations to be surprising. Looking at those over 80 questioning the status quo and expecting to continue maintaining their responsibility for themselves does not fit with the late WWII-ers, or even the early Ikes, described by JWT. I asked Hobson how he could explain this discrepancy. The answer was clear to him:

The 80-year-olds have learned over the years from the younger generation, the Leading-Edge Boomers, to challenge and to keep control of their lives. Their 50- and 60-year-old kids have been pushing them to ask questions. Now it is second nature to them.

I have my own experience with this push from the kids. I see my wife coaching her 88-year-old father on how to deal with the health care bureaucracies, manage his money, and keep current on his latest computer. The boomers' thinking has migrated into their parents' generation. Our parents are preparing the service providers for our rush into life beyond work.

THE BOOMER GENERATION IN 2030

I will conclude this survey of our history and its effect on our retirement with a look into the future. Keith MacDonald, another of my interviewees, was a research director with First Consulting Group (FCG), a U.S. health care and technology consulting company when, in the spring of 2007, he completed a report for a large health care association. As part of this project, MacDonald and his research team compiled this comparison of the differences he found among different age groups.

MacDonald's comparison closely mirrors JWT's research and Harry Hobson's experience of the differences between the previous generation's

Baby boomers look and behave differently than their parents' generation across many dimensions.

Generational Profiles: Yesterday, Today and Tomorrow		
Baby Boomers' Parents	**Baby Boomers Today**	**Baby Boomers in 2030**
65–85 years old today (April 2007)	43–61 years old today (April 2007)	66–84 years old in 2030
Less active, sedentary lifestyle	Active, working lifestyle	Retired but active—experiencing travel, leisure and social activities
Less likely to have advanced education	Many highly educated	Dedicated to continuous learning
Focus on value and practicality	Focus on comfort, convenience, and service	Higher expectations for service
Focused on family	More self-focused, balancing work with family/home life, exercise, social activities, and self-improvement	Continued focus on self-improvement, looking and feeling younger
Less likely to be engaged in own health care	Learning to navigate new health plans and insurance models with higher out-of-pocket costs	More disposable income, though spending more of it on out-of-pocket health care costs
Receiving significant percentage of care in hospital setting	Receiving majority of care in outpatient settings, including physician offices	Receiving care in a variety of settings (home, out-of-area, active care residences)
Take physicians' word as "gospel" Cared for by children and/or in tertiary (greater than family care and less than long-term care) or long-term care facilities	Moderately engaged in health care and wellness/prevention Managing early stages of chronic disease Accessing Internet for health care diagnosis and treatment options	Participating in chronic disease management programs online or in local community Monitored remotely for signs of changing health status

"When I'm 64: How Boomers Will Change Health Care," produced by First Consulting Group for the American Hospital Association, May 2007.

retirees and ours. Not surprisingly, as with previous generations, our future will see us continuing to be who we are, only older.

The next chapter will look at how we change as we grow from our career-focused lives to our new adulthood.

SUMMARY

In this chapter we looked at:

- The idea that retirement is a big deal. It is much more than just leaving a job. It is about taking on a new stage of life and making this new life work.
- What you will find in this book, including
  - The description of an accomplished person
  - The importance of choice and how to use it wisely
  - Learning what is important to you
- The shared experiences that have helped to create this baby boomer generation and what impact this will have on our retirement.

CHAPTER TWO

DECADES OF CHANGE

"The childhood shows the man, as the morning shows the day."
—John Milton, 17th-century English author

Why does understanding our past help us with our future? Consider this: Experience, good or bad, (1) generates meaning, which (2) generates judgments that (3) guide our actions. The better you understand your experience, the better you control your current actions and your future.

As we saw in the previous chapter, we are all heavily influenced by our shared cultural experiences. We have each used those experiences in our own way, and these experiences have shaped who we are today. In this chapter, I will briefly review what we experience at each different stage of life. Understanding what we have experienced can inform our future in our new era beyond work.

Looking back at our experiences also helps us to gain perspective. A new perspective can update your thinking. Those who hang on to the past and try to maintain the old ways of doing things are rarely successful or satisfied as they move beyond work. Assuming that you are in your mid-50s to early 70s, you are motivated by many needs and desires that either did not exist or were not primary in the earlier eras of your life. For example, as we get older, work income takes on new meaning as we become more engaged in our own financial planning. We also have growing medical needs that generate concerns and can affect our finances. Therefore, it is important to gain an understanding of where we have been, so we know what is still relevant and what is no longer relevant as we go into the future.

Adult development theory is a well-researched and written-about topic. Books such as Daniel Levinson's *Seasons of a Man's Life* and Gail Sheehy's *Passages* are well known for helping people gain perspective on life. A search for "Adult Development" books on Amazon.com yielded more than 13,000 titles. A search for "Lifespan Development" books returned more than 28,000 entries. I am definitely not plowing new ground here, but I do hope to communicate the basic ideas of adult development in a way that helps you understand what you have gained in each previous era of your life. I will then introduce a new way of thinking about this age, *new adulthood.*

LIFE IN THREE ERAS

Some say that all experience can be described in three parts: the beginning, the middle, and the end. Many people, including myself, see adulthood as having three distinct stages but I prefer not to use the beginning, middle, and end structure. Here are the ways three lifespan researchers define the adult life stages, age 18 to 70 and on:

Researcher	First Era	Second Era	Third Era
Erik Erikson—His 1950 landmark book, *Childhood and Society* (Vintage; New Ed edition, 1995), brought psychology into a new age. He defined eight life stages, three of which were about adulthood.	Young Adulthood: Intimacy vs. Isolation 20–45 yrs	Middle Adulthood: Generativity vs. Stagnation 45–60 yrs	Maturity: Integrity vs. Despair 60+ yrs
Daniel Levinson—First published in 1978, his book, *The Seasons of a Man's Life* (Ballantine Books, 1986), described the research he conducted at Yale University. Building upon Erikson's work, Levinson focused on how adults (men at the time, and later women) developed over their lifespan. He defines three "eras," each including a transition into and out of each stage.	The Early Adult Transition (17–22 yrs), followed by the Early Adulthood Era (22–40 yrs)	The Mid-life Transition (40–45 yrs), followed by the Middle Adulthood Era (45–60 yrs)	The Late Adult Transition (60–65 yrs), followed by the Late Adulthood Era (65+)

| Gail Sheehy—Her 1974 book, *Passages,* caught the attention of the general public and created a virtual "Passages" franchise. In her updated book *New Passages* (Ballantine Books, 1996), she describes "three adult lives," each marked by a passage. | Provisional Adulthood (18–30 yrs), followed by the Passage into First Adulthood | First Adulthood (30–45 yrs), followed by the Passage to the Age of Mastery | Second Adulthood (45–85+ yrs), including the Passage to the Age of Integrity |

My own understanding of adult development over the lifespan draws from each of these three researchers' theories and uses my 35 years of work as a psychologist and my 40 years as an adult to inform my thinking.

	First Era	**Second Era**	**Third Era**
Beyond Work's Three Eras of Adulthood	Definition and Growth (20–40 yrs)	Consolidation and Fulfillment (40–60 yrs)	Knowledge and Reward (60+ yrs)

WHAT HAVE YOU GAINED WITH AGE?

Estrid Geertsen (b. August 1, 1904, Denmark) made a tandem parachute jump on September 30, 2004, from an altitude of 4,000 m [13,100 ft] over Roskilde, Denmark, at the age of 100 years, 60 days.
—Guinness World Records 2007

Ms. Geertsen provides us with an example of what can be done after people move beyond work, as does the California great-grandmother who gave birth at age 62. It is good to know what is possible and even better to know what makes sense for you.

Looking back at our 20s from our perspective of 55 or more years, we can easily see what we have lost, but we sometimes forget to notice what we have gained. Back then, we had lots of enduring strength, energy, and stamina. We miss that stamina and the excitement it provided in our lives. Now quickness of thought has slowed, sexuality has receded, and stamina has declined. "Slowed," "receded," and "declined" are words that relate to loss of functioning. If this were all that aging was about, we would be reduced to a rocking chair, a shawl, and mild tea.

Fortunately, aging also provides gains in experience, knowledge, and wisdom, which we use to accomplish more while using less strength and energy. As the saying goes, "Work smarter, not harder." These gains in experience and wisdom create a fuller life by giving us an understanding of how our world works and what we find enjoyable or burdensome. The more experience we have, the more knowledge we have available to define who we are.

Here is a chart depicting our comparative stores of stamina and knowledge over the three eras of adulthood.

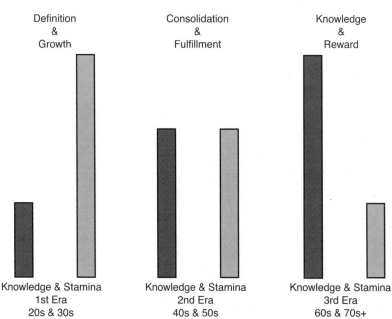

The 3 Thematic Eras of Adulthood

Definition & Growth	Consolidation & Fulfillment	Knowledge & Reward

| Knowledge & Stamina 1st Era 20s & 30s | Knowledge & Stamina 2nd Era 40s & 50s | Knowledge & Stamina 3rd Era 60s & 70s+ |

When I show this chart to clients who are planning their third era, I ask them if they would trade their current knowledge for their past stamina. While they all would enjoy more youthful stamina, none of them would trade it for their hard-won knowledge. Muhammad Ali said it well: "The man who views the world at 50 the same as he did at 20 has wasted 30 years of his life."

LIVING A MEANINGFUL LIFE: A MATTER OF CHOICE

To understand these three eras, you need to know what makes up each era and how each era builds upon the preceding era (the first adult era, Definition and Growth, is a product of the many preceding childhood eras, which I will not describe). On any given day, week, or month we engage in many activities to satisfy our needs and desires. These activities are rarely random behaviors that have no organizing theme. Our choice of how we spend our energy and time is closely related to what we consider meaningful. How do we translate what is meaningful to us to what we do every day? Here is an example.

Franklin is a member of a management team at a large corporation. He is 45 years old, is successful in his career, and has a good family. He lives a busy, sometimes hectic, but good life. He knows that life is good because it supports what he feels is important to him. The things that are meaningful to him include these six factors, listed here in the order of importance to him:

1. *A good marriage. He loves his wife and feels loved by her.*
2. *Good and happy kids. He has two boys, a 20-year-old in college and a 13-year-old getting ready for high school.*
3. *Retired parents. His parents feel secure and connected to each other and to his family.*
4. *Success at work. He feels good about his company and his role in it. He feels he has viable career paths ahead of him and opportunities to pursue his career.*
5. *Community. Even with little discretionary time, he believes it is important to participate in and support his community. He does this by actively participating in his younger son's school activities whenever he can. The family actively participates in their religious congregation.*
6. *Happiness. This broad feeling includes his life working well, as determined by the factors described above. It also includes feeling healthy and enjoying bike riding and other preferred activities, including spending time with a few good friends.*

Such random activities as commuting to work, helping his son with homework, paying bills or spending time with his wife are seen by Franklin as supporting what is meaningful to him. His various activities are organized around an understandable purpose.

Franklin can link his activities to what is meaningful in his life. Some people are not so fortunate. They do not feel that their lives have meaning, and they feel stuck in a cycle of chores over which they have no control. For them, daily life consists of meeting different sets of responsibilities that

drag on, day after day. It is likely that retirement will be no more meaningful for these people than their current life is today.

For your life to have meaning and purpose, you have to know why
you do what you do every day. You know that you *choose* to go to work
or do the laundry. The key word is that you *choose* to do what you do.
When you have choice in your life, you have control of your life. Feeling
in control of life is a strong indicator of happiness with life.

THE THREE DOMAINS OF LIFE

In our adult years before retirement, we tend to organize our life into
three domains: family, work, and self. Throughout our lives, the amount
of energy and attention we give to each domain varies. Here is a description of the three domains:

1. **Our Work Life**. Work is what we do to support ourselves and meet
   our responsibilities. This can include both income-generating and
   non-income-generating activities. The common feature is that we
   are productive. We often use work to define our schedule.

2. **Our Family Life**. Family consists of our spouses and our children
   (most directly), along with our parents and other extended family
   members. It can also include our friends, colleagues, neighbors,
   and members of the community. This domain of life is strongly
   determined by our own definition of family. The common feature
   is that it involves other people who share our life. The responsibilities we share with our family members can provide support but
   they can also create stress and strain.

3. **Our Self**. Thomas Mann, an early 20th-century writer and winner
   of the Nobel Prize, referred to the power of knowing one's self: "No
   man remains quite what he was when he recognizes himself." The
   self refers to the attributes that make us unique; how someone else
   would describe us; what we enjoy or dislike; and our knowledge
   of what we consider to be good or bad, right or wrong. Self also
   acts as a framework upon which we can hang ideas, beliefs, values,
   hope, and desires. The common feature to self is that it ultimately
   defines what we do and why we do it. The more you know of your
   self, the more you can control the world around you and generate
   satisfaction.

Daniel Levinson, in his 1978 book, *The Seasons of a Man's Life*, described what he saw contained within the self:

> *The self includes a complex patterning of wishes, conflicts, anxieties, and ways of resolving or controlling them. It includes fantasies, moral values and ideals, talents and skills, character traits, modes of feeling, thought and action. Part of the self is conscious; much is unconscious; and we must consider both parts. Important aspects of the self, initially formed in the pre-adult era, continue to influence a man's [sic] life in adulthood. We have to see how the person draws upon the self, or ignores it, in his everyday life. The self is an intrinsic element of the life structure and not a separate entity.[1]*

More simply, the self is made up of all your experiences and the meaning you give to each.

The meaningful things in Franklin's life, in our example above, naturally fall within these three life domains:

Life Domain	Factors	% of Time Franklin Spends on Each Factor During a Typical Week: 7 Days = ~ 112 Waking Hours
Family	Wife, Kids, Parents, Community	50 hours, or 45%
Work	Success at Work	50 hours, or 45%
Self	Happiness	20 hours, or 10%

In the different stages, or eras, of life, each of these three domains shifts in priority, as do the demands on our time and attention. These shifts explain why, for example, issues of self predominate in our early 20s and why the early 40s can be a time of crisis.

The best way to describe how each domain relates to the others in each era of our life is through illustration. In the diagrams below, each Work, Family, and Self domain is represented by a circle labeled W, F, or S. The circles vary in size according to the relative amount of energy we use to reach the goals and the priorities of each domain in each era.

For each era, I will display two sets of the diagrams. One set displays the life domains of a person who is primarily involved with building a

---

1 Daniel Levinson, *The Seasons of a Man's Life* (New York: Knopf, 1978), p. 42.

career—*Work Focused*. The second set looks at the same period of time for the person who has decided to focus on the family—*Family Focused*. Each chosen focus has a major effect on personal development. In the not-too-distant past, these choices were gender specific. Men pursued career (work) and woman raised families. Today, society is more accepting of either gender pursuing either course.

Consider these illustrations of adult growth a framework on which you can hang your own personal experience. They do not display the correct way to move through each decade, but rather the way our shifting priorities typically push, shove, and eventually balance each other during our lives.

An Overview of the Three Adult Eras and the Decades within Each

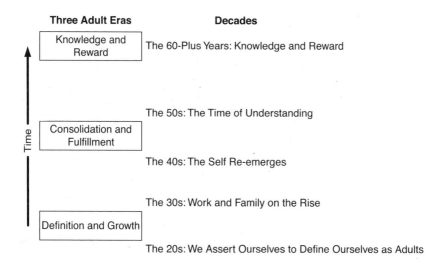

The 20s and 30s: The Definition and Growth Era

When I was a child, I spake as a child, I understood as a child, I thought
as a child: but when I became a man, I put away childish things.
—Bible, King James Version: 1 Corinthians 13:11

In our 20s, we are just leaving adolescence and our future awaits—a daunting prospect for someone whose life up until now has been fairly structured by school and family. We look to define our self and also to find compatible work and/or a family. This focus on self can be seen in both

The 20s: We Assert Ourselves to Define Ourselves as Adults

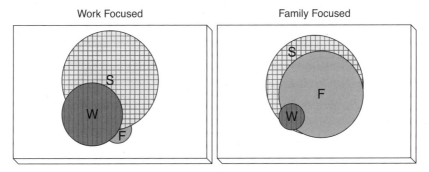

diagrams. The family-focused person often finds his or her self dominated by family priorities. The work-focused person uses work to define part of the self but has energy to pursue other interests. Culture, spirituality, sports, dating, and learning tend to be the main interests at this stage of life.

The early 20s, the novice adult years, are marked by an almost conscious effort to become an adult. We do what we can to put the trappings of childhood and adolescence behind us. It becomes important to feel like an adult. We experiment with new ideas and behaviors, at times succeeding and at times failing. I recall my excitement when I received my first telephone bill for my new apartment: I was an adult listed in the computers of the telephone company! This excitement waned very quickly.

Whether work- or family-focused, people at this stage expend a great deal of their energy defining their self as an adult. The work-focused person tends to reduce the energy spent on family. The family-focused person is nonetheless primarily working on defining the domain of his or her self. At the same time, their family life is requiring a great deal of their energy as well. Family can be defined in many ways, including involvement with the family of origin when their presence is needed. Most often, the family focus begins with having a child. Whether this is a planned or unplanned birth, the effect is to maintain the focus on family responsibilities.

No matter what our focus, this is the time when we define our self through experience. We can then use our knowledge of our self to move ahead on life's paths.

As we move out of our 20s, most of us have learned that we are adults. We have experimented and followed a path into our adult lives. Paths from the 20s to the 30s are usually either chosen, predestined, discovered, or poorly defined.

Those on a *chosen path* have a fixed goal of becoming something—a lawyer, an actor, a parent, an electrician, a soldier, or another desirable role. These goals are often set in high school or before. A memorable experience may catch the imagination and focus a person's interest.

Those on the *expected path* may be joining the family business or starting their own family. The family path was the expected path for women until the women's movement challenged the expected paths for us all. I once heard a woman say that when she was graduating from college in the late 1950s, "Women were expected to marry, or you were doomed to work."

The *discovered path* is the riskier path because those on this path enter their 20s without a clear idea of what they want to become. The uncertainty of what to do weighs heavily, and parents often increase the pressure: "What are you going to do? When are you going to make something of your self?" Making your *self* is exactly the point of this path. Experimentation is the tool used to discover what captures your attention and then works to define who you are. You might at first simply look for a job that is convenient and pays the rent. A friend who works at a medical testing lab that is a reasonable bus ride away tells you that the company needs someone to stock the supplies in the labs. You get the job, and then you discover that this medical stuff is interesting and that the other people working there are fun. The work draws you in and you are good at it. You begin to focus on this as the path and you pursue other jobs in the medical field. Maybe you even take courses and become a licensed clinical laboratory technologist or work on getting into medical school. You follow this path into your 30s.

The *poorly defined path* is less chosen than it is an outcome of vague interests and motivation. On this path, people drift into their 30s with little knowledge of what engages or excites them. This drifting could continue through the following decades, or something could catch an individual's imagination at any time. This is a high-risk path that can create an unfocused and often dissatisfying life.

The 30s: Work and Family on the Rise

At this point we can recognize most people as adults, responsible and driven. The search for self—"Who am I?"—gives way to a focus on the adult career, whether it's building a successful work career or building a successful family career. In the past 20 or so years, many people have been trying to combine these two, and many have succeeded. This career focus drives us right through our 50s and early 60s. At that point, the focus of life dramatically changes.

The 30s: Work and Family Overshadow the Self

Work Focused

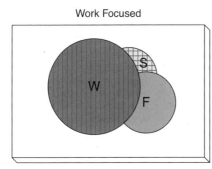

Family Focused

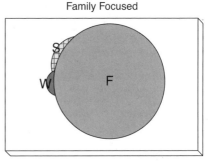

The 30s begin with the legacy of the 20s. A typical person in his or her early 30s has built a sense of self as an adult and can shift his or her energies to build other domains. Those who are work focused move from having a job to building a career. They have succeeded at the entry-level job and are now considered an experienced person.

The career path may or may not be exactly what they want, but pressures from growing responsibilities begin to limit choices. Marriage and children may be an important part of life. Unattached women and men may feel the pressure of starting a family or they may set that option aside. Renting gives way to owning a home and paying a mortgage. Changing jobs is no longer a way to try out new work choices; it is now considered "job hopping" and is not seen as leading to experience gained, but as wasting time.

Those who are family focused may be in the midst of raising their family. For these people, the work domain is mostly contained within the family domain. In many ways, family is their work. They may have a paying job, but their family is their main focus. This focus on family can be very rewarding, but it can also cause a person to wonder if they are able do anything else. As work and family responsibilities grow, the self is relegated to grabbing scraps of energy not otherwise consumed. Welcome to the 40s.

The 40s and 50s: The Consolidation and Fulfillment Era

In our 40s we attempt to consolidate our gains and mitigate our losses. Most of us have been working toward the goals we set for ourselves when we were in our 20s. We may redefine our goals and continue on our path or we may decide to set very different goals that promise a better life. This midlife reevaluation is grounded in the setting of new goals that have grown from our 20 years of adult experience.

It is in our 50s that most adults hope to fulfill their goals and to find satisfaction with life. Some accomplish their goals and many come close, while others find that life has not been kind.

The 40s: The Self Re-emerges

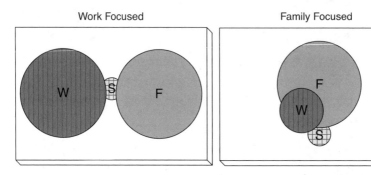

Accomplished people can now consolidate the base of work and family built during their previous 20 years as an adult. In many ways, they have attained the goals they set for themselves in their 20s and worked toward in their 30s. The 40s is the time when we can recognize and relish our success as adults. The simple fact is that our opportunities and our responsibilities peak at about this time of life. If work and/or family are going well, we take on bigger tasks. We consolidate gains from the first era and move on to live a fulfilling second era. But it can still be a bumpy ride.

The task of the 40s is to reassess our self and determine our needs and desires for the next 20 years. Our work and our family responsibilities continue, but we can now pay attention to "who we are" and enjoy what we have built.

The lives of many in their 40s rocket forward, fuelled by their 20 years of previous experience. They are on track to fulfill their new goals.

If work is not going well, we might look for a better work situation. We are also dealing with our children as they deal with their adolescence. The family-focused parent may anticipate the forthcoming empty nest, beginning to ponder questions of relevance in the self domain. And then we can add to this mix the growing responsibilities for our own parents. The idea of the "sandwich" generation, feeling pushed from below and above, becomes real for many.

Many of the questions regarding our quality of life that surface in our 40s are our response to the decisions we made 10 to 20 years ago. We are living the dream of the 25-year-old we used to be, but that dream may now feel like a burden. It is time for our pursuit of our first adult era goals to shift focus to the goals relevant to a person in their second adult era. Many of us find ways to navigate through this time, and most of us question whether our priorities support our own midlife interests. It is worth noting that in midlife all of us, to some degree, face the question "Who am I and am I the person I want to be?" Some find this to be an interesting and refreshing experience, a summing-up of the first 20 years and a midlife re-evaluation of purpose that allows for the setting of new goals. Others find that this questioning uncovers repressed dissatisfaction and unhappiness. This is the root of the ubiquitous term "mid-life crisis," which unfortunately gets all the press. We all re-evaluate at this stage, an evaluation that can trigger a crisis of purpose for some.

I recall a woman who had spent a dynamic 20 years as the wife of a successful doctor and as the mother of two children. As she entered her 40s, she saw great opportunities to pursue the interests she had cultivated during her first adult era. As her family responsibilities subsided, she completed a master's degree in business in her field of interest—art. She quickly landed a just-above-entry-level professional job at a prestigious consulting firm—a job that would usually be given to a new MBA 20 years younger. However, this woman's life experience and maturity overshadowed the younger MBAs' stamina. Within five years, she was a senior professional and by age 50 she was made a partner.

As this example shows, the 40s can be a time of recognized success. But the 40s can also be a time of growing dissatisfaction and exhaustion. If you look at the diagrams of the life balance for the 40s, you can see that the self domain has become minuscule. The work-focused person talks of feeling crushed by the sheer volume of the responsibilities generated by work life and family. People in this situation can also feel pulled apart by the competing needs of work and family. The family-focused person often describes himself or herself as "lost." Children have become more responsible for themselves, but their demands and problems escalate. If the working partner seems distracted by work, the family-focused person can feel lonely and uncertain. Self-value can sink, and uncertainty can rise. At this point we become vulnerable to a midlife crisis.

Working through the questions of midlife requires some introspection—the ability and courage to examine your feelings and your thoughts. Those who are able to be introspective can use midlife as a time to question their priorities and reset their goals. This produces the feeling that their self is being refreshed and made ready for the future—as in the example of the woman who got her MBA and a new career. Those who lack the skills of introspection either bury their dissatisfaction and unhappiness deep within themselves or seek the superficial "ax" cure, lopping off one major set of responsibilities (in either the work or family arena) and replacing it with something (or someone) new.

Introspection can reveal doubt and anxiety: life should be working for you instead of you working for your demanding life. This can raise the question of what we have accomplished, often with accompanying feelings that what we have accomplished is not enough. This is the root of a 40s midlife crisis. A person in crisis may feel a dearth of energy and boredom or even anger with their work or their partner, which fuels the desire to make changes and make them quickly. There is a sense that time is being wasted on an unfulfilling life. It is often the first realization that time is limited. This is a truly painful and unhappy experience.

The 50s: The Time of Understanding

"In youth we learn; in age we understand."
—Marie von Ebner-Eschenbach, Austrian novelist (1830–1916)

At this age accomplished people can feel fulfilled even when they do not feel completely satisfied with their lives. To do this they look past the actual results of their decisions and actions throughout their life and look at what has been learned. They then combine their learning with the

The 50s: Cresting the Consolidation and Fulfillment Era

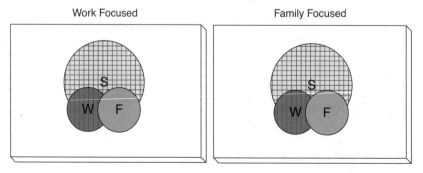

perspective gained from more than 30 years of adulthood to understand their life and what is of meaning. It is their knowledge of what is meaningful that acts as a guide, replacing the goals that drove them.

We reassert ourselves in our 50s in a more balanced way than we could have before. If we feel accomplished in our work and family domains, we see the energy needed to maintain them being reduced to a manageable level. This does not mean that work and family lose their importance or that we are turning away from them. It simply means that:

1. Our experience has built a store of knowledge that we can tap as needed.
2. The value of this knowledge at work and at home is that we can use it to anticipate what is needed. Less strain, more gain.
3. The family domain may require less energy as the children grow. If we are lucky, the kids may even supply energy as their adult lives take shape.

Until this time, 40 years of adulthood had been made up of the three life domains. We have peaked as Second Era adults and we are ready to enter the next adult era. The Second Era peak does not mean that it is all downhill from here. It does mean that we have completed the 40-year climb and we are positioned for the next adventure. We take what we have learned to date and prepare for the next adult era.

The 60-Plus Years: the Knowledge and Reward Era

As the diagrams show, the 60s see a diminishment of the work domain to a level not seen since adolescence. This does not necessarily mean that work ceases, but rather that it now supports ourselves and our growing

The 60s: Work as a Distinct Domain Changes, Timeframes Shorten, and Questions of Self-Satisfaction Ascend

Work Focused

Family Focused

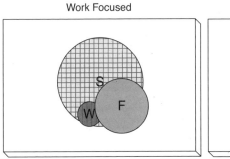
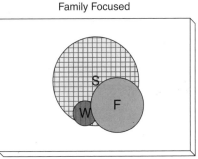

interest in family. At this point, family can include more social relationships than we previously had time to enjoy.

What I have found is that at this time of life the three domains that have served us well begin to lose their relevance. They are not as useful in describing our priorities as they once were. They feel old, and we feel old if we continue to try to make our new life fit into this old structure.

The 60s: The New Adulthood

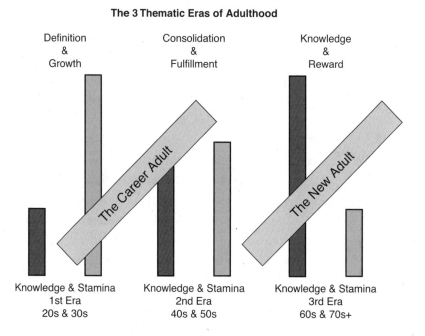

The 3 Thematic Eras of Adulthood

The 60s take us from our career adulthood and bring us into our *new adulthood* as we move beyond work. Here, in our new adulthood, we re-create our life domains. In our first and second adult eras we defined ourselves (self domain) and consolidated our gains (work and family domains). When we enter the third adult era beyond work, the three domains of our career adulthood become less valid and are transformed into four new domains:

- Financial
- Physical
- Social
- Personal

These four domains now structure our life and motivate our living.

Restructuring the Career Adulthood to Meet the Needs of the New Adulthood

You can see from the "fan effect" figure on the next page that the first two eras create a bundling effect and tie the three domains together. Almost any change in one domain will affect the other two.

The third era reduces and even cuts the bundling constraints and allows for freer movement. Now, what you do in regard to your family may not affect your work. You can rent a place in Pittsburgh for a month to help your daughter with her move to a new house, or you can join a friend next week for skiing because he just won a trip for two at a charity raffle.

As a new adult, you have fewer constraints and more freedom to pursue your interests. You are less tied to work and family demands, which leaves you time for your self. You can now live life on your terms. This is great, as long as you are comfortable with less structure and as long as you know what you want.

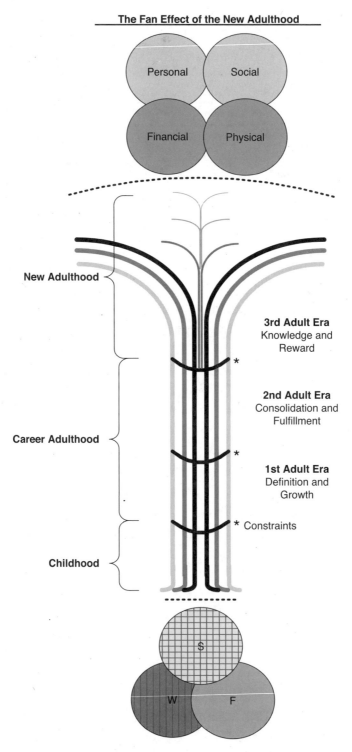

The Fan Effect of the New Adulthood

Personal

Social

Financial

Physical

New Adulthood

3rd Adult Era
Knowledge and
Reward

2nd Adult Era
Consolidation and
Fulfillment

Career Adulthood

1st Adult Era
Definition and
Growth

* Constraints

Childhood

S

W   F

As I have read the research on retirement and on aging, I have found that various labels are applied to different age groups to differentiate the experiences and views of a 95-year-old from a 65-year-old. This type of categorization is a positive step in separating old age from aging. In the past, you retired at 65 and you were seen as the static entity of "retired." I have looked at the Knowledge and Reward era and see that moving beyond work stimulates the transition from the Career Adult to the New Adult. New adults grow and develop just as we previously had done. Here is how I see the typical chronological ages for a relatively healthy and financially secure New Adult. Note that there is overlap as not everyone will proceed at the same pace.

The Stages of the New Adulthood

1. Beyond Work—55 to 65. The initial transition from work to beyond work. This transitional time usually lasts one to two years within this decade.

2. Establishing the New Adulthood—60 to 70. This stage is characterized by lots of experimentation with the expected successes and failures as we test our options and enjoy our life. Now is the time to reacquaint ourselves with who we are. This is often done by learning what we enjoy and what works for us. The process can take an interesting three to five years.

3. Enjoying the New Adulthood—65 to 75. This time may remind us of our 30s and 40s when we were full of energy and confidence, but without the growing burden of work and family responsibilities. When managed well, this is a time of enjoyment and meaning.

4. Consolidating the New Adulthood—70 to 85. Having now lived 10 to 20 years as a new adult, we use our experience to guide us through this time when the meaning and appreciation of life grows. Resilience is a key skill to help us accommodate to physical and social changes as they occur. Independence becomes our focus and concern.

5. Mastering the Knowledge and Reward Era—80 to 90. Having had 20 to 30 years of new adulthood experience, we can find time for peaceful reflection and active enjoyment. This is also a time when our bodies limit our choices of how we live. Some may become disabled, while many will find that they slow down and are more deliberate and realistic about what they do. Health and well-being are not a given, and therefore are greatly appreciated. Maintaining as much independence as possible becomes a central goal.

6. The Revered Elder Years—85+. We begin to free ourselves of attachments to things and are more concerned with our social and personal connections and well-being. I suppose this can be considered old age as our dependencies grow.

Note - As I am sure you know, our health and the health of loved ones is a wild card that can change our sense of well-being at any time and change our development during our Knowledge and Reward era.

THE NEW ADULTHOOD'S FOUR DOMAINS

"Happiness is nothing more than good health and a bad memory."
—Albert Schweitzer

Understanding the four new domains can smooth the path into your new adulthood. The financial and physical domains are the two "foundation" domains. Even if we are not as healthy as we may have been, at least our hazier memory can maintain this happiness equation.

You might think of the combination of the financial and physical domains as your "hard" assets, while the combination of the social and personal domains make up your "soft" assets.

An analogy may help to fix the concept of hard and soft assets in your mind. Most of us are familiar enough with computers to understand the idea of hardware and software. Computer hardware is the box and the gadgets inside the box that contain the whiz-bang technologies that make up the computer. My friend Daniel Behr, of Harvard University's Office of Technology Development, has founded several hardware companies and is fond of saying, "The difference between hardware and software is that when you drop hardware on your toe it hurts." Without the hardware, we would not have a way to store or access the information (software) that we keep on a computer (hardware).

Hard(ware) Assets

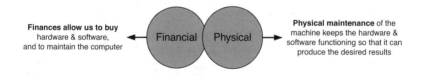

Finances allow us to buy hardware & software, and to maintain the computer ← Financial Physical → **Physical maintenance** of the machine keeps the hardware & software functioning so that it can produce the desired results

Software is the complementary part of computing that allows us to put that good hardware to work. Without the software, the hardware is just a large paperweight. The software is a set of instructions produced to allow you to use your hardware in various ways. The range of software is enormous and growing; it includes programs for everything from e-mail and personal banking to writing a book, creating a dress pattern, and protecting Earth from alien invaders. My own perennial software favorite is still Solitaire.

Soft(ware) Assets

Personal aspects of software dictate how we use what we have available. It determines what software we use and how we use it. Ultimately, it determines our satisfaction and happiness with our computing.

Social aspects of software help us to decide what software (Internet or games, etc.) we will have on our computer and how we learn to use it and discover new uses and ideas.

Our hard assets—finances and physical state—provide the base from which we can operate. If either is compromised, we must deal with the situation before we can use our soft assets to engage the world. Satisfaction, meaning, and happiness spring from our soft assets, as do dissatisfaction, meaninglessness, and unhappiness.

MEETING OUR NEEDS

Another way of looking at the four new life domains is according to our needs. Many people are familiar with Abraham Maslow's hierarchy of needs, in which he defines the needs that motivate people throughout their lives. The needs are presented in a hierarchical order; you must satisfy at least the basics of one need before you can begin work on satisfying the next. His definition of human needs has withstood the test of time. The new adulthood's four life domains are built upon Maslow's framework.[2]

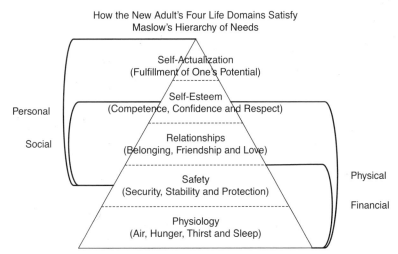

The financial and physical domains, our hard assets, support our basic need to sustain our physical well-being. Our physical domain also reaches into the self-esteem needs, since an illness or disability can affect our competence

---

2 Abraham Maslow, *Motivation and Personality*, 3rd edition (New York: Harper & Row, 1970).

and confidence. Our social and personal domains, our soft assets, use the foundation of the hard assets to help us reach toward fulfillment.

A HOLISTIC APPROACH TO A NEW AND BETTER ADULTHOOD

This four-domain set is very workable as the new adult plans and lives life. It is less role-focused and more meaning focused: it is based on a holistic model of the good life. *You are no longer defined by what you do; you are now defined by who you are.* This is one of the reasons that knowing yourself, the personal domain, is more important than it might have been in your career adulthood.

The new and better four-domain structure can include aspects of our career adulthood. For instance, you can continue to generate income but be less career-driven. You can combine work activities with more socializing. I know of several new adults who had executive positions and are now working three days a week at gardening stores. I also know several former executives who now fill part-time senior roles in their old business or in their industry. Some work on projects, some consult, and some are on the payroll part-time. People who had their own businesses or professional practices often just slow the pace of their work and increase activities that support their social and personal desires. Travel, community, volunteering, athletics, hobbies, and learning are some of their favored activities. In the next chapter, we will meet Erdman Palmore, who has created a new life—and several new careers—for himself in his new adulthood.

SUMMARY

In this chapter we looked at

- The three eras of adult life. Adults under 55 structure their lives around their work, their family, and themselves.
- How the adult's priorities shift as they incorporate their experience during the decades of the career adulthood. The career, whether work or family based, takes center stage and defines many adult goals.
- How the career adult shifts into the new adult. After 40 or more years as a career adult, the career focus diminishes, preparing people for their new adulthood.
- The new adult's move away from pursuing goals to finding meaning. The new adult finds that the pursuit of meaning in life is very satisfying.

CHAPTER THREE

THE NEW ADULTHOOD: LIFE ON YOUR TERMS

"I have not quite figured out yet in my own mind whether I'm apologizing for thinking I'm going to work, or I'm apologizing for thinking I'm not."
—John Kimpel, retired corporate attorney

The best way to begin your new adulthood is to understand that creating a great retirement is a challenge that you can take on. You can be passive and let retirement happen, or you can be active and shape it into what you want it to be. Do you want to be a retired person or a new adult?

Retired people are passive and in decline; new adults are active and evolving. If you choose to actively create your life beyond work, it is helpful to understand the nature of the challenge—the challenge of becoming a new adult.

You have probably heard these new clichés: "Fifty is the new 30" or "Seventy is the new 50." I find these comparisons a little sad and somewhat dismissive of the people, often our children, who inhabit these age groups today. If 50 is the new 30, what does that say about our 30-year-old friends? Are they no longer relevant because we want to be 30 again? The comparisons also have the ring of the older generation trying to stay relevant. In 1971, I was 21, and I remember the enjoyment of attending college classes with good-looking women wearing hot pants. I also recall the distaste of visiting my parents and seeing my mother's 55-year-old friend decked out in hot pants and high white boots. That image seared itself into my memory. The new adult does not try to reclaim an age better left to those of that age. Part of the transition to becoming a new adult is leaving your younger self behind and getting on with the new era, which has its own rewards and challenges.

The transition into the new adult era is not the same as our transition from our first adult era to our second adult era. Now we are fortified with decades of experience and maturity. We use this experience to make our plans, try new things, and learn what works for us. The potential problem with experience and maturity is that it may limit our thinking and reduce our willingness to try on new behaviors and to take reasonable risks. The challenge is to use our experience while not being ruled by it. You cannot live a new life without trying new ways to live. When you understand what the important aspects of life become for people moving beyond work—the four new domains of financial, physical, social, and personal—you gain more control of your life and you make better decisions.

WHAT ARE YOU AFTER YOU RETIRE?

Jack Rosenthal, writing in the Sunday *New York Times Magazine*, explored the inadequacy of the words *retire, retiree* and *retirement* as used to describe people as they move beyond work. He writes: "Boomers, describing those born when the population started to bulge in 1946, are only now starting to enter their 60s. Retirees is an imperfect generalization because, for one thing, many people retire young and, for another, many older people continue to work, whether for the money or the satisfaction."[1]

I agree with Mr. Rosenthal, as did every person I interviewed for this book, that at best the "retiring" words are inadequate. I prefer to think of us as New Adults living in our Knowledge and Reward era. "New Adults" is another imperfect term describing our varied age group, but I like it. I will use it when I can to replace the retiring words. The act of retirement is what we may do or what we have done; it does not describe who are.

DEFINING YOUR TERMS FOR THE LIFE YOU WANT TO LIVE

One person who has defined his own terms for his new adulthood is Erdman Palmore, former professor of gerontology at the Duke University Center for the Study of Aging and Human Development.

1 Jack Rosenthal, Wellderly, *The New York Times Magazine*, July 22, 2007, p. 14.

At age 77 in 2007, Erdman had 15 years of living in retirement. He described himself as having been one of the first research-focused gerontologists. He has published many papers and books on the subject, including the *Encyclopedia of Ageism*.[2] As he completed his chores around his North Carolina home, he spoke to me about what he tells people who are considering retirement.

"It's important for accomplished people to develop new interests, new careers, and sometimes I call them new purposes in life. Now that your children have grown up and you've established your mark and your career, when you retire, you can re-create yourself."

Practicing what he preaches, he has found new purpose since his own retirement.

"I'm 76," said Erdman, "but I'm getting ready for my 77th birthday, which includes my birthday triathlon."

At 76, he was training to complete a triathlon for his 77th birthday. "I ride my age in miles," he explained, "and do push-ups and sit-ups that equal my age. I'm trying to prove that you can improve with age by adding one mile, one push-up, and one sit-up each year. So, each year before my birthday, some friends and I go out and we ride my age in miles on the bicycle. We have a good time, stop for lunch, stop every hour, take a break, have ice cream on the way home, and beer when we get back. So, that's become sort of an annual event among my friends."

He admits to not being very athletic before he retired. "I tried out for the basketball team but never got beyond the junior varsity. I played some tennis, but I never won any championships with it. It was only when I retired that I re-created myself and became an athlete.

"So now I bike a lot, and I hike a lot, and then there is this triathlon. I think this year I'm going to add doing knee-bends and squats to equal my age."

I was a bit skeptical. How could a 77-year-old do this triathlon? I pictured him getting up at 4 a.m. to begin a 77-mile bike ride and not stopping until he had done his 77th sit-up. In thinking he could not complete such a task in one day, I discovered my ageism (my own prejudice about New Adults). My limited thinking caused me to assume his timeframe was

2 *Encyclopedia of Ageism*, Binghamton, NY: Haworth Pastoral Press, 2005.

similar to an Ironman competition in which everything is completed in as fast a time as possible. Why put a deadline on something that you enjoy?

When I expressed my skepticism to Erdman, he explained with equanimity, "Well, I don't try to do them all in one day. I do one thing each day. One of the parts I like about the bike ride is the ice cream on the way back home. I've burned up enough calories that I can have it guilt-free."

What Erdman did was set a challenge for himself on his own terms. He took the idea of a triathlon and used it to frame a set of physical challenges to mark his birthday. He succeeds not because he has made things easy—his triathlon is not easy—but because it is challenging enough to be meaningful. He marks this time by demonstrating to himself that age is mind over matter. For him, age does not matter; capabilities matter.

This physical challenge is but one meaningful part of Erdman's life. Since retiring from Duke, he still contributes to the ageism field with research, writing, and lecturing, but his participation is now more sporadic, which gives him time to enjoy the other parts of his life, as he explained.

"Let me tell you about my other new careers besides being an athlete. One of them is that I went into the home repair business. I got this idea from my brother, who became a home repairman when he retired from the ministry. And he's been making more money as a home repairman than he ever did as a minister. I fix leaky faucets, and repair broken windows, and whatever else I can do that needs doing. Like a handyman, I do nothing that requires a license, no major plumbing or electricity in the walls, that sort of thing.

"My third career is that I became a human celebrant. I'm authorized by the American Humanist Association to celebrate weddings and funerals and other rites of passage. All of these things have re-created my interests in life and given me recreation and kept my life interesting.

"I'm also very active in our church, and have an extensive social network there. I do other volunteer works. I do Meals on Wheels, I'm secretary of the local United Nations association. So, what I suggest to other people retiring is that they get into some volunteer work or whatever provides them with a purpose to their lives.

"The only people who usually don't adjust well to retirement are people who never had any life outside of their work. If they've been workaholics, then they're in trouble and they need to find a new life. It is

---

Two Tips for Workaholics or Others Worried about Retiring

1. **Respect your view of what you enjoy doing.** Retiring does not have to mean leaving work altogether. Consider taking on part-time or project work or explore other ways to "keep your hand and mind in." Find activities that can feel like work. Use some time to learn new skills or expand your knowledge. Consider this a project—create a project plan, with goals and tasks. You may not do it forever, but managing your life by mimicking work is a fine way to enter into this new era. Erdman Palmore might come across as a retirement workaholic, but so what? He knows that what he does serves his purpose and that his purpose helps him define what he does.

---

2. **Find help.** You may not like the idea of getting help. But think of it as similar to going to the dentist when you have a bad tooth. Why suffer needlessly when you retire when you can improve your circumstances by seeking some help? Begin by talking privately with someone you respect and trust. This will help you to clarify the specific problem. Then find people who specialize in your problem area. If it's finances, check with your financial advisor to find out what financial options are available. If it's physical or personal, check with your doctor or clergy. Get a few ideas and see which ones make sense to you. The simple message is this: don't stew in your own juices, get help.

---

especially important for workaholics to identify a purpose [or meaning] in their life."

Three Thoughts from Erdman Palmore for Life Beyond Work

1. Aging and retirement are usually better than most people expect. There are a lot of negative images about aging—negative stereotypes that it's all downhill, that you fall apart as soon as you retire and so forth. Those are mostly myths. Most people are quite happy in retirement, unless they have some major problem like not enough money or ill health.

2. It's important for people preparing for retirement, or people of any age actually, to educate themselves about the facts on aging. Learn some of the basic facts and myths about aging and fears that people have about aging.

3. Stay active.

THE BEST YEARS OF YOUR LIFE

Like Erdman Palmore, you can make your retirement years—your new adulthood—the best years of your life. You can do this by defining the terms of your life, that is, by deciding how you want each of the new adult's four domains (your financial, physical, social, and personal life) to be. If I ask you, "How much money do you need for retirement?" or "What do you find enjoyable?" I am asking you to define the terms of life as you want them to be. As new adults, we have unprecedented freedom to define our terms. Previously, many of the terms on which we based our lives were determined by our parents, our work, our spouse or partner, and our children. You are now free of many of these restraints and can make your decisions based on what you want. Do you know what you want?

The rest of this book is designed to test your ideas and your illusions about aging to see if they hold up. As we explore life as new adults in the next chapters, you will be able to determine if your beliefs are accurate or mistaken and discover what it takes to manage your quality of life.* The next four chapters will look in depth at each domain of new adulthood. They will help you to decide what you want and to determine whether you can get it. None of us can master every part of life, but we can all learn about how life beyond work can be organized. This knowledge allows us to use our strengths to their maximum and to find ways to support our weaknesses.

SUMMARY

In this chapter we looked at

- The terms that define the new adult and how you can discover your own terms. Because we have spent so much time living as career adults where our terms for living were often defined by our responsibilities, we can expect it will take us time to clear the fog to see what we want as a new adult.
- Tips for workaholics or others worried about retiring. New adults develop new, and often surprising, skills for living. Those who enter this period of life ready to learn, to ask questions, and to discover answers find their way sooner than others.
- Three thoughts from Erdman Palmore for life beyond work.
- Living the best years of life by defining how you want to live it.

---

* There is an online assessment tool that estimates your confidence in each of the four domains described in the next chapters. You can use this confidence measuring tool to pinpoint ideas that you may choose to focus on as you continue with the book. You are welcome to complete it now or at another time. The Estimate of Confidence in *Beyond Work's* Four Domains tool is available at www.beyondwork.net.

PART

2

THE NEW ADULTHOOD

CHAPTER FOUR

THE FINANCIAL DOMAIN

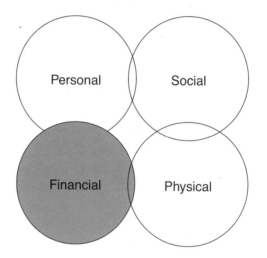

"When it's a question of money, everybody is of the same religion."
—Voltaire, 18th-century French philosopher

Financial security is the threshold we must cross to feel that retirement can work. Not surprisingly, finances occupy the minds of people considering retirement. If you do not have enough money to support yourself comfortably in retirement, you will either have to postpone your retirement or look at how you can fill any money gaps during retirement. You can't spend much time thinking about how to live when you must think only of earning a living. And even in relatively comfortable circumstances, it's often hard not to be preoccupied with concerns about security.

Becky Thompson is a good example of how accomplished people can think about retirement. I met Becky when I called her to arrange an interview with her boss. I told Becky why I was calling and she said, "You should be talking with me. I just turned 60 and I am retiring soon. Retiring is all that I think about." I thought that her invitation was great, so I scheduled an interview.

Becky and her husband own an old farm and farmhouse in a "little bitty town at the end of a road that goes nowhere." It is about three hours north by car from where they currently live and work. Becky happily told me that "that's where we'll move to" when they retire.

Neither has roots in the town but they have friends who had a summer place near there; when their friends retired, they moved up there.

"We would come up and stay with them, and there was a house behind them that went on the market, and we liked it and put a bid on it. But it turned out it had already sold. We had the bug; we wanted to buy in the area.

"We didn't start out looking for a house, and it was just sort of an accidental plan. We didn't know what we wanted, but the realtor kept showing us houses and then we saw this farmhouse."

I thought that it seemed like a big step to move from a suburb to a rural town.

"I see this as a process, trying things out and making decisions as we go along," she replied. "We've gone through as much planning as we can, yet there's always the thought of what you do without a paycheck. We've gone to financial advisors, we have quarterly meetings with our investment people, so that part should be okay, even though there will be some anxiety. I think that we are ready.

"I expect that everyone is anxious about their finances when they retire but I'm a pretty frugal person by nature. The things that I will spend money on are going to see my children, books, and things for the garden, and then the rest of it is just what it takes to live."

Becky and her husband have taken stock of their situation and planned accordingly. They have a combination of a good financial base and thoughtful planning. They have a tolerance for understandable risk. But risk, in spite of everything, remains a worry for them.

Many of my clients have told me that they do not actually understand that they are retired until months after they receive their first retirement check. A client described it this way:

> *I have worked for more than 45 years and a regular part of work was to save a little money each month for retirement. One thing I always knew, retirement savings were sacrosanct, untouchable. Of course, I knew that the money was there but I never thought of it as money I could use.*
>
> *So 45 years suddenly passes and then I did it: I "retired." My time was now my own, which took some getting used to. Then the paychecks [making up for accumulated vacation days not used] stopped. Again, no surprise, but what a shock! I had been getting a paycheck since I was 18. I suddenly felt displaced, sort of vulnerable. When the first "retirement" check arrived, I felt shaken. I was no longer productive; I was not earning my way. On top of that, I was now drawing off the savings I had spent years accumulating. Honestly, it felt like I was doing something wrong. I guess it took me about six months to get over the feeling that I was not making my own way.*

In retirement, learning to feel at ease can be a struggle. Most of the accomplished people I spoke with are reluctant to say that they are financially secure, even if they are, because experience has taught them not to tempt the fates. A measure of doubt keeps them vigilant. Voltaire approved of doubt: "Doubt is not a pleasant condition, but certainty is absurd." So much of our thinking and planning for retirement focuses on our finances because we continue to doubt.

Every person I asked about their number one concern for retirement told me that they worry about their finances. And why not? In our world, money buys security and we want to feel secure as we age. The best approach to calming financial worries is to learn as much about your situation as you can absorb and work with a financial advisor you trust. This will not guarantee a carefree retirement but it will significantly improve your decisions about money and about your life.

AN AGE-OLD QUESTION

What kind of income do I need to retire? It's a question that comes up again and again. In fact, it's a question that has been asked for as long as retirement has been an option. Consider this article published in the *Star News* of Pasadena, California, on July 19, 1971:

One thing we can count on: [retirement's] going to be expensive.

If we estimate that there will be an average rise in the cost of living of 3 percent a year for the next 25 years[1] (and some experts would call this conservative), you can see where you'll stand 25 years from now.

Say, for example, that you could get by on $500 a month if you retired today. That means you'd need the following monthly amounts for each of the next 25 years to live the same way—not better. (Each year is figured on the previous year's expected cost of living rise. Figures are rounded.)

1971	$500	1984	$734
1972	$515	1985	$756
1973	$530	1986	$779
1974	$546	1987	$802
1975	$563	1988	$826
1976	$580	1989	$851
1977	$597	1990	$877
1978	$615	1991	$903
1979	$633	1992	$930
1980	$652	1993	$958
1981	$672	1994	$987
1982	$692	1995	$1,016
1983	$713	1996	$1,047

Source: Martha Patton, "Money in Your Pocket," Star-News, Pasadena, California, July 19, 1971.

Extending Martha Patton's calculations to 2010, the equivalent of her 1971 "get by" amount of $500 a month would be $1,583 per month or $19,002 per year. Add about 20 percent for taxes and, according to Patton's estimate, you would need to generate approximately $23,000 in retirement income. At an 8 percent investment return, but wait! I am on the brink of confusion.

---

1 The actual inflation rate from 1971 to 1996, as measured by the yearly change in the Consumer Price Index (CPI), was +5.8 percent. This rate includes a high one-year change of +13.5 percent in 1980 and a low change of +3 percent in 1992, 1993, and 1996. An item costing $1 in 1971 would have cost $3.87 in 1996. By contrast, the CPI rose an average of 2.6 percent from 1997 to 2006.

For many of us the financial information that is crucial to our future security quickly becomes mind-numbing. I could go on by describing how a mix of pension, social security, Canada Pension Plan (CPP), Old Age Security (OAS), work income, and income from savings could cover this amount. But that is not really the point, is it? For a start, no matter what the accepted wisdom was in 1971, most accomplished people expect to live on more than $20,000 a year, often much more. In addition, if you followed this 1971 advice on saving for retirement, you would be in bad shape today.

At this point you may wonder what you can do to secure your finances, if you have not done already. First, recognize that retirement finances need more sophisticated planning than we may have done in our career years. At that time generating more income was the typical way we chose to fund our expenses. Retirement finances are different as they depend mostly on the money and assets you have accumulated while working and the income that it produces. Second, unless you are very wealthy most of us need professional advice on how to best secure our future. Discovering what you need to retire comfortably is no simple matter. The bottom line is this: learn what you want to have available to you in retirement and stay current with the experts' advice.

WHAT ARE OTHERS DOING?

You will notice that much of the information for this section comes from Fidelity Investments. I have worked with Fidelity Investments for more than ten years as an outside management consultant and executive coach. I know the quality of the people at Fidelity Investments, and I knew who to ask for assistance with my book. They were very forthcoming with their help and have provided much of the information I needed for this chapter. Fidelity Investments is an excellent financial company, one of many in the marketplace. While I know the quality of Fidelity Investments, and it is the only financial products company mentioned, my intent is not to suggest that you should only consider Fidelity Investments as your financial products provider. Be thoughtful about which companies and people you use to plan and manage your financial future.

Do you ever wonder what others are doing for their retirement financial planning? I do. What others are doing and where they stand might help me to evaluate my own actions and position. My usual rather pessimistic thought, however, is that I'm not doing nearly as well as my peers, my basic assumption being that I have not saved enough or that I am spending too much. My friends and I are comfortable talking in general terms about our money, but we are always vague and always want to sound smart and on top of our finances. I just don't know if I'm ahead or behind the curve. Am I doing the right things to secure my retirement, or am I way off base? Do my peers have answers that I don't?

A recent study by Fidelity Investments provides some insight into what others are doing. Polling nearly 3,000 American retirees and pre-retirees, the study found that pre-retirees are on target to replace an average of 61 percent of their pre-retirement income. In other words, full-time workers earning $100,000 annually today are likely to see their income drop to $61,000 when they retire. Could you afford to live on 39 percent less than you live on today?

To gain a more complete understanding of where our peers stand, let's look at some of Fidelity's other findings on the financial status of the people polled.

In addition to retirement savings, pensions, Social Security or Canada's CPP, the three most frequently cited sources from which people expect to receive additional income in retirement are these:

- Working at least part-time in retirement (63 percent) and /or their spouse working in retirement (25 percent)
- Inheritance for self or spouse/partner (23 percent)
- Sale of current home (21 percent)

Overall, Fidelity Investments found the two sources on which people intend to rely most for income in retirement are these:

- Personal savings, including IRAs, 401(k)s, RRSPs & GICs (in Canada) and other workplace plans to which they have contributed (39 percent of all workers polled).
- Social Security (20 percent of all workers and 33 percent of pre-retirees expect Social Security to be their greatest source of income).

- In Canada, this would the Canada Pension Plan and Old Age Security.

Thirteen percent of those polled expect a "very comfortable" lifestyle in retirement, while nearly half (44 percent) expect a "somewhat comfortable" lifestyle. Nearly one-third (29 percent) expect to be able to make ends meet but not much more, while nearly one in ten (9 percent) believe it will be difficult to make ends meet at all.

Most of us (77 percent) believe that we are not saving as much as we should for retirement. The good news is that this is down from 83 percent in 2006, just a year before.[2]

Most people approaching retirement live in hope and fear. A few live in confidence. Of those of us who live in hope, more than half (57 percent) expect to live at least a somewhat comfortable or better life in retirement. Yet 77 percent of us who live in fear do not think that we are well prepared for our retirement. Only 13 percent live with the confidence that they are on solid financial ground for retirement. Where do you reside on this continuum?

DENIAL: I DON'T BELIEVE IT!

"I can't think about that right now. If I do, I'll go crazy.
I'll think about that tomorrow."
—Scarlett O'Hara in *Gone With the Wind*

Scarlett used denial in its most noble manner, to put today's reality out of mind to be able to focus on what must be done now to free one's self from a predicament. The problems with denial come when we deny the realities of our situation to protect ourselves from worry or responsibility by blocking our awareness that a problem exists. We distort reality to avoid the pain that an uncomfortable truth may contain. That may work today but tomorrow we will probably continue denying until the pain grows from a worry to a throbbing pain that requires massive doses of denial.

---

2 Fidelity Investments, "Retirement Index," *Fidelity Investments Research Insights*, March 2007.

How do you know if you are on track for a comfortable retirement? Do you base your assessment on factual knowledge, intuition, hope, or good old-fashioned denial? My experience has led me to believe that the worse a person's financial position, the more likely he or she is to indulge in denial. This tendency is highly unfortunate yet often understandable.

Psychologists think of denial as the usually unconscious effort to reduce anxiety associated with life's demands by not acknowledging these demands. In our case, retirement finances cause anxiety. Will we have enough to live at least a "somewhat comfortable" lifestyle? Will medical expenses drain our resources? Will our investments perform as hoped? Talk about anxiety! These questions connect with the basics of Maslow's hierarchy of needs: physiology and safety.[3] Many people are so worried that they would prefer not to know. That is classic denial.

I believe that denial is a normal and understandable response to a potentially frightening scenario. What if I discover that I am financially unprepared to retire? Knowing this will make me feel worse, while not knowing at least allows me to hope that I am better off than I fear I might be.

Avoiding the facts is understandable but it is not smart. When it comes to your finances, flying blind almost always guarantees a crash. I spoke with Perry Chlan, a Senior Vice President of Fidelity Investments, and Steve Feinschreiber, also a Senior Vice President of Fidelity Investments and who has developed Fidelity's retirement planning methodology, authored numerous research papers on retirement and developed the Fidelity Investments Retirement Index. Not surprisingly, they recommend that you begin today to plan for tomorrow:

A simple place to begin is to look at where you're at today. Begin by understanding where your money's coming from and where it's going. That's really powerful when looking into the future. Once you start from that baseline, you can make changes. You can say okay, I'll retire in a couple of years. This transportation expense, driving to work, that's going to go away. And my work clothes, that's probably going to go away. And then you could think of things that you may want to do. Maybe you want to

---

3 Described in Chapter 3.

travel some more. Or you want to give money to an organization. You experiment with incremental changes and see what your spending pattern might be.[4]

When information about important life decisions is available but not accessed, we are essentially denying ourselves the ability to make the best decisions we can make. Hope and fear, tied to unchallenged belief, allow us to continue to live in ways that are comfortable but do not support our goals. I have attached a simple budget in Appendix 1 to help you assess your finances today.

FACE FACTS AND CREATE A PLAN

According to the Fidelity Investments Retirement Index report, 77 percent of working Americans do not have a detailed, formal retirement savings plan that outlines how much they need to save and builds in periodic reviews. Why is it that only 23 percent of Americans have a good retirement savings plan? One reason, we know, is denial. The other reason is despair. Two of the top three reasons given to Fidelity by pre-retirees who had done nothing to prepare for retirement in the previous six months (and they accounted for 58 percent of those pre-retirees polled) were that they

- barely had any money left over after paying basic living expenses (33 percent) and
- any extra money was being used to pay off credit card debt (27 percent).

Unfortunately, it is precisely people like these who are most in need of a reality check and a plan. No matter what their situation, planning will improve it, but they have to face reality. You can choose to be one of the majority, one of the 77 percent without a plan, or you can join the 23 percent minority and take control of your financial future.

Fidelity Investments found that 42 percent of the people in their survey had taken action in the previous six months to improve their "Retirement Readiness." What that 42 percent did may give you ideas on what you might consider.

---

4 Personal interview, June 12, 2007.

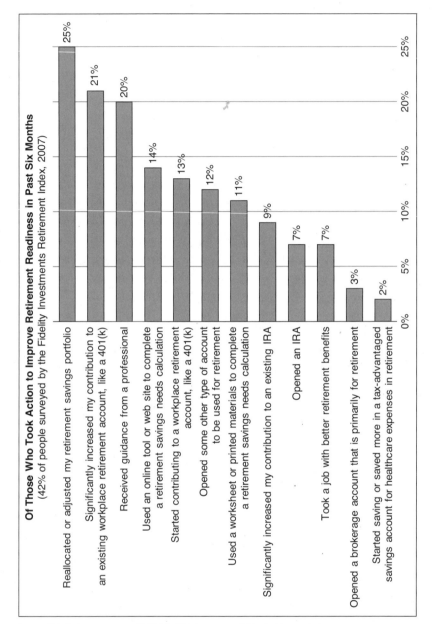

Of Those Who Took Action to Improve Retirement Readiness in Past Six Months
(42% of people surveyed by the Fidelity Investments Retirement Index, 2007)

Reallocated or adjusted my retirement savings portfolio — 25%

Significantly increased my contribution to an existing workplace retirement account, like a 401(k) — 21%

Received guidance from a professional — 20%

Used an online tool or web site to complete a retirement savings needs calculation — 14%

Started contributing to a workplace retirement account, like a 401(k) — 13%

Opened some other type of account to be used for retirement — 12%

Used a worksheet or printed materials to complete a retirement savings needs calculation — 11%

Significantly increased my contribution to an existing IRA — 9%

Opened an IRA — 7%

Took a job with better retirement benefits — 7%

Opened a brokerage account that is primarily for retirement — 3%

Started saving or saved more in a tax-advantaged savings account for healthcare expenses in retirement — 2%

At this point you may feel the discomfort rising and decide it is easier to cast the matter aside. I have heard people give any number of excuses:

- "My head hurts when I think about this stuff."
- "Math is not my strong suit."
- "My employer takes care of all this."
- "I don't have any extra money to put away, so why bother?"
- "I expect that the news won't be good. I would just rather not know."

Why should you push through any discomfort you have and take a look at your situation now? Here are two good reasons:

1. It is much easier than you think.
2. Knowledge is power.

A simple online tool you can use to get an initial understanding of your financial situation is the "myPlan Snapshot" made available by Fidelity Investments. Many other financial service and product firms have excellent tools as well, but the Fidelity tool is one of the best. This three-minute tool is free of charge and anonymous, and it's available at www.fidelity.com/myplan (look on the opening page for "myPlan^{SM}" or search for "Fidelity + myPlan" on a search website).

Chris McDermott, vice president of product development for Fidelity Investments, explained the thinking behind myPlan.

> *Our objective was to make planning for retirement easier and more accessible to everyone, whether they are a current Fidelity customer or not. Our tools are available to help build awareness, engage and motivate people to improve their retirement planning situation today. Whether you do a formal retirement plan now or in five years, you do need to get started on that path to success.*
>
> *Retirement planning can be a three- or four-hour exercise if you do it from a comprehensive perspective and you really weigh the different options and directions from a product perspective and an asset allocation perspective. We ask you to take three minutes and just understand what it might take and whether you're on track with our myPlan Snapshot. In*

three minutes of completely anonymous work using the myPlan Snapshot you will have taken the first step to understanding your retirement finances. You can then continue work with the more comprehensive Fidelity myPlan tools, bring the information to your own financial advisor, or file it away until you are ready for the next step.[5]

The myPlan tool asks these five questions, which you answer with your best estimate:

1. How old are you?
2. How much do you make?
3. How much have you saved for retirement so far?
4. How much do you save each month?
5. What's your investment style? ("Your investment style" is explained to you. No need to know this ahead of time.)

The tool then generates a chart displaying your financial retirement situation as of the time you answer the questions. But more than that, it also allows you to change your numbers to see what choices you have to secure your financial future. You can experiment with variables to see what works the best.

But a word of caution: Using online tools should only be a starting point in understanding your situation and creating a plan. We are blessed with Internet resources galore—so many tools that the problem may be too much information, rather than too little. I tried an experiment to see what variety there was among online retirement income calculators. I used three very reliable sources (not including Fidelity Investments) to calculate the financial outlook in retirement for an average single person:

Current age	60
Number in household	1
Yearly income	$75,000
Salary increases until retirement	4 percent
Yearly savings (15 percent) of pre-tax income	$11,250
Age to retire	65
Expected longevity (20 years)	85
Estate upon death	$0

5 Personal interview, July 12, 2007.

Expected rate of inflation	3 percent
Current retirement savings (assuming no home equity)	$200,000
Expected pension	None
Social Security or CPP (Canadian Pension Plan) beginning at 65	$24,948 (this may be less for the CPP)
Rate of investment return until retirement	8 percent
Rate of investment return during retirement	8 percent
Yearly earned income during retirement	$15,000
Health insurance and medical expenses would come out of yearly income.	

Based on this information, here are the results from each retirement calculator:

- **Calculator 1:** My retirement savings will run out when I am 76, leaving me with $25,000 per year in Social Security / CPP and whatever portion of $15,000 I can earn.
- **Calculator 2:** I will need to save an additional $2,422 each year for the next five working years. Once retired, I will have $62,715 available to me yearly until I am 90, five years past my expected longevity. I would leave some money in my estate.
- **Calculator 3:** This calculator gave lots of interesting information but I ended up more confused than when I began. It told me either that A) I will have about $50,000 a year to live on from age 65 to 85, or that B) I need to save an additional $357,899 in the next five years to generate a yearly income of $50,000. I vote for option A, but I would worry that option B is accurate.

These results present a wide spectrum of possible outcomes, from no retirement income after age 76 to $62,000 a year, or maybe $50,000 a year. I want to restate that the tools I used are provided by very reputable sources who are not selling any product. Why is there such discrepancy in their conclusions? To be honest, I do not know and I am not sure that it really matters. These tools are useful to help you organize your thinking about retirement finances, much like online medical tools can help you understand an illness. But just as online medical advice is no substitute for talking with a skilled doctor, online retirement tools are no substitute for seeking the advice of a skilled financial advisor. The moral of this story: find a good financial advisor who understands you and whom you can understand.

SEEK SOUND FINANCIAL ADVICE

> *"It is too difficult to think nobly when one thinks only*
> *of earning a living."*
> —Jean-Jacques Rousseau, 18th-century French-Swiss philosopher

Some of our friends and peers thrive on immersing themselves in financial intricacies and consider managing their money as part of their retirement career. Some, but not many. My friend Ned Riley has spent more than 40 years in the financial industry, including the last 15 as the chief investment strategist for two multinational businesses, one of which manages over $1 trillion. I asked Ned what he would recommend to someone considering how best to manage his or her own finances. He told me, "I would tell them to farm it out to a good financial advisor, that is what I would do. This is all the guy does each day, every day; he worries about your money so you don't have to worry. A good advisor knows personal finances better than you do."

Albert Einstein once admitted, "The hardest thing in the world to understand is the income tax." Einstein was a renowned genius but he still needed assistance with his taxes, and I assume with managing his money. So don't feel so bad about your perceived lack of financial clarity. Unless you are an expert investor or tax accountant, or unless you manage your money almost full time, you should consider getting expert advice.

You might believe that if you do not have enough money for retirement, there is no point in getting an advisor. Consider the example of Don, a respected and accomplished professor and author, whom I was helping to create a retirement plan. While talking about what he was hoping to do as he moved beyond work, we were beginning to frame the picture and add some detail when I asked about his financial status. Don told me about the rock-solid home he owned in a very desirable town and about some savings. It appeared that he was in decent shape, until he confessed that he was living from paycheck to paycheck, his credit cards were maxed out, and his house was highly mortgaged. Don told me that he was in this situation because of a divorce and his own reckless spending habits. At this point, he was ready to give up on any retirement planning: he was embarrassed, self-loathing, and very worried. He told me that he just "wanted to hide from all this" and let his "life crumble as it may."

I asked that we pull back and regroup and begin with an assessment of his finances, after which we could decide to continue the planning or end it. Don grudgingly agreed. I referred him to a good financial advisor. Don and I started our work together after that, incorporating what we now knew about his finances. The financial advisor discovered that Don was in worse shape than he feared. He worked with Don to restructure his debt, to create an understandable and useful budget, and to change his retirement savings investment plan. Don is now paying less on his loans, the budget allows him to understand how he is spending his money, and his investment return has tripled. Don also knows that he will be able to move beyond work just a few years later than he had hoped. He will also have to generate some income during the early years of retirement. This is not exactly what Don was hoping for but at least he knows that his life will not crumble away.

What do you do if you are in a position similar to Don's? Robert Bodio, Jr., a registered investment advisor (RIA), makes a simple case—get advice as soon as possible:

> It's important to get to an adviser earlier rather than later. You have more time and choices to rectify the situation. Let's say you're 55 and want to retire at 60 but you fear that your finances are in bad shape. If you wait until 60 to come in and get that bad news, you're not a happy camper at all. You come in at age 55 and tell me what you want to do at age 60. From now until age 60, we can do a lot to make things work. I then can break the finances down to the penny—what the person or couple need to save per year to get them from A to B, or offer other solutions. They might downsize the house, work two additional years, or think about using a reverse mortgage to finance that time of retirement. . . . The sooner you plan your retirement finances and link them to your objectives, the more options you have.

As I said before, the people most in need of financial advice are often the least likely to seek it. It may be that it is too painful or that being strapped for money makes the use of a financial advisor out of the question. Remember that if looking into your financial future is painful now, living in it will be more painful. Get help so that you can improve your situation as much as possible. If you just cannot afford the expense, look for a qualified advisor within your bank, your tax service, or even credit counseling services. I would begin by asking at my local bank about low-cost community services they could recommend. They may offer to help you, which is fine as long as you are clear on what they expect in return. Make sure that they know you want a clear and objective plan without any products or services built in. Once you understand the plan then you may want to talk with them about what they can offer.

Consider that the financial industry has worked hard for years and invested billions of dollars to create viable alternatives for even the worst-case financial picture. There is a good chance that there are alternatives that can help you. Denial may feel like it keeps the wolves at bay, but it also keeps you from improving your situation.

FINDING A GOOD FINANCIAL ADVISOR

"If I were two-faced, would I be wearing this one?"
—Abraham Lincoln

"Can I trust my financial advisor?" That is the question I hear from almost all of my clients. Trust is at the heart of determining a good financial advisor, so let's consider who we can trust and why. We may be surprised that training, credentials, and resources are not the first or best criteria for determining the trustworthiness of someone. Trust is not given, it is earned. It requires both good actions by, and experience with, the person. It is a fallacy to think that we can look into a person's eyes and know that the person has a good heart. Better to trust with your eyes wide open.

Henry L. Stimson (1867–1950), U.S. statesman and secretary of war during World War II: "The chief lesson I have learned in a long life is that the only way to make a man trustworthy is to trust him; and the surest way to make him untrustworthy is to distrust him."

Stimson's point, I believe, is not to trust blindly (we have to keep our eyes open) but that trust has to be built and we ourselves must contribute to the building of it. When questions surface—ask; when concerns arise—challenge. Building mutual trust is a two-way street.

Six Steps to Assessing an Advisor and Building Mutual Trust

1. **Begin by being trustworthy yourself.** Be truthful about what assets and liabilities you have, what you want for your financial future, and what you are willing to do to create that future (your risk profile). At this point, you may not know exactly what to say or how to say it; a good financial advisor will help you understand and communicate these basics.

2. **Determine if the financial advisor understands you.** How? Ask! Ask that the advisor tell you what he or she understands are your resources, what you want, and what you are willing to do. Then listen to what the advisor has to say. This means *stop talking and let the advisor talk.*

3. **Does the advisor provide you with a clear picture of your situation?** If the advisor seems to understand about 75 percent of your situation, he or she is listening to you and understanding you pretty well. It would be worth investing the time to fill in the gaps. An advisor cannot tailor plans and advice to your needs and desires if he or she doesn't understand you. If the advisor does not understand you, consider trying another one.

4. **Is the advisor qualified?** Consider how you came to approach this person. Was it on a recommendation from an already trusted advisor or from family or friends? A referral from an employee benefit service? Did he or she work for a firm you trust? Did a sales call or sales material impress you? Did you meet the person at a party? Referrals from trusted people are often the best way to find a trusted advisor.

5. **Does your advisor do the work you are looking for day in and day out?** Are you looking for a financial planner, accountant, life insurance agent, or an estate planner? Is that your advisor's full-time job?

6. **Trust your advisor and keep your eyes open.** Keep asking questions to clarify what your advisor is doing and why. Remember, part of the job of financial advisors is to communicate plans and actions to you clearly. If you do not tell your advisor when you are uncertain or confused, he or she cannot do a good job.

In their book *The Trusted Advisor*, authors David H. Maister, Charles H. Green, and Robert M. Galford seek to educate the professional advisor about the meaning and benefits of building trust with their clients. It is instructive to us, the clients, to understand how they describe a trusted advisor:

> *The highest level, the pinnacle, is that of trusted advisor, in which virtually all issues, personal and professional, are open to discussion and exploration. The trusted advisor is the person the client turns to when an issue first arises, often in times of great urgency: a crisis, a change, a triumph, or a defeat.*[6]

---

6 *The Trusted Advisor* (New York: The Free Press, 2000), pp. 7–8.

Bobbi White Smith, whom you met in Chapter 1, described how and when she knew that her financial advisor was not only competent but also trustworthy:

> *I had, and still have, my investments managed by my financial advisor, but I watch the numbers closely. At one point, I went to him and told him that I thought we should sell some investments and he said, "No, no, no, we're fine." It turned out that in fact my recommendation was a good recommendation. His was not. And I remember him calling me and saying, "You know what? You were right. I blew it on that one." He was so honest. Trust is not about being right as much as it is being honest, taking responsibility for the losses and sharing the credit for the gains.*
>
> *Also, he is genuine; he is a great listener. In a lot of ways, he's not just a financial advisor. Every time my husband and I meet with him he understands what our situation is in relation to how we're living, what our life is like. For example, when we were thinking about buying a second home we talked with him. More than just could we afford it, we talked about did it make sense for us. He is one of our inner circle of advisors, if you will.*
>
> *The other reason why I trust him so much is that I knew someone in dire financial straits and he helped her. I could tell that he wanted to help her.*

Jerry Nilsson-Weiskott lives in Columbus, Ohio, where he has a management consulting practice. He trusts his financial advisor and describes what this trust is built upon:

> *I know that I trust Rick [Rick Schuster, his financial planner] but I am not sure that I can tell you exactly why. I think that it began with word of mouth. People I respected spoke highly of Rick; that was an important first step. Respecting the person is important to me. I like to know about a person, their own life, their business, their family.*
>
> *When my wife Susan and I first began working with Rick, it was long before any real retirement plans so we worked on the plans for where we were at the time and what we thought would make sense for the future retirement. As we did our work, we got to know Rick, his plans, and his family, just as he got to know us.*
>
> *Also, Rick was not easy on us. He would challenge our thoughts when they did not fit well with what we had told him we wanted in our financial*

life. He would even urge us to get other opinions. I could see that he was confident in his ideas and welcomed our challenging him.[7]

Rick Schuster on Financial Advisors

Jerry suggested I talk with Rick Schuster. He is an attorney and a Certified Financial Planner ™ (Certified Financial Planner Board of Standards, www.cfp.net), and is Chief Operating Officer & Financial Planner at Chornyak & Associates, Ltd. in Columbus, Ohio (www.chornyak.com).

Although Rick trained and practiced as a lawyer, he took this experience and began to work with people planning their finances for retirement.

While Rick had a law degree and experience, he did not feel qualified to advise people on their finances. In the past three years, he studied for and earned his General Securities license, his Uniform State Securities Representative and Investment Advisor Representative license, his General Securities Supervisory License, and CFP® designation.

He spent three years studying and passing rigorous credentialing criteria for these licenses and certifications because he knew that his clients trusted him with more than just their money, they trusted him with their future.

Rick had some advice about what an accomplished person should look for when seeking a financial advisor and what to be wary of:

> *There are some licenses and certifications but anyone can say that they are a financial advisor whether they have valid credentials or not. The most well known credential is the Certified Financial Planner designation (www.cfp.net). To obtain the CFP requires both a certain level of experience and ten hours of testing on 89 different topic areas. There is also a certification for the insurance industry called a Chartered Financial Consultant. The Financial Planning Association is a professional association that provides information for people looking for a financial advisor (www.fpanet.org for the US and www.cfp-ca.org for Canada). A number of designations are now being given directed toward the financial advising of seniors. I would encourage a client to ask about the content and length of these certification processes. Some require only a weekend workshop in order to hold oneself out as a trained seniors advisor.*
>
> *As with any professional service, the hard part for an individual is that you don't know how good that service is until you have received it. And so consumers do tend to look for different types of certifications to increase their comfort level with their decisions. I encourage people to make sure that they ask about the person's background and the content of their certifications.*

Rick explained the difference in financial advising for someone who is about 60 and people who are already retired and in their 80s.

> *We have retirement clients of all ages. We have a number of clients who are in their 80s. What tends to happen in that period of time is we begin to have more involvement with the next generation, with their children. I have a woman that I'm now working with who is beginning to experience dementia,*

---

7 Personal interview, February 16, 2007.

*and so the kids are much more actively involved. We go through the process
of advising the children while their mother still has full use of her faculties.
They may want to look at setting up a trust and at least a power of attorney
so that her needs can be taken care of should she continue to decline. . . .*

*We also talk with the client about the estate part of it, including if there
are legacies they would like to leave, charitably or otherwise.*

*Because we do comprehensive financial planning, one of the things that
we deal with in the estate area early on is to have people obtain a general
durable power of attorney (a document in which you appoint someone else
to act on your behalf on matters that you specify, usually legal and health
matters, when you are not capable of doing so yourself) for when an elderly
individual might experience some dementia, and, when they're in the midst
of it, they may not recognize it until it's too late.*

Choosing a good financial advisor is easier when you know what to look for.

*There are a number of things that we think are really important when choos-
ing a financial advisor. First, people should look for someone who does comprehensive financial planning. You want someone who's going to help you
look at not just the retirement planning and the investment planning piece,
but someone who also talks to you about income tax planning, education
funding planning, risk management, and estate planning.*

The financial advisor probably will not be an expert in all these areas but he or
she should know where you stand on these planning issues. They may work with
other professionals who are expert in particular areas.

*The estate planning area entails the setting up of wills, trusts, health care
powers of attorney, living wills, and durable powers of attorney. We always
have these discussions as part of our services. But we work with either the
individual's personal lawyer or a lawyer with this specialty to whom we
will refer our client. What's important is not whether we perform the work
ourselves; it is having it done well.*

*An important part of my role as a financial advisor is to oversee the
process for my client. Although I maintain my law license, I don't have the
opportunity to stay on top of all the nuances of estate planning, wills, and
trusts. I want my clients to have the best, and that means having someone
who specializes in this work every day. It is not my job to do all the work; it is
my job to ensure that all the work is done well.*

*Estate planning is important because how people own assets determines
whether they're going to have an estate tax issue and whether their assets ultimately are passed on the way they wish. How people want to distribute their
money upon their death becomes an important issue when you're planning the
different types of investments, the vehicles for those investments, the titling of
those investments, and the beneficiary designations of those investments. And
all of that [is part of] the estate planning area. It is also important that a person
find a financial advisor who gets involved with income tax planning. And, again,
the advisor may coordinate that with an outside CPA (accounting) firm . . . .*

*The reason that income tax planning is important for the retirees is
that their tax situation is often very different from their work-based income.
Consequently, we want to be able to do income tax projections with them for
regular retirement expenses. We can determine what amounts should*

be coming out of any taxable accounts, and what should be coming out of tax deferred accounts. Within those taxable accounts, how much should be coming from income-oriented investments or from capital gain investments in order to minimize the overall tax liability.

Rick is describing much more than a plan to decide which mutual funds to invest your money in. As he said, he is describing a comprehensive financial plan that includes investment planning but also covers much more. Like me, you may think that this is a good idea for people with millions of dollars. Rick assured me that many of his firm's clients have very modest assets and they benefit from this comprehensive planning as well.

Rick had more advice on what to consider when choosing a financial advisor:

Another thing that is critical for people who are going to retire is to look for an advisor who has been around long enough to have worked on retirement distribution planning. Most people are very familiar with being in the accumulation phase; we're saving toward retirement. How that then gets paid out is actually a separate art and science. And so they should get a good feel for how many of that advisor's clients are retired and how long have they been retired because it's a different process. And that's what I mean by working with someone who is very comfortable with, familiar with, and experienced in the distribution phase.

You want an advisor who is experienced with properly selecting the distribution rate and the asset mix. We often hear people say, well, I'm at retirement therefore I should do a major shift of assets into more income-oriented items and out of equities. Understandably, they want to reduce risk and build income. This is a good strategy to enhance comfort but it reduces the longevity of their finances. They don't know, and I certainly don't know, the date that they will die. It is prudent to plan based on a long life span balanced with a good income stream during that long life. Simply reducing investment risk does not allow for this balanced approach.

We have to plan this distribution process as if you're going to live forever. Consequently, we still have to have a proper mix of equities with fixed income items and we have to have a proper withdrawal rate that can sustain those investments and allow them to continue to grow so that during the down market cycles you can maintain most of your withdrawal rate. In the up market cycles, you're building up your reserves. As you see, we do spend time with people walking through that process. And my guess is that those firms who are more experienced in the distribution side would do the exact same thing.[8]

Rick's guidance on how to choose a financial advisor included understanding the credentials, experience, and service orientation of the advisors you interview. He also added a valuable concept that many pre-retirees fail to consider— does the advisor have experience after the planning stage is completed and the distribution stage begins? We can be so focused on accumulating our financial assets that the actual use of them seems like an afterthought. The last thing that you want is to work hard for years and then mismanage your rewards.

For financial guidance in Canada, readers may want to read Sandra Foster's book *Who Is Minding Your Money?* (Wiley, 2002). It provides

---

8 Personal interview, May 31, 2007.

detailed information on Canadian investment tools and how to select the best financial advisor for you.

MISTRUST

Some people will misuse the trust you have given them. In a *New York Times* article, Charles Duhigg described the abuse of one client's trust by a "certified senior advisor."[9] This CSA credential cost $1,950 for a correspondence course and an unsupervised multiple-choice exam. The advisor is only one of 18,700 other applicants since 1997 to have paid for and passed this exam. Many other such credentials exist.

The advisor sold his clients unnecessary, complicated, and expensive insurance products from reputable insurance companies, collecting $720,000 in product commissions within a year of his certification as a senior advisor. Yet one client, a 73-year-old widow, had so much of her money tied up in these products that she could not pay her dental and home repair costs.

Why would she have given her $75,000 in savings to a man she met once at a free seminar? Duhigg quotes her as saying: "All these insurance companies had trusted him, so I knew that I could trust him, too. And when he became a certified senior advisor, I felt good, because he had gone to school for a long time."

The advisor in question believed he had done nothing wrong. He simply "did what [he] was told" by the companies paying him money to sell their products and by his correspondence course credential program. Taking the trouble to assess accurately a financial advisor's credentials is an absolute must. Trustworthy financial advisors will want you to do no less. They too bear the burden of the malintentioned and unregulated advisors who buy a credential and then harm clients. The trustworthy, well-trained, and ethical advisors support their professional organization's attempts to work with regulators to set and enforce standards. It is an uphill battle.

Here are 12 simple questions you can ask yourself to determine how much you trust your advisor or how much you may trust an advisor you are considering using. Read each statement and mark how true it is for you.

---

9 Charles Duhigg, "For Elderly Investors, Instant Experts Abound," *New York Times*, July 8, 2007.

Twelve Questions to Assess an Advisor's Trustworthiness

Trust Component: My advisor is	To what extent is each statement true for you?	Not true	Somewhat true	True	Very true
Trustworthy	1. I can trust my advisor.	1	2	3	4
Attentive	2. My advisor listens to what I have to say.	1	2	3	4
Understanding	3. My advisor understands what I tell him or her.	1	2	3	4
A clear communicator	4. I understand what my advisor tells me.	1	2	3	4
Thoughtful	5. My advisor knows my situation and does not think of me as a general "type of client."	1	2	3	4
Interested in my well-being	6. I believe that my advisor cares about me (is not just focused on the fees I pay).	1	2	3	4
Open to my ideas	7. My advisor welcomes my questions and discusses them with me.	1	2	3	4
Competent	8. I feel that my advisor is skilled in his or her specialty.	1	2	3	4
Reliable	9. My advisor follows through on the plans we create.	1	2	3	4
Honest	10. My advisor quickly takes responsibility for mistakes or problems.	1	2	3	4
Available	11. My advisor is available when I need him or her.	1	2	3	4

(continued)

Compatible with me	12. I like my advisor as a person.	1	2	3	4
Sub-total for each column:					
Total of the four columns' sub-totals:					
Interpreting your score:					

12 = No trust

13 to 24 = Some trust

25 to 36 = Trust

37 or above = Strong trust

How did you rate your advisor? The higher your score, the better. If your score falls between 20 and 36 you can look at the statements with the low scores and talk with your advisor about your concerns. You can use this Advisor's Trustworthiness tool for all your advisors, not just your financial advisors.

UNDERSTANDING FINANCIAL ADVISOR CREDENTIALS

Rick Schuster recommends that a person considering a financial advisor should review the advisor's credentials carefully. Charles Duhigg counsels that we look for credentials that require "years of study, difficult tests and extensive background checks" of those applying for the credential. You can usually acquire much relevant information on the credentialing authority's website, or you can ask friends or other, already trusted advisors such as lawyers or accountants. Truly qualified *and experienced* advisors will be proud of their background and training. They may have their credentials hanging on the wall and will be happy to describe what stands behind them. They will even encourage you to ask them questions and check their backgrounds.

Here are some excellent sources to help you understand the credentials that financial advisors use:

- AARP has reference material at www.aarp.org. Search for "Understanding Financial Credentials."
- Canadians can find information at www.carp.ca or the Investment Planning Council at www.ipcc.ca.

- You can find a description of many financial industry credentials at the Financial Industry Regulatory Authority's "Understanding Professional Designations" at apps.finra.org/DataDirectory/1/ ProDesignations.aspx. FINRA is as a non-governmental regulator for the securities industry. Their data directory of professional designations is a great resource to use to understand what your financial advisor's credentials mean.

Here is the FINRA description of a Certified Financial Planner:

CFP—Certified Financial Planner	
Designation	Certified Financial Planner
Acronym	CFP
Issuing Organization	Certified Financial Planner Board of Standards
Prerequisites/Experience Required	Candidate must meet *one* of the following requirements: • 3 years of personal financial planning experience and a bachelor's degree, or • 5 years of personal financial planning experience
Educational Requirements	Candidate must complete a CFP-board registered program, or hold one of the following: • CPA • ChFC • Chartered Life Underwriter (CLU) • CFA • Ph.D. in business or economics • Doctor of Business Administration • Attorney's License
Examination Type	• Final certification exam
Continuing Education/Experience Requirements	30 hours every two years
Investor Complaint Process	Online at Submit a Complaint
Public Disciplinary Process	Online at Public Disciplinary Actions
Check Professional's Status Online	Online at Search for a Certified Financial Planner Professional

Source: Financial Industry Regulatory Authority http://apps.finra.org/DataDirectory/1/ProDesignations.aspx.

FINRA specifically prohibits financial professionals registered with FINRA from "referencing nonexistent or self-conferred degrees or designations or referencing legitimate degrees or designations in a misleading manner."

Also be aware that *Financial Analyst, Financial Adviser (Advisor), Financial Consultant, Financial Planner, Investment Consultant* or *Wealth Manager* are generic terms or job titles, and may be used by investment professionals who may or may not hold any specific designation.

When I ask an advisor, any advisor, a question and he or she says, "Trust me," I know that he or she is not answering my question. My response is to open my eyes wider and ask more questions.

THE FINANCIAL ADVISOR SELECTION CHECKLIST

Richard C. Salmen is a senior vice president and senior advisor with GTrust of Topeka, Kansas, which specializes in trust and asset management services (gtrust.com). He is a Certified Financial Planner (CFP®) and is on the national board of directors of the Financial Planning Association (FPA).

Like Rick Schuster, Richard has some good advice about choosing an advisor. He highly recommends that people look for a Certified Financial Planner practitioner when they're looking for a planner, as it is one of the criteria for entry into the profession of financial planning. A CFP designation is awarded by the CFP Board of Standards Inc. (www.cfp.net), which tests and manages the professional standards. According to the CFP Board, "Individuals authorized by the CFP Board to call themselves CFP professionals have completed the established and rigorous education, examination, experience and ethical requirements of the CFP certification process. The CFP Board takes seriously its enforcement of ethical requirements and recently adopted an updated and strengthened set of ethical standards designed to make sure the public has access to ethical financial planning services."

When you look for a qualified financial planner, your best bet is to work with a person who has earned the CFP designation. This does not mean that those without a CFP are to be avoided, but you should question them on what makes them qualified to work with you.

The Financial Planning Association and the Certified Financial Planner Board of Standards Inc. have developed a comprehensive Checklist for Interviewing a Financial Planner which is available in Appendix 2. You can also access this tool online at www.fpanet.org/public/tools/ten-questionschecklist.cfm.

THE FINANCIAL MANAGEMENT TEAM

A truly comprehensive financial plan, as described before by Rick Schuster, covers many more areas than an investment plan can cover. Many areas can be covered well by one professional but other areas may require that you add specialists to your team. Here are eight areas of professional expertise you should include in a team to build and maintain your financial plan.

The Eight Professions that Work Together to Build and Maintain a Comprehensive Financial Retirement Plan

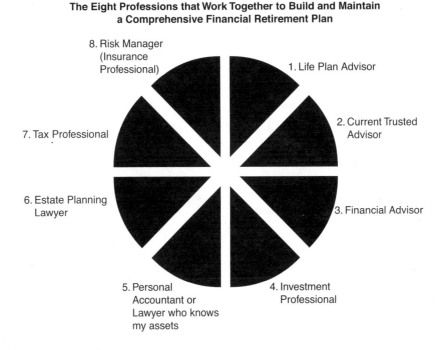

8. Risk Manager (Insurance Professional)
1. Life Plan Advisor
2. Current Trusted Advisor
7. Tax Professional
3. Financial Advisor
6. Estate Planning Lawyer
5. Personal Accountant or Lawyer who knows my assets
4. Investment Professional

Now you may feel that you know your assets and do not need an accountant or lawyer to create a list, or you may enjoy managing your own investments and therefore do not want an investment professional. The purpose of this list is to inform you about what a comprehensive financial retirement team should include. It is your choice how, or if, to include these eight categories. Mostly, I want you to know what is involved.

Here is who each professional may be and what you may want to discuss with them:

1. Life Plan Advisor (spouse, family, friends, clergy, or a psychology professional with a mature life planning practice): *What do I want during my early retirement? What will make me happy?*

2. Current Trusted Advisor (good friend or colleague; current accountant or accounting service, lawyer, banker, life plan advisor, etc.): *How do I find trusted professionals in each area?*

3. Financial Advisor (this person often helps you to find other professionals and manages the process from planning to periodic reviews): *How do I build a plan that will support what I want?*

4. Investment Professional: *How do I invest my assets as my plan guides?*

5. Personal Accountant or Lawyer who knows my assets: *What are all my assets and how do I manage them?*

6. Estate Planning Lawyer: *How do I want my estate to be managed and how do I ensure that it is handled as I want?*

7. Tax Professional: *How do I pay the least amount of taxes for which I am responsible?*

8. Risk Manager (Insurance Professional): *What are my risks and how do I protect my assets against loss?*

What's the Purpose of a Life Plan Advisor?

Chris McDermott, vice president of product development for Fidelity Investments, identified a major problem that occurs when working with customers on their retirement: "They cannot say what they want in retirement or what will make them happy. The typical descriptions are more free time, travel, and family. They can't really define what they need, what's going to make them happy, what they value, what's going to keep them challenged."

Marc Byrnes, chairman of the board and chief executive officer of the Oswald Companies, one of the largest privately held insurance risk management consulting firms dealing in the areas of financial services, employee benefits, property casualty, and retirement plans in North America, considers a person's life plan critical when taking on retirement. As he and I were talking about risk and risk management, he asked, "Are people mentally truly prepared for their own retirement? I ask because that is to me the highest level of risk. And I think many are not, especially those that have served in the military, and top-flight executives and professionals. A lot of them have not done a decent job in emotionally managing their own behavior surrounding the day that they're no longer in charge."

A life plan advisor can help you define what you want and set clear goals for the time beyond work.

There are a number of ways to build your retirement financial management team. One is to identify and check the expertise and credentials of each team member. Another is to choose one person you trust and have him or her recommend the others. The second option is the easiest, and it is likely that this team of professionals has worked together before.

Financial Planning

At the center of your plan, you need a financial advisor or planner to oversee your planning and your regular reviews. At a minimum, you want the financial planner to be in contact with your estate planning lawyer and your tax accountant or service. You should also include your insurance agent or broker as part of the team. The more inter-team communication, the less you need to be responsible for communicating complex information. Your financial advisor should then pass on to you the compiled recommendations.

Should you use an independent financial advisor or work with someone who is part of a larger firm? There is no right answer to this question. I think that the first step is to identify a well-credentialed advisor by talking to people you respect about who they use. An advisor who is part of a firm has more resources directly available and has more oversight. A good independent advisor can be skilled enough to be able to maintain his or her own clients and can typically provide a more customized service. Independent advisors typically have a group or network of expert resources available to provide the services that are outside their areas of expertise. As we saw earlier in this chapter, it is important to confirm that the advisor has valid credentials that have required intensive study, proctored licensing/credentialing exams, continuing education, and adherence to a publicly available code of ethics and standards.

The financial planner I use is part of a small planning and investment firm. A work colleague of my wife recommended him to us. My wife and I worked with him to review our situation and to build a plan based on our needs and desires. He manages our investments, which was our choice. We continue using an accountant who has served us well for the past 25 years, and our insurance agent as well. Our planner referred us to an estate lawyer, who updated our wills and restructured the way we hold some assets to minimize taxes. These are the kinds of services a good financial planner should offer.

Estate Planning

That's about writing a will, right? Every financial planner and accountant I spoke with emphasized the importance of estate planning as you build your financial plans. Estate planning ensures that the assets you have so carefully accumulated over a lifetime do two things:

1. Provide for you if you become disabled, ill, or no longer competent.
2. Ensure your wishes are followed after your death.

Without a well-crafted estate plan you cannot be assured of either. A good estate plan will complement a good financial plan, and a financial plan is incomplete without the estate component covered.

Frank Yunes, a lawyer whose legal practice (www.yunes.org) focuses on the areas of estate planning, estate administration, and corporations, advises that you use a lawyer with a specialty in both tax law and estate law. These are very complicated and always changing areas of the law on which general practitioners find it hard to keep current.

Most of us tend to think of estate planning as preparing a simple will. This is an important part of it but there is more to it, as Frank explained.

> I think that the most valuable commodity an estate planning lawyer can provide is the ability to explain what planning needs to be done and why it needs to be done. It's not a pile of papers that I throw in front of my client and say you need this, this, and this. I want people to walk out of my office understanding why they made the decisions they made, and what they need to look out for on an ongoing basis that might impact their estate in the future. It is as much education as it is legal paperwork.[10]

Frank also explained that estate planning is not just about who gets your stuff when you die. It also protects your interests if you become incapacitated. It is difficult for loved ones to accurately recall what guidelines you want them to follow in such a situation. Even if they do know, the caregivers may not be able to work with the family members if you have not made your wishes clear. Setting out your wishes in a living will or preparing clear directives in your power of attorney for personal care document can prevent your family from arguing among themselves

---

10 Personal interview, July 20, 2007.

about what you might want. Choosing the right health care proxy to make the right decision for you, putting together a living will that sets out your wishes about your end of life and your wishes about extraordinary measures ensures that your thinking is known and respected. I have clients who say, "Hey, pull the plug. I don't want to be a financial burden or emotional burden." I also have some clients who are religious, and they say, "My religion doesn't allow me to say pull the plug, and under no circumstances do I want you to do that." And there are a lot of people in the middle. So out of love for yourself, your spouse, and family, do this planning.

Risk Management

Risk management is the most often overlooked component of financial management. Bob Joyce, chairman and CEO of the Westfield Group (www.westfieldgrp.com), an insurance, banking, and financial services group of businesses, talked to me about various aspects of financial planning and of retirement in general. During our conversation, Bob asked me a question that sparked my interest:

> When was the last time you talked with your insurance agent and reviewed your whole package of insurance? I would tell you that too many accomplished people have not paid enough attention to their personal insurance plans. With property insurance, you have very different sets of risks today than you had 20 years ago. Yet most people have not had a conversation with their agent about what their needs are today. Nor has the agent likely called them.

Bob told me of a friend of his who recently retired, and he and his wife moved from their hometown with mild weather to a coastal town that was susceptible to large storms. When they bought their new house, Bob's friend had budgeted $1,000 annually for homeowners' insurance, the same as he was paying for his midwest weather-safe house. He was shocked when he learned that the estimate to insure his new home was closer to $10,000. Times and needs change.

> What happens if there are mechanical breakdowns, power outages, and those sorts of things in a storm, and backup of sewer and water, how do

you respond to that? Consider flood coverage today and then look at the flood and wind damage of Katrina or the damaging 1998 ice storm in Canada. Too many people take it for granted that this is covered in their insurance policy and have never read it. I have seen too many literally left out in the cold when they read their policies for the first time after the damage is done.

In today's litigious society, you face financial vulnerability. Take identity theft—not a big issue 20 years ago. Older, accomplished people are a desirable target for these crimes. You may be in the right but you still have to pay to defend yourself. God forbid you cause physical injury to someone while you are driving. It is a very expensive proposition.

Simply put, you never know how you are going to lose your money. You may have liability today that can come at you from a lot of different places and unless you've known somebody who's been caught in it, or you've been somewhere where your business has been exposed to it, it's not something you think about.

I asked Bob what a smart retiree should ask his or her insurance agent to confirm that he or she has the right insurance coverage. Bob suggested I speak with Marc Byrnes, chairman and CEO of the Oswald Companies, which provides its clients with insurance-based risk management (www.oswaldcompanies.com). Marc told me that a good agent would be proactive and identify areas their 55-plus clients should consider:

A solid insurance package should include coverage for personal homeowner's liability, automobile and what we call boats, toys, planes and trains—really, any area of potential risk of loss or liability.

As we gather the client's information, we consider their insurance needs as well the other areas that they need professional advice to reduce risk. A good financial plan is a significant risk-reduction tool.

As you assemble your financial management team, keep in mind that what is important is that this team of professionals can work together smoothly and keep your best interests foremost in their minds. The result should be an understandable plan and improved investment performance.

The Best Piece of Advice on Financial Advisors and Planners

John Kimpel is a lawyer and an expert on retirement finances. Here's his advice on looking for an advisor:

> *The best piece of advice to give to somebody looking for an advisor is that if you can't understand what your financial planner is telling you, get a new one. I used to always think, that's how some financial products were sold, by confusing you. And people's ego not allowing them to say, "Well, hell, I don't understand a word you said." Instead, they think, "Well, he or she's showing me all these fancy charts; he or she must know what he or she is talking about." Some prey on your ego, your inability to say, "What? I don't know what you're talking about."*

WORKING WITH YOUR FINANCIAL ADVISOR

Once you begin work with a financial planner, you will be asked many questions about what you want and what you are comfortable doing. You will also have many questions yourself. Many of my clients have stopped working with a financial planner because of a situation like Mary's. Mary, a client for whom I had helped develop a retirement life plan, was a senior tenured professor at a well-known university. For almost 40 years, she had been putting 15 percent of her salary into a university-sponsored retirement savings plan. Now considering retirement, she suspected that she had saved enough money to live in comfort. Off she went to a financial advisor whom a number of colleagues were using. After only three meetings, however, she stopped going. Mary had become frustrated by the advisor's habit of answering "It depends" to every important question she asked:

Q: Will I have enough money to travel?
A: It depends.
Q: Should I sell my home and move to a smaller place?
A: It depends.
Q: Can I help with my granddaughter's college tuition?
A: It depends.

In defense of Mary's advisor, the answers to these questions do depend on Mary's investment plans and her personal goals. On the other hand, her advisor failed to see that Mary needed help in understanding what the "it depends" response really meant. Mary was left feeling that the advisor was not using her expertise to help Mary make decisions; she was just pushing the responsibility back onto Mary.

When you ask a question of your financial advisor and the response you receive is "It depends," you should respond with this question: "It depends on what?" "It depends" is an inelegant way of saying "You have just asked a good question that highlights a decision point that we should explore together." Consider, for example, the question "Can I help with my granddaughter's college tuition?" This depends on a number of factors:

- How much money you will have when your five-year-old granddaughter turns 18?
- Are you thinking of a direct payment to the college or are you thinking about a monthly amount transferred into a savings account for the next 15 years?
- How will this affect your estate plan and what you want to leave to your granddaughter's mother and your other daughter, who does not have a child?

A good financial advisor will tell you that plans depend on a number of interrelated ideas, desires, and goals. The advisor should not leave you to puzzle out the decision yourself, but rather use the opportunity to discuss more broadly what you want and what is important to you. You should always leave a discussion with your financial advisor with more clarity, not more confusion.

The best financial advisors are not only experts in their field; they are also great communicators of complex ideas. Consider Albert Einstein's standard for understanding: "You do not really understand something unless you can explain it to your grandmother." It is your advisor's responsibility to explain the financial concepts to you; it is not your responsibility to understand everything said without explanation. When questions surface, ask; when concerns arise, challenge.

If you are thinking that this all sounds like hard work, you are both correct and wrong. It does require some focused thinking but it is not nearly as hard as you may think; in addition, the payoffs are well worth the effort involved.

ARE YOU CAPABLE OF MANAGING YOUR FINANCIAL DOMAIN?

This chapter has presented a great deal of information that can feel close to overwhelming to many people. The simple approach to creating a financial management strategy is to find that knowledgeable advisor who can guide you through what you need to do.

Also, most people fare well as they move beyond work. Here are some findings from Fidelity Investments' research that confirms what I hear from most accomplished people who have retired: retirement is great.

- Satisfaction and enjoyment in retirement is fairly high, with 49 percent of retirees extremely or very satisfied in retirement overall and 40 percent reporting their retirement to be more enjoyable than expected.
- Seventy-six percent of retirees said they are living fairly or very comfortably.
- Those who find retirement more enjoyable than expected cite a range of positive aspects of retirement, most often the ability to travel (26 percent), freedom (22 percent) and the opportunity to run their own schedule (21 percent).

SUMMARY

In this chapter we looked at

- The idea that financial expertise does not always mean that the expert will be proven right. The advisor should be capable of describing ideas and plans in a manner that you can understand. You need to keep asking questions. Expect to understand.
- How secure finances require more than just a qualified financial advisor's plan. It requires a team of professionals to insure you obtain the results you define in the plan.

Remember, our retirement begins with finances but that is hardly where it ends. Another of Albert Einstein's comments puts it well: "Not everything that can be counted counts and not everything that counts can be counted."

CHAPTER FIVE

THE PHYSICAL DOMAIN

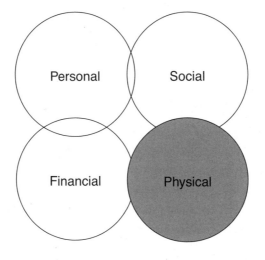

"For every person who claims retirement made their health worse, roughly four retirees maintain that retirement has improved their health."
—George E. Vaillant, M.D.

This observation can't be right, can it? You retire and you get older, yet your health improves? It seems counterintuitive. After all, once you get past 60, isn't aging all about deterioration, the inextricable slide into disability and dependency?

Health issues are often seen as life's "wild card"—an unpredictable factor that causes or influences an outcome. Health issues for someone aging seem even more of a wild card. But new adults are healthier than we believe we are; we are just not as robust as we once were. In this chapter I will challenge the assumptions we have about aging and our health, and provide some ideas and information for managing our health.

How can four out of five retirees feel healthier? As they approach retirement they are concerned about "getting older"—about losing physical and mental functioning. But when they actually retire, many find that there is no precipitous drop in their functioning and that their more comfortable pace of life, combined with more time to focus on their physical and mental self, actually improves their view of their health.

The concerns we have about aging stem from assumptions we make about it. As American author and speaker Marilyn Ferguson commented, "Of all the self-fulfilling prophecies in our culture, the assumption that aging means decline and poor health is probably the deadliest."

John Rowe and Robert Kahn, in their book *Successful Aging*, report on the findings of their 10-year MacArthur Foundation Study of Aging in America. They set out to study what enables people to "preserve and even enhance their mental and physical vitality later in life":

> *Older men and women are sensitive, sometimes overly sensitive, to any sign that they may be losing functional capabilities. Every lapse— misplaced car keys or a forgotten name—brings to mind the looming fear of Alzheimer's disease. But the MacArthur Foundation research has three reassuring messages on the subject of maintaining functioning in old age: First, many of the fears about functional loss are exaggerated; second, much functional loss can be prevented; and third, many functional losses can be regained.[1]*

If the authors of *Successful Aging* are right, many of the assumptions held by people aged 55 to 70 about losing their functional abilities are at least exaggerated, if not just plain wrong.

CHALLENGING OUR ASSUMPTIONS ABOUT AGING

Let's begin by finding out what *you* think about aging. Take this simple true/false test.[2]

---

1 John W. Rowe, M.D., and Robert L. Kahn, Ph.D., *Successful Aging* (New York: Pantheon Books, 1998), p. 42.
2 Used with permission of the author, Susan Nilsson-Weiskott.

Circle true or false in response to each statement.

1.	Memory loss is a natural part of growing old.	True	False
2.	Heredity plays a big role in aging—I will age in the same way my parents do or did.	True	False
3.	Personality development is mostly complete in childhood and finished by early adulthood; few changes can take place after that.	True	False
4.	By and large, older adults are stubborn, set in their ways and have no flexibility.	True	False
5.	Moving out of active involvement in society is a natural adjustment to advancing age.	True	False
6.	The more we ignore aging, i.e., don't admit our real age and make cosmetic changes, the better off we are.	True	False
7.	People die of old age.	True	False

This set of questions is used by psychologist Susan Nilsson-Weiskott in her work with older adults. She uses this test to start a talk with them about their beliefs of what aging is and what it isn't.

> We talk about aging, because it is fear, denial and anxiety that keep people from doing the things that would actually help make a difference. This creates a self-fulfilling prophecy: "Oh, well, I'll get old, and I won't be able to do anything," so you don't do anything, because you're "getting old." It's the old, "Oh, my hip hurts, I'm getting too old." I respond by saying, "Your other hip is the same age, and it doesn't hurt. Maybe it's not age. Maybe it's that you've got a problem with your hip."[3]

One of Susan's specialties is working with new adults who are having difficulty adjusting to the realities of their new age. When she runs groups, she has the participants answer the seven true/false questions above and then discusses the results. Susan estimates that most people get two to

---

3 Personal interview, July 22, 2007.

three questions wrong and that very few provide all correct answers. The answers to these seven questions are all false. Conventional wisdom provides the reasons many believe they are true:

1. Why did I come into this room?
2. I figure that I will live into my early 80s, just like my parents did.
3. You can't teach an old dog new tricks.
4. The older you get, the more set in your ways you get.
5. What? I don't hear as well as I used to.
6. Seventy is the new 50, and I look 50.
7. My goal is to die of old age.

These harmless ideas and sayings may describe some of the people some of the time, but they do not describe all of the people even some of the time. The last one is just plain wrong: no one dies of "old age."

AGING VERSUS OLD AGE

The term "old age" is a remnant of an old reality, when aging was considered the equivalent of debilitation. It has often been used to refer to everyone in their 70s through their 90s. Today, aging is thought of in two ways: aging and senescence.[4] Senescence is the process of growing older and showing the effects of age. Aging is the simple count of years from date of birth; it is a fixed number that is not changed by your health status. Senescence, however, is a highly variable assessment of your functional abilities, which can vary widely due to your health status. For simplicity, I will refer to senescence as the effect of your chronological aging on how well you function.

"Old age," therefore, is an out-of-date term that incorrectly uses your chronological age to describe the impact of your aging on your ability to function. You have probably heard someone say, or said yourself, "She is young for her age." This phrase at least separates out the chronological and functional ages, but it makes a negative assumption about our capacities when we get older. It is akin to another outdated phrase, "She is a credit to her race," which acknowledges the person's abilities while

4 Rowe and Kahn, *Successful Aging*, p. 208.

diminishing her racial forebears. For the young-for-her-age person, it would be better to say something like, "She's eighty and she still beats me at tennis."

So if old age does not automatically encompass everyone in their 70s through 90s, what does it refer to? I searched through the research and could not find an adequate definition until I came across the following quote by Rowe and Kahn in their report of the MacArthur Foundation study: "Older people, like younger ones, want to be independent. This is the principal goal of many elders and few issues strike greater fear than the prospect of depending on others for the most basic daily needs."[5] By implication, then, "old age" refers to a loss of function and the dreaded *loss of independence*. Have you or someone you know had to take away an aging parent's car? If so, you know the visceral fear of dependency. Each time independence diminishes, the person feels diminished. This, I believe, is what transforms "aging" into "old age."

It is likely that you are either considering retirement or have retired within the past few years. So old age is not even on the horizon, but it is interesting that today old age is looked at as a functional state and not a chronological landmark. I am sure that you have known people who developed a debilitating illness or experienced a trauma in their life, and they seem to have aged ten years in a month. They suddenly enter old age—that is, they begin to depend on others for what before their illness or trauma they could do themselves.

It is difficult to shake the ideas of aging that we have and not build up expectations of loss and disability. You can always find someone to support any of Susan Nilsson-Weiskott's seven incorrect ideas of aging. You can also look for examples of people who challenge old assumptions about the new adulthood.

IMPROVE YOUR HEALTH BY MANAGING YOUR EXPECTATIONS

Dan Cashman is a good example of a new adult who both challenges the assumptions of aging and manages his expectations about his new adulthood.

---

5 Rowe and Kahn, p. 42.

I never thought that I'd still be playing basketball with a bunch of guys who are now in their 60s. I mean, how ridiculous is that? When we started, we didn't know each other. We started playing together in our mid-30s, almost 30 years ago. But we had a guy on the court playing with us who was 50 years old. We could not believe it. A guy was still playing at 50! Now, we have a whole group of guys, and not one of them is under 50—the youngest is 54 or 55. We've all slowed the game down together, but the competition is as intense.

We play on Sundays at this huge court where there are younger guys playing too. We stay away from these guys. Playing with them would make us nuts; it would be no fun. I would feel like I was in a track meet. I would just get to one end of a full court; I'd think I was in a different time zone. I'd probably hurt myself. The idea is to finish so you can go have beer, not to get hurt.

Playing a good competitive game of basketball on Sundays is the triumph of optimism over realism. So, optimistically, will I be playing ball when I'm 80? Probably not. I don't think I'll even be playing golf at 80. But we're very active in the workout and try to take care of ourselves—except when we eat corned beef sandwiches and potato chips. On the other hand, three guys have been diagnosed with cancer at one time or another and they are still playing . . . So who knows?[6]

As well as challenging the assumptions about older people (they are "too old" to play basketball), Dan Cashman's story highlights the realistic expectations he has for his game—he does not play with the younger guys because he knows their game is too fast-paced for him and that he wouldn't be able to keep up—and might even get hurt. The reality, as Dan Cashman knows, is that unless you are quite a remarkable 65-year-old, if you attempt to ride a bike, solve a problem, or even have sex the way you did when you were 35, *you will fail*. And it is therefore your choice to fail.

We cannot turn back time, but we can certainly be a great bike rider, solve difficult problems, and have enjoyable sex. We can do these things if we use what we have to the fullest extent. We can even improve over

---

6 Personal interview, January 15, 2007.

our 40-year-old self's performance. Biking can be more enjoyable when you have the time to do it, and you can still compete if you choose and be faster than your peers. New adulthood problem solving is much more effective, since we can bring our experience into play and use our "knowledge shortcuts" to quickly narrow the volume of options to the best few. Sex, well, sex is really up to you. Many couples have told me that they know each other well, enjoy the lack of time pressure, and don't worry about being interrupted by the kids. Sex can become more of a pleasure than just an act. Is 35-year-old sex better than 65-year-old sex, or is it just different?

Right now, I expect that a good number of readers are rolling their eyes, thinking, "Here it is: reduce your expectations to increase your satisfaction. That defeatist approach to life stinks." If you recoil at the idea of managing your expectations to enjoy more of life, I suggest that you skip this section. But before you do, let me tell you about my aunt Adele.

My 80-year-old aunt, Adele Shectman, is a visual artist. I have many of her watercolors displayed around my home and office. She is, as you would expect, a very visual person. About ten years ago, she was diagnosed with macular degeneration, which is the leading cause of severe vision loss in people 60 years of age or older. There is currently no cure to improve vision loss from macular degeneration, but appropriate treatment can slow future vision loss in some people who have the disease.

When I attended the 65th anniversary of my aunt's marriage to my uncle Sid, I asked Adele about her eyes. Her response: "Billy, I am so happy that the progression is slow. I have lost vision in one eye and the doctors tell me that the progression in my other eye is slow. I enjoy what I see more today than I have before. I am blessed."

Here is a visual person losing her eyesight and she talks about her life using words like "happy," "enjoy," and "blessed." In the same way, Dan Cashman knows very well that his basketball games are "competitive" and "intense." These are not defeatist or even compromising people. They expect, and demand, the best from themselves.

You can choose to manage your expectations and be happier, or you can decide that your 20-year-old view of your capabilities is what you should continue to aspire to. As they say about the dinosaurs, they could not adapt and they died. Your subjective measures of health have as much to do with your expectations as your actual physical functioning does.

Three Rules of Expectation Management

"If a young man forgets his hat after a party, nothing is said about it.
But if an older man forgets his hat, people say,
ah, yes, he's losing his mind."
—Samuel Johnson

The first rule of managing expectations is "Don't look back," except to enjoy the memories and recall the lessons learned. If you build an expectation on what you used to be, you will not see what is, and you will lose whatever was. Respect who you are today and don't long for the person you were 20 years ago. If you do, you will make yourself unhappy by choice.

Rule number two is "Look ahead." Aging is scary when you are ignorant of the future. Learn about the future and you will reduce your fears. Learn what the future can hold and how people like you have learned to enjoy it. Talk with others in the know, people who have retired a few years before you. Find out what they have learned and what they would do differently. Discover how they have fun and what makes them happy. Talk with the winners, the people who appear to be enjoying themselves, and learn from them. Also, learn the baselines: what can you expect physically as you age? Talk with your doctor and read what you can. Fight assumptions with facts.

Rule number three is "Get past negative assumptions." The more you learn, the fewer assumptions you will have. We tend to suffer from our assumptions. They can create an expectation that things will be worse than they may actually be, causing us to feel pain and worry when there is no need, resulting in a loss of enjoyment and competence. Assumptions can also raise expectations so that even a good result can feel bad if it does not match our high expectation.

Assumptions also play an important, positive role in managing expectations. When you understand that an idea you have may not be based on facts and clear thinking, it can motivate you to explore the topic more. Assumptions can therefore stimulate critical thinking, as well as kill it.

Managing Expectations about Aging

1. Don't look back.
2. Look ahead.
3. Get past negative assumptions.

INCREASE YOUR LIFE SATISFACTION BY MANAGING YOUR EXPECTATIONS

A study examining life satisfaction and positive emotions was undertaken by Errol Hamarat of Georgia State University. The findings describe how our Western culture views the new adulthood.

> *Old age has been described as a time of physical, cognitive and social loss, and ageism. Most Americans view old age negatively and believe that aging makes people unattractive, unintelligent, asexual, unemployable and senile. In spite of these conditions and beliefs, many older adults report that they are happier, experience fewer stressful events, and have fewer negative emotions than do their younger counterparts. In fact, old age [new adulthood] is reported by many as a time of elevated satisfaction, marked by the pursuit of new endeavors and an increase in meaningful relationships.*[7]

The Hamarat study goes on to state "that for healthy adults, the oldest old (75 years and older) cope at least as effectively as their younger counterparts (45 to 64), despite their likelihood of encountering increased levels of stress, and psychologically, old age may be viewed as a time of resilience and fortitude."[8]

The study also provides a partial explanation for this sustained coping ability as being due to a shift in the new adult's priorities and satisfactions. It states that adults

> *cope with changes with age as a gradual style shift from an assimilative or tenacious goal pursuit [a hallmark of our 20s – 50s] to an accommodative or flexible, way of coping [our new adulthood]. Although tenacity in pursuing goals is likely a beneficial attribute for younger adults, flexibility permits the older person to successfully adapt to the inevitable losses of old age without sacrificing satisfaction with life.*[9]

---

7 Errol Hamarat, "Age Differences in Coping Resources and Satisfaction with Life Among Middle-aged, Young-old, and Oldest-old Adults." *Journal of Genetic Psychology* (2002), 163(3), p. 360, Heldref Publications.
8 Hamarat, p. 360.
9 Hamarat, p. 362.

The ability to manage our health and to cope with health issues as they arrive provides us with a sense of control over our future health that ultimately increases our satisfaction with life. Life satisfaction is one of the main ingredients in our assessment of our well-being and quality of life. How satisfied are you with your life?

DEFINING SUBJECTIVE WELL-BEING

"Most folks are about as happy as they make up their minds to be."
—Abraham Lincoln

Ed Diener and his co-authors at the University of Illinois at Urbana-Champaign describe *subjective well-being* as "how people evaluate their lives" and explain that it "includes variables such as life satisfaction and marital satisfaction, lack of depression and anxiety, and positive moods and emotions."[10] The authors go on to describe well-being as a combination of thoughts and feelings. The thoughts occur when a person judges his or her satisfaction with life as a whole, as well as specific aspects of life. An example of a specific thought is "I just had dinner. Was it a good meal?" Feelings then modify what we think: "Did I enjoy that meal?" "Enjoyment" doesn't just apply to the food itself but to the circumstances surrounding the meal. I am sure that you can recall a time when you had bad food and a good time. While having good food and a good time is the preferred experience, a good time can forgive bad food. Good food, however, cannot mask a bad time.

Diener and his colleagues go on to explain that people have "high subjective well-being when they experience life satisfaction and frequent joy, and only infrequently experience unpleasant emotions such as sadness and anger. A person is said to have low subjective well-being if he or she is dissatisfied with life, experiences little joy and affection, and frequently feels negative emotions such as anger or anxiety. The

---

10 Ed Diener, Eunkook Suh, and Shigehiro Oishi, "Recent Findings on Subjective Well-Being," University of Illinois (1997), http://www.psych.uiuc.edu/~ediener/hottopic/paper1.html.

thoughts and feeling components of subjective well-being are highly interrelated."[11]

Subjective well-being is defined as your internal experience. How you measure your own well-being is for you to determine. I could say that by all objective measures you should be feeling pretty good, or pretty bad, about your life, but that is not relevant. Facts are not relevant except when they affect your thoughts. Thus you feel good about your life if you feel good about your life.

How else would you explain Eugene O'Kelly's response to his cancer? In 2005, O'Kelly was 53 years old and chairman and CEO of KPMG, one of the largest accounting firms in the United States. That year, he received a diagnosis of late-stage brain cancer with a prognosis of three to six *months* to live:

> *I didn't have a summer to adjust. I barely had a summer, period. I would need to make the quickest, most dramatic costume change of my life. If I was going to emerge from the misery of my condition and somehow make something positive from it, I would have to do it fast and efficiently—and get it right the first time.[12]*

Near the end, Eugene O'Kelly told a friend, "I've had a great life."

I hope that I will be able to be that noble as I die. I hope that I will have had a life of high subjective well-being so that I can understand and appreciate that "I had a good life."

I urge people with a major illness to read O'Kelly's book, *Chasing Daylight*, to learn what they can do to help themselves. I also urge people who are ruled by their dark and negative thoughts to read the book to learn what they might do to improve their subjective well-being.

How can you know if your subjective well-being is positive or negative? Here is a tool you can use to measure your life satisfaction:

---

11 Diener, Suh, and Oishi, "Recent Findings on Subjective Well-Being."
12 Eugene O'Kelly, *Chasing Daylight: How My Forthcoming Death Transformed My Life* (New York: McGraw-Hill, 2006), p. 45.

Measuring Subjective Well-Being

Satisfaction with Life Scale

Using the 1–7 scale below, indicate your level of agreement with each of the five items by placing the appropriate number on the line preceding that item. Please be open and honest in your responding.

7 Strongly agree
6 Agree
5 Slightly agree
4 Neither agree nor disagree
3 Slightly disagree
2 Disagree
1 Strongly disagree

1. _____ In most ways my life is close to my ideal.
2. _____ The conditions of my life are excellent.
3. _____ I am satisfied with my life.
4. _____ So far, I have gotten the important things I want in life.
5. _____ If I could live my life over, I would change almost nothing.

Total your scores and compare your score to this subjective well-being scoring template:

31–35	Extremely satisfied	15–19	Slightly dissatisfied
26–30	Satisfied	10–14	Dissatisfied
21–25	Slightly satisfied	5–9	Extremely dissatisfied
20	Neutral		

Source: Diener, Suh, and Oishi, "Recent Findings on Subjective Well-Being."

Is your subjective well-being score consistent or inconsistent with your thoughts about yourself? Does this information support, modify, or change your expectations for healthy aging? If you are not happy with your score, I recommend that you take this scale and your results to a trusted personal advisor to discuss. Help is available, and it begins by asking for that help.

IS HEALTH A WILD CARD OR MANAGEABLE?

Wild card: an unexpected occurrence or an unpredictable factor that causes or influences an outcome.

We are all beset with health problems, whether acute or chronic, hereditary or accidental. We can approach this reality in one of two ways. We can live our life, hoping that we dodge the bullet(s) as best as possible, or we can actively manage our health so that there are fewer and less damaging bullets. I think the best approach is a combination of the two. Health problems are a wild card in retirement, but actively managing your health and health problems reduces their negative impact. Just ask Jerry Nilsson-Weiskott, husband and business partner of psychologist Susan Nilsson-Weiskott.

On January 17th I thought I had a heart attack. I was flying to Florida on business, for a two-day seminar. I was on the plane and my chest felt like an elephant was sitting on it. My arm went numb and I was sweating profusely—all the signs I had heard about.

What did I do? I went to work. I got off the plane, did my keynote address and my seminar for the next two days, then drove from Cape Canaveral to Sarasota, picked up my wife Susan at the airport and said, "Before we go to visit these friends and do these other two days of seminars, I think I need to go to the hospital."

My wife told me I was an idiot for waiting so long, and I had to agree. We got to the hospital and they immediately ran heart attack tests—they took it very seriously. It turned out I had a virus that had attacked my chest wall. They gave me a cortisone shot right into my chest wall. The doctors told me that I have a very healthy heart, but that I have something called costochondritis, an inflammation of the chest wall.

My advice to others? Get a physical, and really make sure that you're preventing as much as you possibly can, rather than being reactionary.

My plan is to live till 90 at least. Since my "episode," I think I'm doing a better job of taking care of myself. But as importantly, since my wake-up call I have more things that excite me; I enjoy life more. And I really do think that that's part of what gives people some of that longevity; they have passion that makes life worth living.

Jerry told me that as a result of his heart experience, he has moved his retirement planning from a second-tier priority to the first tier. Nothing drastic has changed, but he and Susan have put dates to their retirement ideas, they are looking at how best to manage the future of their business, and they no longer take their health for granted: it is now a top priority.

You can affect your health before it affects you. You can actively manage your health, or you can wait and see. Which approach you choose has less to do with your physical health and more to do with who you are. As a successful new adult, actively managing your health is the preferable option. All you need to know is how to do it well.

MANAGING YOUR HEALTH

> *"Be careful about reading health books.*
> *You may die of a misprint."*
> —Mark Twain

What does it mean to actively manage your health? First, it does not mean complete adherence to a specific health regime. While perfect health maintenance is an honorable expectation, I have seen it make people anxious, dull, rigid, and non-compliant. Reducing high-risk behaviors and following a middle-of-the-road self-care plan can dramatically increase your current and future health.

The answer to how to actively manage your health is relatively simple. First, take care of yourself. I expect that you know this information, but it bears repeating:

1. Know your physical and emotional weak spots.
2. No smoking.
3. Be thoughtful about what you eat, and eat well.
4. Watch your weight.
5. Exercise regularly.
6. Drink alcohol moderately or not at all.
7. No illicit or non-prescribed drugs.
8. Balance your life.
9. Taking a multivitamin is encouraged. (Check with your doctor to confirm this idea for you.)
10. Protect yourself from the sun.
11. Work with your chosen doctor or dentist and have regular contact.
12. Build a social network of healthy people.

Your Health Risk Profile

Managing Your Health Begins with Good Information
Many doctors and researchers recommend the Harvard University School of Public Health's "Your Disease Risk" tool to provide you with your individual risk profile and information on the nature of your risks. This online tool is available at www.yourdiseaserisk.wustl.edu. www.yourdiseaserisk.wustl.edu. or http://www.yourdiseaseriskindex.harvard.edu/.

The most important single choice you will make to manage your health is your choice of your primary care physician. Managing your health also means finding the best doctor who is affiliated with the best hospital in your area. You may prefer a doctor who does his or her work without explaining what will be done, but most people prefer to know what is planned and why. Many doctors view educating their patients about health management as an important part of their work.

There is an overwhelming amount of information available on the Internet to help you select the best doctor, as well as find up-to-date information. Among sites I found to be comprehensive and understandable are those of the U.S. National Institutes of Health, National Institute on Aging (http://www.nia.nih.gov), WebMD (www.webmd.com), and AARP (www.aarp.org). In addition, see Appendix 3 for a list of suggested questions to ask when selecting a doctor.

A Good Doctor Works Best with a Good Patient

Good doctors can do only as well as their patients allow. You can invest time and energy into finding a good doctor only to learn that you are not a good patient. Consider your responsibility for successful health care.

The August 24, 2006, issue of the *New England Journal of Medicine* carried an article by Dr. Robert Steinbrook about personal responsibility for health. It included this on what makes a good patient:

> *The concept of personal responsibility in health care is that if we [the patient] follow healthy lifestyles (exercising, maintaining a healthy weight, and not smoking) and are good patients (keeping our appointments, heeding our physicians' advice, and using a hospital emergency department only for emergencies), we will be rewarded by feeling better and spending less money.*[13]

13 Robert Steinbrook, M.D., "Imposing Personal Responsibility for Health," *New England Journal of Medicine*, 355 (8), August 24, 2006, p. 754.

Notice that in Dr. Steinbrook's brief description of the patient's responsibility for his or her health care, there is no mention of always agreeing with the doctor or any other passive acceptance. A good patient is engaged with his or her doctor, agreeing with what makes sense and questioning what appears odd or counterproductive.

Maintaining personal responsibility and taking prescribed medications are part of being a good patient. Just as you want a good doctor with a good "bedside manner," the doctor wants a patient with good patient manners. In an article titled "How to Talk with Your Doctor," the AARP provides information on what people can do to hold up their end of the doctor-patient relationship.

> *Your relationship with your doctor, including how well you talk with each other, affects your care. A good relationship—where you and your doctor share information and work together to make the best decisions about your health—will result in the best care. You'll also feel more confident in your doctor and the quality of care you're getting.*

This article has other recommendations for building a good relationship with your doctor. You can read the whole four-page article on the AARP website: www.aarp.org/health/staying_healthy/prevention/a2003-03-13-talkdr.html.

HEALTH INSURANCE IN THE UNITED STATES

> *"My doctor gave me six months to live, but when I couldn't pay the bill he gave me six months more."*
> —Walter Matthau

I would be remiss if I did not talk about health insurance. In the United States what to do about health insurance is a major open question that people face. Your health insurance policy is the gatekeeper of your medical plan. What your insurance will pay, if anything, for some procedures can significantly influence your health care decisions.

It would take an entire book just to cover the topic of new adulthood health insurance. I am not the person to write that book. In my research, I tried to understand the best options for health care coverage and I came up empty. I did learn that it is up to you to find the best coverage that is available to you, at a cost you can afford. This is made very difficult by the interplay of state and federal laws, Medicare rules, confusing insurance industry language and varied employer policies. My research came up with very few professionals expert enough in this area to advise you. Frankly, our health insurance situation in the United States is disgraceful. The US could learn from Canada, the Commonwealth countries and Western Europe where everyone has basic coverage. While not perfect, these systems offer a comfort level unknown by most in the States. When talking with Canadians about their health care, I was startled by their calm and secure feelings about their care as they age. Quite the opposite of the US citizen I spoke with. In Canada, people may have to wait longer for a knee replacement or other scheduled procedures, while their preventive, standard and critical care is very good, timely, and dependable. Unfortunately, in the US health care is not only a political issue but is a major concern for people preparing for, and in retirement.

The Commonwealth Fund, "a private foundation that aims to promote a high performing health care system" (www.commonwealthfund. org), has published a survey of older adults that explores the extent and quality of health insurance coverage for baby boomers. The survey's emphasis is on the impact of health care on people who have low or moderate incomes, but the baseline data can be of use to compare your health care costs with those of others.

The survey found that "in the United States older adults with low income, with individual coverage, or with no insurance spend substantial shares of their income on coverage and health care.

- **Premiums.** More than half (55 percent) of older adults with coverage on the individual market spend $300 or more per month, or $3,600 or more annually, on premiums. In contrast, only 16 percent of older adults with employer coverage spend in excess of $3,600 per year on premiums. Nearly two of five insured working older adults with household incomes under $40,000 spend 5 percent or more of their income on premiums, and nearly one quarter (23 percent) spend 10 percent or more. More than three of five (62 percent) older adults with individual coverage said that it was very or somewhat difficult to afford their premiums compared with about one quarter (26 percent) of those with employer coverage.
- **Deductibles.** Nearly half (48 percent) of older adults with individual coverage have per-person annual deductibles of $1,000 or higher, despite

their higher premiums. In comparison, about 8 percent of older adults with employer coverage face deductibles of $1,000 or more per year.

- **Out-of-pocket costs.** Thirty-eight percent of uninsured older adults and 37 percent of older adults with coverage through the individual market spent $1,000 or more per year on out-of-pocket health care costs, including prescription drugs. In contrast, 21 percent of older adults with employer coverage spent $1,000 or more. Older adults in low- and moderate-income working households are also more likely to spend a large share of their income on out-of-pocket costs than are those in higher-income households."[14]

The first consideration when buying health insurance is to learn what your doctor recommends regarding coverage for problems that your risk factors flag. The second is to learn what your coverage options and costs are, and what will actually be covered. You are in a much better position to modify coverage before you need it. Third, locate a non-commissioned advisor who can work with you to make your decisions. Look to your trusted advisors for recommendations in this area. This is an important part of your financial plan.

If you have no coverage options available, you will have to buy your own policy. Find out from a doctor what you can expect to pay for routine health care and also what he or she recommends for coverage based on your health care risks. Then locate a policy that will cover what you need and buy a high-deductible policy that will have you pay for your routine care yourself while protecting you from treatment costs for major problems. Build this expense into your financial plan.

FEELING OLD VERSUS FEELING OUR AGE

We have looked at our incorrect assumptions of aging and the issues of managing our health, but what do we actually face? What is our physical domain's future? A good place to start is with a medical doctor who can give us an accurate picture of what physiological changes we will face as we age.

Feeling Age: What Do We Feel and Why?

What does aging feel like to the new adult and why? I asked this question of Dr. Bruce Cohen, professor of psychiatry, Harvard Medical School.

---

14 S. R. Collins, K. Davis, C. Schoen, M. M. Doty, and J. L. Kriss, Health Coverage for Aging Baby Boomers: Findings from the Commonwealth Fund Survey of Older Adults, The Commonwealth Fund, Januray 2006.

BR: *What does it feel like to age, and why?*

DR. COHEN: *As you get older, you lose cells in the brain, but what everybody notices is that they lose energy. And the brain is particularly compromised when you lose energy because it requires ten times as much energy to function as the average of the entire body. It's a very energy-expensive endeavor to run a brain, and one of the parts of your body that does not do well with age is called mitochondria. These are the little parts in cells that do what is called oxidative phosphorylation.*

These particular parts of the cell, the mitochondria, are what produce most of your energy. When you breathe in oxygen, the oxygen is used by the mitochondria to finish burning the sugar that you've eaten. The mitochondria burn the oxygen, leaving carbon dioxide, which you then exhale.

Think of this as a little mitochondrial engine in the cells. It's an energy-producing device in there. The mitochondria get damaged with age because they're producing toxic byproducts in part. They get gummed up. In making energy, burning the oxygen, parts of each mitochondria also get oxidized, so, if you will, they "rust." That's why they tell you that antioxidants will extend your life and your tissue health. It works to a degree, but it's not enough. The mitochondria still get broken.

BR: *If I have followed your line of thinking correctly, you are saying that as we age our body produces less energy, and that has a direct effect on the brain because it's such a large consumer of energy.*

DR. COHEN: *Yes. One of the reasons people feel that with age they get physically weaker in their muscles is that they can't produce energy the same way. It's not the only factor, but it's one factor. Physiologically our bodies have less energy available to them—it's not just a feeling. The mitochondria aren't as efficient; they're not as good at making energy. That's one factor that's making you feel more tired, and making you feel less strong, and making your brain not work as efficiently.*

BR: *What is it like to age?*

DR. COHEN: *It's around age 60 that people start to seriously notice change in muscle power. Now consider George Forman. When he was still boxing, competing successfully in his 50s, I remember wondering: How long can you box and be at the top of your game? The answer seems to be that you can do it until you're 50 years old. It's going to fail you in your 50s, because you're going to be slower in blocking the punch or making your punch. That's because you can't react as quickly, and you can't react as quickly because you do slow down, and your nerves slow down in the passage and processing of information. You're not going to be as strong as you get into your 50s, and by the time you're 60 you're going to notice that.*

We also begin to notice that we can't multi-task as well as we used to. When I was young, and I was giving a lecture or having a conversation like this, I was thinking about five things at once. I now think about maybe three things at once. Twenty years ago, I could literally have taken this conversation in five directions and been able to manage all of them. So you do lose. But doing three or two things at once, you are still more than functional.

Having patience helps a lot. If you make an older person do a test under a time constraint, they will not do as well as a younger person. But if you take off the time constraint, they can do as well as or better than younger people with most intellectual tasks until they become very old.

One of the ways of dealing with these changes is to rethink what time means to you. You can honor the change in your body and give yourself more time to do things. Two very important people in history commented on aligning your goals with your capabilities. Sigmund Freud said, in essence, that if you set yourself up to do things you can't do, you'll fail and you'll be unhappy. And much, much before Freud ever said it, the Buddha said, if you want things you can't have, if you try to control things you can't control, you will just create suffering.

If I don't set myself up to have to do more than I can handle as I get older, I'm likely to be happier. Instead of being involved in ten research projects, why shouldn't I be involved in five or three, or one, depending on how old I get to be? Similarly, if you're going to read or solve the crossword puzzle or whatever you're going to do, give yourself a little extra time, and don't make it compete with a lot of other things, because you're not going to balance as many things in your head.

The truth is that you are going to lose muscle strength, you're going to lose visual acuity, you're going to lose acuity of your hearing. Your remembrances are going to slow down, so you have to find the balance. Find things to do in life that keep you exercising your muscles, and exercising your mind. But if there are things that frustrate you, you're not going to do them, so choose activities that you enjoy.

Other changes occur that frustrate many people. Our ability to handle sugars changes, our storage of fat changes, and of course you're quite aware of skin changes and hair changes. There are probably similar changes in the processing of spatial information. I'm not talking about dementia. I'm talking about people having more trouble learning a new neighborhood, just as they have more trouble learning new words. They may be slower in orienting themselves; they may more easily get lost when they're walking or driving, to small degrees.

As Dr. Cohen makes clear, changes occur as we age that, for the most part, we cannot stop. We can, however, choose how we respond to these changes, and we can manage our expectations.

THE FACTS ON AGING

Let's look at what research has found about the physical effects of aging.

- Less than 5 percent of the population over 65 years old dies each year. This translates into 4,050 deaths per 100,000 people over 65 in a given year. The six leading causes of death for this segment of the population are heart disease, cancer, stroke, chronic obstructive pulmonary diseases, pneumonia and influenza, and diabetes.[15]
- Living to the age of 90 is not the exception that it once was. The life expectancy for a person who is 65 is another 17.8 years, or 83 years old. If you live to be 83, you have a good chance of living to 91, or another 6.2 years. Northwestern Mutual Life provides a life expectancy calculator you may want to try on its website: http://www. nmfn.com/tn/learnctr-lifeevents-longevity.

---

15 National Vital Statistics System, Center for Disease Control.

- According to research conducted and reported by Dr. George Vaillant in his book *Aging Well*, there are six common variables that most of us incorrectly believe to be predictors of healthy aging. Dr. Vaillant also lists seven factors that do predict healthy aging.

Following is a summary of Dr. Vaillant's variables and factors as presented in his book.

Here are the six variables that were *shown not to predict* healthy aging:

1. The longevity of your parents
2. High cholesterol
3. Stress
4. Parental characteristics
5. Childhood temperament
6. Ease with social relationships[16]

These variables continue to affect your well-being, just not your healthy aging.

The seven variables that were *shown to predict* healthy aging:

1. No heavy smoking
2. No alcohol abuse
3. Stable marriage
4. Some exercise
5. Not overweight
6. Adaptive coping styles (mature defenses)—how you manage problems and anxiety
7. Years of education—more years of education can increase longevity[17]

Does this information challenge your thinking about how many people die after age 65, life expectancy, physical aging, and predictors of healthy aging?

THE "YOU HAVE ..." MOMENT

We do not die of old age, but ultimately we do die of something. You may live into your healthy 90s but if you contract the flu, which triggers pneumonia, you could be dead in a month. You can also

---

16 George Vaillant, *Aging Well* (New York: Little, Brown and Company, 2002), pp. 203–211.
17 Ibid., p. 203–213

contract cancer at 72 and be dead within a year. Many of us may also develop a chronic disease that creates degrees of disability (diabetes, heart disease, or manageable types of cancer) and live 10 or more good years.

I know as I age, each visit to the doctor is accompanied with the worry that the appointment will end with that dreaded statement, "I am sorry to tell you this but the tests confirm that you have (insert your own personal disease fear), but we have many treatment options available."

My own "You have" moment came early. I was 43 when I was told that I had atherosclerosis, hardening of the arteries. This basically meant that my arteries are prone to collecting cholesterol, which can either clog an artery and cause a heart attack or break off in small pieces and cause a stroke. This simple statement "You have atherosclerosis" was shocking but not surprising. At age 45, my father had died of a heart attack. With the medical advances since his death in 1959, he would probably have survived today. Learning that I had the same disease that killed my father was not a surprise; since I was nine years old I had believed that I would die as my father did. This diagnosis just confirmed my beliefs. I was, however, shocked. It's one thing to carry a death sentence mentality; it's another to have that idea confirmed.

At 43, I believed I was about to die—to widow my wife and abandon my son. I was not taking the diagnosis well. As time passed and I lived past my father's age of death, I survived several physical challenges, and my health actually improved. I learned that my doctors had pardoned me and my death was not imminent. However, I do believe that someday I will die of this disease.

Fifteen years after first learning of my health situation, I have had two heart attacks, four stents inserted, and a quadruple by-pass. At age 57, I feel pretty good and I am thankful for the earlier diagnosis, excellent emergency care, remarkable medications, and, most of all, a great team of doctors. At my most recent checkup, my cardiologist told me that I am in "excellent health."

I know that my health status is excellent for a 57-year-old man with my health history. I comply with 90 percent of my doctors' recommendations. I am perennially 10 pounds overweight, which I consider not too bad for a person who loves to cook and eat. I am not the youngest 57-year-old in my neighborhood, which is an assessment of my health status compared with my number of years on this earth. I am also not the oldest.

Since my heart problems surfaced, I have been dogged by the "Why me?" question, and I began to take a fatalistic approach to life. I was to die of heart disease, so what could I do? I had, in a sense, given up to the disease. About a year ago, I got fed up with this point of view. My wife had recently retired, and our retirement finances looked reasonable. The future looked bright and exciting, except for my inescapable disease. I asked myself, "Am I going to enjoy the rest of my life or am I going to wait to die?"

My wife, Jane, answered the question for me: "I am enjoying retirement and you are a big part of my retirement plan. I expect that we will be doing lots of things together, so figure out how to live long and enjoy yourself." She had set up a challenge for me—how to give up my mild self-pity and get on with a great future. I began to think about what really bothered me, and I realized that I felt like a health-burdened 57-year-old. It took me more than a month to peel away my thinking and to recognize this feeling. Compared with my friends, I was debilitated. How could I change that reality?

Here is what I did. I kept my chronological age at the time, of 56 (no real choice there). I then thought about my functional, or sentient, age. At what age would I consider myself to be healthy? I realized that my health status made me feel about 10 years older than my chronological age. If I were 66, I would feel okay, even good, about my "health age." I began thinking about what I would do if I actually *was* 66. I realized that a form of retirement made sense: less focus on my work and more focus on my wife and me. I saw that I would be a young 66 instead of an old 56. This started to look pretty interesting. I actually felt freed to pursue my next 10 to 20 years the way I wanted, instead of the way 56-year-olds typically do.

Then I hit a brick wall. I had just given away 10 years of my life. That just seemed reckless and unfair. Why should I have to compromise my life? When I heard my self-pity again, I rebuked myself for lapsing back into old thinking. I now had to come to grips with this loss-of-10-years idea.

In preparation for writing this book, I completed many online life expectancy calculators. I found, to my surprise, that I could expect to live until about 83, even with my health history. I had always thought I could expect to live only into my early 70s. Eighty-three years of life expectancy actually added 10 years to my estimates. At 56, I expected another 15 years of time to enjoy life. If I saw myself as a healthy 66-year-old who could live another 17 years or more, I would actually add at least two years on top of feeling healthy, and I could enjoy my years ahead. Of course, this is a mind game that really changes nothing except my sense of well-being, and that is what it is all about.

A year later, I have lived 57 years and I am a happy 67-year-old, with many great years ahead of me. My wife and I are making plans for the next five years that include time together, travel, family, friends, and the variable enjoyment of golf. These are ideas that most 57-year-olds may not see as imminent but are prime ideas for a 67-year-old. The result of all this thinking, which is called cognitive restructuring, is that I am a happy 57, with the priorities of someone 67. It works for me.

THE RISKS OF AGING

I have spent some time in this chapter telling you that aging is not equivalent to old age and that our health can be better than we anticipate. This does not mean that we will not be ill or saddled with a chronic or even a terminal disease. We will all die of something at some time. Aging does have its problems.

How Do You Manage a Disease?

Jon Walker considers himself a lucky man. In the early 1970s he spent more than 10 months in heavy combat along the DMZ in Vietnam. He felt lucky to have made it out alive. He has also recently retired from a successful career with the US federal government as an environmental engineer. He expects to enjoy his pension and do the many things he has been preparing to do. He owns a few apartments that he rents to tenants; one plan is to buy more rental property.

Regarding his health, he says, "I'm kind of lucky that I'm healthy, given all the hazardous materials I have been around." A few years ago he learned that he had diabetes. He took it in stride; he exercised more, lost some weight. He could handle it. Then he went for a regular appointment with his endocrinologist.

She came in the exam room and said to me, "You're in denial" and she was serious. Honestly, I didn't understand what she meant; I knew I had Type 1 diabetes and I was doing what I thought was the right stuff. She went on to say, "How would you like to be playing tennis with one arm? How would you like to play basketball with one leg?" She got my attention; of course I don't want that. But sugar is a daily thing. It's up and down, so it's hard to manage.

The truth was that I was living a little healthier than I did before the diagnosis and I was therefore a little healthier. To truly manage my diabetes and remain healthy, I had to accept that this was more than just an inconvenience; I have a life-threatening disease that I had yet to fully incorporate into my life. I had to accept that my diabetes was a reality that I had to manage. That was a few years ago and I still have all my arms and legs. I do what I need to do and I feel healthier than I have in years. I wouldn't recommend diabetes to anyone but I have won this challenge.[18]

If you have been diagnosed with a disease, you are probably scared, angry, edgy and quite possibly moody even though you have a great medical treatment team applying all the best medicines, procedures, and devices that medicine has to offer. Simply put, you are not adapting well to this new reality, and you know it.

Take the example of rheumatoid arthritis. Fifty percent of people over 65 have some form of diagnosed arthritis. Overweight or obese people are at higher risk for arthritis than are normal or underweight people.[19]

Patricia Katz, a professor of medicine and health policy at the University of California, helped me understand how people adapt to a degenerative disease such as rheumatoid arthritis.

When Dr. Katz began working with an arthritis research group, it was clear that many of the group members were depressed. She found that the rates of depression were a lot higher among disease-disabled people than in healthy people and that this was a remarkably consistent phenomenon across the diseases she studied. Much of this depression was likely due to the loss of function and the growing sense of dependency.

To adapt to these diminished physical circumstances, Dr. Katz suggested that people should keep themselves mentally healthy by maintaining activities that are important to them. She said, "In my research, I call those 'valued life activities.'"

---

18 Personal interview, January 8, 2007.
19 Centers for Disease Control and Prevention, *Prevalence of Doctor-Diagnosed Arthritis and Arthritis-Attributable Activity Limitation — United States, 2003–2005.* MMWR 2006; 55: pp. 1089–1099), http://www.cdc.gov/mmwr/PDF/wk/mm5540.pdf.

Dr. Katz pointed to the advertising for drugs and health care products that focus on valued life activities. Advertisers understand that new adults want to choose what they want to do and not have to limit their choices. They want to be able to engage in activities such as work, to socialize, to think clearly, to play with their grandchildren, or to play tennis or golf. Says Dr. Katz:

> *People want to do the things that add some spice to their life, that add some interest to their life, and importantly, that have some sort of intrinsic value to them. So the nugget is that the people who can maintain those activities are the ones who tend to stay mentally and psychologically in better shape. Research has shown that maybe you don't maintain the same activity that you had before, but if you become disabled, you need to find a substitute. You find something that is at least a cousin to the valued activity. The idea of value is transferable.*

Take the example of a person who has been diagnosed with rheumatoid arthritis who loves to cook. People with this progressive disease often have problems with their hands. For the cook, this would mean no longer being able to lift heavy pots or to manipulate the knives and the ingredients to cook. So how do you get around that problem? Dr. Katz has found that people can be really creative. For example, they can buy their vegetables already cut up, buy lighter pots, and store the pots in a place that is easy to reach. These are simple solutions that are legitimate adaptation strategies. The problem arises when the cook feels that buying pre-cut vegetables, for example, is "cheating" and is not the right way to cook. Dr. Katz goes on to say:

> *The less the person can accommodate to simple changes, the more they will struggle with their disease. It's this lack of flexibility—almost "it's my way or the highway" thinking—that can trigger depression. If you choose to fight a disease like arthritis, you should remember that the disease does not care if you fight or adapt. If you set up this battle, the progressive disease will win and you will lose. If you use covert methods to undo the disabilities as they come, you will very likely win.*

Dr. Katz works with her clients to find adaptations that allow them to maintain their valued life activities. "My clients may not be able to do these activities as quickly, but still being able to do the activities allows them to maintain important life roles and to maintain their ideas about themselves. In many cases, it allows them to maintain important social connections."

Dr. Katz sees a pretty strong drive in her clients to maintain their independence. When she talks to people about their fears of what their disease will cause, she finds that they are most afraid of becoming dependent on their family. They don't want to be a burden. Loss of independence can also lead to loss of self-esteem and emotional well-being. For this reason, she believes that depression should be treated aggressively and as part of the overall disease syndrome. "For one thing, there is an increased likelihood that people will be able to manage their treatment better. Depression is associated with a lack of adherence to treatment, and it can also magnify symptoms, particularly pain."

Unfortunately, many physicians do not screen for depression, says Dr. Katz.

> Some physicians don't really associate physically disabling disease with depression. This may be because when people think about disability, they're thinking, "Can you get out of a chair?" But I think that our generation has higher expectations for aging. We see that in people with chronic disease. Because of better available drugs, people with rheumatoid arthritis no longer think that treatment has been successful only if they stay out of a wheelchair. They think they're successful if they can continue going to their salsa class. I think that, generally, as we age, we have those expectations, too.

Dr. Katz has good advice for new adults who are dealing with an illness. "If your treatment team does not screen you for depression, ask to be tested. If you are asked why, tell them, 'I would rather know that I am not depressed than be depressed and not know it.'"

She also highlights the importance of asking and answering the question "Can I do the things I want to do?" "Don't assume that you can't dance because of a painful back. Find someone to teach you to dance with the assets you have available. If you do not ask the question, you will probably not get the answer."

What Diseases Afflict People 65 and Over?

What kinds of diseases are new adults most prone to? The American Hospital Association (www.aha.org) regularly looks at health in the United States 10 to 20 years or more into the future. This analysis is done to help their member hospitals plan for what will come. Here are the highlights of its May 2007 report.[20]

- The over-65 population will nearly triple as a result of the aging boomers.
- More than six of every ten boomers will be managing more than one chronic condition.
- More than one out of every three boomers—over 21 million—will be considered obese.
- One of every four boomers—14 million—will be living with diabetes.
- Nearly one out of every two boomers—more than 26 million—will be living with arthritis.
- Eight times more knee replacements will be performed than are performed today.

Canada is facing a similar challenge. In 2002, the public health agency of Canada reported the results of research that includes information on the costs of health care by age.[21] The data showed that in 1998 people 65 and over were responsible for 28.4 percent of the cost of adult health care. This cost will grow as the baby boomers enter their 60s and 70s and almost double the percentage of people and health care costs in that age bracket.[22]

There are many health issues that can arise as we age—everything from high blood pressure to cancer, osteoporosis to depression, and it is likely that at some point you will become more than familiar with some illnesses or conditions.

The good news is that health care has improved dramatically over the past 20 years and is primed for even more dramatic growth over the next 20 years. Cancer is no longer a death sentence, heart disease can be managed, and osteoporosis can be prevented, to name a few improvements.

20 American Hospital Association (www.aha.org) and First Consulting Group (www.fcg.com), "When I'm 64: How the Boomers will Change Health Care," May 2007, http://www.aha.org/aha/content/2007/pdf/070508-boomerreport.pdf.
21 Health Canada (2002), Economic Burden of Illness in Canada, http://ebic-femc.phac-aspc.gc.ca/
22 Statistics Canada, http://www40.statcan.ca/l01/cst01/demo23a.htm

LOOKING AHEAD: REMARKABLE TRENDS IN HEALTH CARE

As industry reinvented invention in the 1800s, medicine is now reinventing the search for medical solutions to illnesses, diseases, and various conditions. The result is that progress across medicine is gaining momentum. Not only have new drugs and procedures been developed, but a whole new way of developing more advances has also been created. Access to our genetic code allows researchers and doctors to do what was impossible 20 years ago. Medical devices have become so precise that new applications are crowding the government approval process. Today we are closer to Dr. McCoy ("Bones") on the *U.S.S. Enterprise* of *Star Trek* than we are to Richard Chamberlain's *Dr. Kildare* of the 1950s.

Dr. Eric Peterson, professor of medicine at Duke University Medical School and director of cardiovascular research at the Duke Clinical Research Institute, is involved in creating public health policy, and he frequently participates on panels that "look ahead" into the future of medicine.

He described to me nine trends in medicine that will be good news for those of us over 55 and less than 100 years old.[23]

1. Prevention

Prevention is very much part of the next wave of medical innovation. Rather than waiting for disease to strike, it is preferable to prevent the disease from coming on in the first place. In the recent past, doctors relied heavily on patients for prevention, lifestyle changes, and treatment plan compliance. The focus today has moved prevention into the doctor's office. Tests and screenings now exist or are becoming available to identify people at risk and then provide better treatment for those high-risk groups. Genome research, for example, is focusing on identifying people with high risks for cancer, heart disease, and other diseases at the genome level. People who in the past had what was called a "family history" will in the future have "markers" that can identify them as high risk. Their situation may then be monitored, and they can also be counseled to modify their life in a manner that will reduce that risk.

---

23 Personal interview, July 27, 2007.

2. Personalized Medicine

You may have heard this term and wondered what it means. The general concept is that your medical care can be tailored to your specific needs and your genetic background. This reduces the need for your doctor to take a "trial and error" approach with your care. Perhaps you have been prescribed a medicine to see if it helps, but it does nothing or, worse, creates bad side effects. Personalized medicine will allow your doctor to better prescribe medicines that will help, while avoiding medicines that may cause problems. Genomic medicine, the study of medicine at the gene or DNA level, is leading the way in personalized medicine.

Genomics—the study of genomes—can be used to identify your genetic predisposition for risk of disease in ways not possible before. Because of this early indication, you and your doctor have a longer period of time to monitor and treat conditions at the earliest possible stage.

When treating a patient with a disease, medicine is just beginning to learn how to better determine who benefits from a treatment and who is potentially harmed. Genetic testing of a patient can determine "markers" that indicate if the drug will be successful or dangerous for you. As Dr. Peterson describes it:

> As we move forward with the better characterization of patients within current and future studies . . . we can begin to ferret out who should be given which drug. And once understood, there is the potential to differentially apply treatments only to those for whom it will work and not harm. [A team] at Duke University is already doing this work with several drugs used currently in the treatment of breast, lung, and ovarian cancers. This group is also pioneering personalized medicine in cardiovascular and infectious disease. The future of personalized cancer care is closer than we think, since doctors will soon have a vast array of genomic tools to select the right therapy for the right patient at the right time.

You may know of the drug Warfarin, which is used to thin the blood of many heart patients. Thinner blood passes more easily through constricted blood vessels but can create unwanted bleeding. The drug can be life-saving but the bleeding can be deadly. Doctors now must "experiment" with the patient to find the best dose of the drug that results in the optimum therapeutic level of the drug in the blood that is also below the bleeding level. Genetic testing is now being used to determine which levels are best for each patient. In August 2007 the FDA added genetic testing to Warfarin's bottle label by placing a black-boxed warning informing both patients and doctors of the recommended use of genetic testing to determine a correct dose. Many deaths have occurred due to bleeding as Warfarin dose setting has been conducted. This Warfarin labeling is an early victory for personalized medicine. Work is also proceeding to determine which anti-depressant drugs work with a patient without dangerous side effects. The result for you is that treatment options will greatly expand while the risks of treatment will be lowered.

3. Self-Care

Self-care will become much more sophisticated. Much screening and treatment that is now done in the doctor's office or at a hospital will be done by the person at home or elsewhere. For example, in the area of identifying markers for the early identification of health risk, genetic testing will be available directly to the consumer through home testing kits. The resulting report would highlight potential markers that could be discussed with your doctor.

There will also be changes in the home treatment of disease using new devices and equipment being developed (such as monitors for glucose, drug levels, lipids, etc.). The costs for these home care approaches are dropping as they become more widely used.

4. Location

The home-based self-care trend combined with Internet access is providing us all, but especially boomers, an expanded definition of independent living. Today, the call for emergency care is a button push away. Sophisticated and non-intrusive home health monitoring will even do away with the button. The increased access to physicians via the Internet will reduce the need for "live" visits, will help people to remain in their homes longer, and will reduce the need to be closer to a specialized clinic.

5. Personal Health Records

Currently, if you want to seek care from another physician or hospital, you have to have your records physically transferred, or go through repeat testing because your records couldn't be transferred. In the future, your records will be maintained on a secure website and you will be in control of your information and how it is used. Your electronic records will be accessible to you, as well as whomever you wish to provide with access to them, and they will contain information on all the drugs you are taking, your history, your allergies, and your tests. You might also carry a credit-card-like device containing critical information such as drug allergies, serious conditions, and contact names and numbers. This would be the equivalent of carrying around your medical records with you at all times that could be accessed during an emergency. (This may wave red flags with people who are concerned about their privacy and who have seen credit card information misused. These concerns are taken very seriously, and protection is an important part of the design of any system.)

6. Implantation

Technology is driving another major change. In the future, many diseases will be monitored and treated with devices in your body. A current existing example is the implantable heart defibrillator and/or pacemaker, which continuously monitors your heart and shocks you when your heart goes out of rhythm. Today's defibrillators have probes that can measure pressures in your heart. If fluid is building up and your heart is not pumping quite as well, you will be signaled to contact your doctor. Devices that monitor heart failure are coming onto the market. Another implantable device under development is one that treats intractable depression that, like a pacemaker, stimulates the nervous system to improve mood.

7. Regeneration

Regeneration is the growing of various body parts to replace ones that are diseased or damaged. Regeneration is still far in the future, but it has the potential to reverse the damage caused by disease. For example, a person with heart damage could receive a new heart muscle that has been grown either from embryonic stem cells or possibly from adult stem cells. The therapy could also be used for the liver and other organs prone to disease. Current stem cell research is focusing on replacing damaged or worn-out tissues.

8. Informed Patients—Information

The Internet has made it easy for the public to research information on diseases. Electronic access to information will continue to grow over the next 10 or 20 years. No matter how rare the disease, people (and their local doctors) can get information from the Internet and consult with experts who may be located far away.

9. Pace of Innovation

Finally, the pace of innovation in medicine has sped up. The current cycle of innovation, the time from early research to use by patients, has been clocked at 17 to 20 years. The National Institute of Health is expending great effort to develop various means of shortening that cycle remarkably, so that innovations in treatment are developed, tested, and made available to the public at a faster pace, within 10 years or less.

Dr. Peterson's advice and information appear to increase the odds that we will live to a healthy 85 and beyond, even if we do have that "You have . . ." moment.

SUMMARY

In this chapter we looked at

- Common negative assumptions we have about aging and health and how most of these assumptions are false. It appears that long-held beliefs about the new adult's predetermined health risks are being challenged and that our ability to influence our sense of well-being is increasing. While there are certain physiological changes that we cannot change as we age, we *can* choose our response to these changes and manage our expectations so that we continue to enjoy the activities we engage in.
- How you are the most important person for managing your health. The most important person after you is your primary health care advisor. The ability to manage your health and cope with health issues as they arrive provides you with a sense of control over your future health that ultimately increases your satisfaction with life. Life satisfaction is one of the main ingredients in our assessment of our well-being and quality of life.

- How medicine is increasing its ability to help you avoid illness, offer better treatments when you do get ill, and even fix or replace parts that are damaged or worn. We have health care choices today that did not exist 20 years ago, and we will have new choices becoming available over the next 20 years. We will age, but old age is being pushed aside.

Take care of yourself. Manage your expectations. Find a good doctor and be a good patient. You have your whole life ahead of you.

CHAPTER SIX

THE SOCIAL DOMAIN

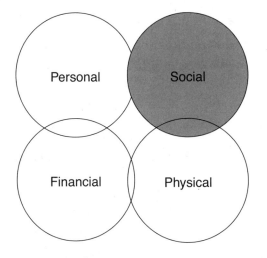

"I define joy as a sustained sense of well-being and internal peace—
a connection to what matters."
—Oprah Winfrey

Let's talk about being happy. In the previous chapters, we looked at money and health, your hard assets. In these next two chapters, we're going to look at your social life and your sense of personal enjoyment and satisfaction, your soft assets. These soft assets help you make use of your hard assets to create the feeling and meaning you derive from what you do.

Here's an example of what I mean. Think about taking a walk in the woods. This is a pretty straightforward activity, but to accomplish it all of your hard and your soft assets need to be in place. First of all, can you afford the time and money involved? The money includes things such as the cost of travel to the woods. It is one thing if the woods are out your back door, but another if you have a long drive each way to get there, and yet another if you want to walk in Germany's Black Forest. If you can afford this walk financially, next you consider whether your physical assets are sufficient to allow you to walk in rough terrain: are you in good enough physical condition?

If your hard assets are in place to take the walk, you consider your soft assets. What will make the walk most enjoyable for you? Will you enjoy the walk more alone or with others? Why are you walking: for pleasure? for exercise? to prove something? These questions are examples of our soft asset considerations—both social and personal.

Loneliness is one of the greatest fears we face as we leave work. I have seen men, in particular, worried about making and maintaining friendships when they move beyond work. They may have many friends or acquaintances but few, if any, close friends. So how do you make friendships in the years beyond work? How do you make sure you feel sufficiently socially connected to others to be happy? In this chapter we're going to consider the social considerations of the new adulthood.

THE ROLE OF YOUR SOCIAL DOMAIN

"Love all, trust a few, do wrong to none."
—Shakespeare, *All's Well That Ends Well,* Act I, Scene 1

Each of us is just one of the 6.65 billion people on our planet, just another face in the crowd. We are, that is, until somebody recognizes us and connects us to their experiences with us and their knowledge of us. The people who recognize us transform us from a face in the crowd of billions into a unique, known person. That is the magic of friends and family (I will use the word "friends" to include both friends and family, unless I indicate otherwise). Friends make our large anonymous world very personal. Friends know us and we know them. When we talk about "setting down roots," we grow friends as our roots.

Roots keep us grounded; they provide us with a sense of our place in this world. They support us and they bind. If we have reason to move, we speak of "uprooting." For those of us who are a generation or more from our immigrant forebears, we may marvel at what it took to leave Scotland and move to Cape Breton, to uproot from the Ukraine and build a life on the Prairies, or to come from China to work on the western railroads. Today, we see many other groups immigrating to North America, as did our families years before. People come, legally or illegally, from Eastern Europe, Asia, Africa, and Central and South America.

Hispanics are but one of many cultures trying to make life work in North America, and their stories ring as true today as those of other immigrants 100 to 200 years ago. Here is one story.

Hispanics Set Down Roots

Cesar Robles was ten years old the first time he saw the Tri-Cities [South-east Washington State]. It was 1980 and his family still lived in the Mexican coastal state of Colima. They had come to visit his aunt, who, like thousands of other Mexicans, had left her homeland in search of a better life in the United States.

Five years later, Robles and his family left Mexico for good and joined his aunt in Pasco [Washington]. It was a drier, more barren place than where Robles grew up playing soccer and visiting the beach.

"It was hard to do it," recalled Robles, now 29, as he sat in the living room of the small Pasco house where he lives with his wife and two young children.

The Tri-Cities was not at all like the beautiful country his family had left behind. He didn't know anyone except his family, and he had to learn a new language in a strange city and school.

Martha, his eventual wife, arrived under similar circumstances a few years earlier. At that time, there were fewer than 3,000 Hispanics in Franklin County, according to U.S. Census figures, and fewer than 10,000 in the Tri-Cities.

But if the Mid-Columbia Valley [in Washington State] was lacking in familiar faces and in what Robles considered natural beauty, it had an abundance of one thing Colima was missing: Opportunity.[1]

---

1 Jason Hagey, "Hispanics Set Down Roots," *Tri-City Herald,* Washington, September 20, 1998, http://archive.tri-cityherald.com/newmajority/roots.html.

A consistent drive among most people is to be known, liked, valued, and hopefully loved. Our friends can protect us from a harsh world and excite us to explore it. Friends also help us to define and support who we are. In Pasco, Cesar Robles' family knew at least one person who already valued and loved them—his aunt. This family connection helped make a big move to a strange land more manageable and less risky.

SOCIAL SUPPORT CORRELATES WITH A HEALTHY AND LONG LIFE!

My career so far has spanned 37 years. A portion of my work includes conducting my own research and learning about the research of others. You may have noticed that researchers are drawn to words such as "tend to," "may occur," "appear influenced by," "could occur," and other words that modify their findings from absolutely certain to likely. Researchers might say, "Our observations suggest that the sun rises in the morning, and usually in the eastern sky." This wording limits our accountability if someday the sun should rise in the northern sky. Highly unlikely, right? But why be definitive when "most likely" will do?

So imagine my surprise when I read the definitive statement by Drs. John W. Rowe and Robert L. Kahn that "people who have a great deal of social support are healthier, on average, than people who lack such support. That assertion, after more than two decades of research, is no longer debated."[2] No equivocating here—it's a flat statement of the importance of social contact and the dangers of not enough.

Why does social contact have such a dramatic effect? Drs. Rowe and Kahn explain that social contact helps people to live longer. They cite many interconnected reasons for this, including the following:

- Close relationships involve support, which has positive effects on health.
- Having people to talk with reduces the damaging health effects of stress.
- The health effects are wide-ranging, including lowering the risk of arthritis, tuberculosis, depression, and alcoholism.

---

2 John W. Rowe and Robert L. Kahn, *Successful Aging* (New York: Pantheon, 1998), p. 163.

- After surgery, people who say they have a strong social support system use less medication, recover more quickly and follow medical regimens more faithfully.[3]

Researcher Lisa Berkman has found that, "for social support to be health-promoting, it must provide both a sense of belonging and intimacy and must help people to be more competent and self-efficacious."[4]

It is no surprise that social networks are positive influences only when they are supportive.

Numerous other studies have also identified social support as a powerful component of personal health and well-being. There is, however, a dark side. Giving or needing too much support can foster dependency. In addition, people can abuse the support they receive in order to control or manipulate the one giving the support. For the supporter, contact with people who are negative, demanding, degrading, or deceitful can be a draining experience. Such people are sometimes referred to as "emotional vampires." Such people, says researcher Albert Bernstein, "stalk you, even as we speak. On broad daylit streets... It's not your blood they drain; it's your emotional energy."[5]

The type of person Dr. Bernstein describes sees you not as a friend, but rather as an opportunity to improve his or her own situation, to suck emotional reserves from you. Blanche Dubois from Tennessee Williams's play *A Streetcar Named Desire* is a classic example of such a person. Blanche was a troubled soul who tried to suck the emotional energy from her sister Stella and her sister's husband, Stanley. When she moved in with the couple, Blanche presented herself as a person of wealth and culture but was actually a broke and damaged person who had been told to leave the town in which she lived. Over time, she destroyed relationships with family and friends, setting the stage for her famous statement "I have always depended on the kindness of strangers."[6] She depended on strangers because people who knew her had been burned by her and were no longer willing to support her.

3 Rowe and Kahn, *Successful Aging*, p. 157.
4 Lisa F. Berkman, Ph.D., "The Role of Social Relations in Health Promotion, *Psychosomatic Medicine*, 1995, Vol. 57, Issue 3, p. 245.
5 Albert J. Bernstein, Ph.D., *Emotional Vampires* (New York: McGraw-Hill, 2001), p. 1.
6 Tennessee Williams, *A Streetcar Named Desire* (New York: Signet, 1986), p. 142.

Dr. Bernstein lists four attitudes that may be expressed by emotional vampires:

- The rules apply to other people, not me.
- It's never my fault, ever.
- I want it now.
- If I don't get my way, I throw a tantrum.

Sound familiar? If you have ever spent time with an ill-mannered four-year-old, you may have encountered this way of thinking. I am not saying that four-year-olds are emotional vampires, but rather that the vampires behave a lot like four-year-olds. The difference is that most four-year-olds will outgrow this thinking.

Enjoy your family and friends, support them, and know that they will support you. Just do this with your eyes wide open.

WHAT IS A SOCIAL NETWORK?

When I think of the power of and possibilities for emotional support, I picture Lou Gehrig on the field of Yankee Stadium. It was July 4, 1939, "Lou Gehrig Appreciation Day," and he was standing before more than 60,000 fans to confirm that he had been diagnosed with amyotrophic lateral sclerosis (now often called Lou Gehrig's disease), a rare disease that causes spinal paralysis.

Fans, for the past two weeks you have been reading about a bad break I got. Yet today I consider myself the luckiest man on the face of the earth. I have been in ballparks for seventeen years and have never received anything but kindness and encouragement from you fans.

Look at these grand men. Which of you wouldn't consider it the highlight of his career to associate with them for even one day?

Sure, I'm lucky. Who wouldn't consider it an honor to have known Jacob Ruppert—also the builder of baseball's greatest empire, Ed Barrow—to have spent the next nine years with that wonderful little fellow Miller Huggins—then to have spent the next nine years with that outstanding leader, that smart student of psychology, the best manager in baseball today, Joe McCarthy!

Sure, I'm lucky. When the New York Giants, a team you would give your right arm to beat, and vice versa, sends you a gift, that's something!

When everybody down to the groundskeepers and those boys in white coats remember you with trophies, that's something.

When you have a wonderful mother-in-law who takes sides with you in squabbles against her own daughter, that's something. When you have a father and mother who work all their lives so that you can have an education and build your body, it's a blessing! When you have a wife who has been a tower of strength and shown more courage than you dreamed existed, that's the finest I know.

So I close in saying that I might have had a tough break—but I have an awful lot to live for![7]

Less than two years later, on June 2, 1941, Lou Gehrig died in Riverdale, New York.

Whenever I read this speech I wonder, who is being supported here? Is Gehrig thanking the people who support him, or is he supporting the people as they prepare for their loss of him? It is a simple, honest, and touching speech. It says more about the man than all his remarkable baseball achievements.

This speech is also notable as an example of Gehrig's social network. He ends his speech with his most intimate friends: his wife, his parents, and (perhaps surprisingly to some) his mother-in-law. Before that, he praises his teammates and the team management. He opens with his fans, acknowledging their concern for him and their importance in his life.

Most of us are no Lou Gehrig, but we have our own social networks. Social networks take three broad forms, and they follow Lou Gehrig's idea of family (including marriage), friendships, and the team. The stronger these positive relationships, the greater the personal benefits.

Over the years, I have had the opportunity to work with thousands of people. I have asked them many questions as I got to know them. One of the questions I often ask is, "Who are your supportive friends and family?" This question helps me to learn about my clients' social network. People typically respond by telling me about their family and their one or two very close friends. Every so often, a person will tell me they have "lots of friends." As I try to pin down what "lots" means, they will say

---

7 Lou Gehrig, "Farewell to Yankee Fans," July 4, 1939. Available at The History Place: Great Speeches Collection, http://www.historyplace.com/speeches/gehrig.htm.

something like "Oh, you know, I must have 10 or 20 good friends." I have learned over time that this type of answer usually means that they have no close friends and only some acquaintances.

Most people define a close friend as someone to whom they can confide their most intimate thoughts and ideas. They may also be the guys I watch football with on Sunday, people I can be myself with when we get together. We usually have frequent contact with our close friends and consider them to be a major part of our life. We also know that these close friends feel the same way about us—that there is mutual support. These people may be members of our family or people we have grown to know and trust over time. What is consistent among most people is that they do not have many true close friends, but do have many good friends or acquaintances.

Having close friends requires the expenditure of a good deal of time and energy to maintain the level of relationship that such friends expect from each other. How many people can you, or do you want to, share intimate thoughts with, be in contact with two to three times a week or more, or depend on? The number for most people is usually between one and three.

My experience is that most people have a social network that is based on close friends and family and then grows from this base. Your social network is made up of people you can count on to have your best interests at heart. In their study on successful aging, Drs. Rowe and Kahn state, "On the average, people of all ages report that their personal networks include eight to eleven members."[8]

Here is how I envision a typical supportive social network:

Broad Definitions of Types of Friends

Acquaintances People who are friends of friends or people you have met at various meetings or gatherings. They may be people you would recognize and who would recognize you at a chance meeting. This is a very broad category.

Friends People whom you enjoy seeing at gatherings or who are friends of good friends. It would be unusual for you and this level of friend to plan on getting together on your own. Work friends are often in this category.

Good Friends People whom you see often, once or twice a month, either together or at gatherings, or whom you talk with on the phone or via e-mail. You would notice if you did not have regular contact. Family members may be included in this category.

Close Friends Very important people in your life whom you speak with and see daily or at least once a week; you each share intimate information and seek reliable support from each other. Family members may be an important part of this category. You can "be yourself with these friends."

---

8 Rowe and Kahn, *Successful Aging*, p. 160.

Social Networks

Circles of Friends and Support

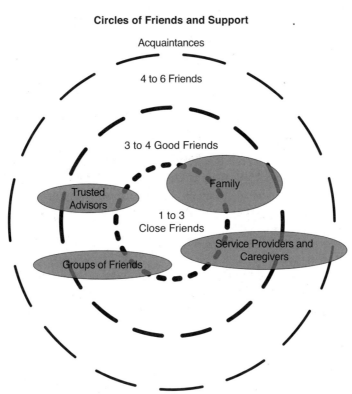

What you see in the diagram is a reasonable balance of friends and family members. Each of us will have our own unique social network that may or may not resemble this picture. Within these categories are groupings of friends that encompass mini-social networks. These cohesive groups can include friends from work; friendships within a congregation, community group, or sports activity; and/or your doctor, clergy, or other service providers. Family members, including spouses, partners, and children, often are also close or good friends. Trusted advisors may be considered friends as well as advisors. A diverse group of people, from doctors and nurses to landlords, grocers, the mail carrier, restaurant staff, and many others, are part of our social networks.

The frequent or infrequent contact you have with these various people, who know you to one degree or another, adds to the social contact most of us crave. Being known confirms our sense of community and belonging. A client told me of a woman who lives in her building who has no social network. She is reportedly pleasant but quiet and hard to get to know. Her family has either died or moved away, and she has lost touch with the small community she had. She creates social contact by having her hair done two to three times per week, arriving early and staying on past her appointment time. The owner of the hair salon has many woman clients like her who use the salon as their social hub. The woman receives hair care, including the physical contact that is lacking in her life, and also gets to enjoy the company of a fairly lively group of staff and customers she considers friends. I am told that this level of contact seems to work well for her.

Most of us likely want to have more social contact than this woman has. But what some people may have in common with her is a sense of loneliness. Loneliness is one of the greatest fears we face as we move into our new adulthood. Some people in retirement are active by nature, and some are more reserved. So how do you make friendships in the years beyond work? To avoid loneliness, more reserved people can determine what activities interest them and use these activities as a way to get to know people. It often helps if you can find someone to go with you. Let me introduce you to Barbara Perry and her friend Lois Sullivan.

Friendship and Social Networks

"Friendship multiplies the good of life and divides the evil."
—Baltasar Gracian, Spanish philosopher, 1601–1658

Barbara Perry retired at age 55 after 30 years of teaching special education students in a large city public school system. She had previously thought about retiring but had never moved from the idea to a plan until she realized that the people she had worked with throughout her career had all retired. Her professional network no longer existed, and her colleagues were now "in their 20s and 30s." She was tired of teaching and ready to move on.

Barbara is a single woman with few fixed expenses and knew that her finances would work. With the numbers working out, she gave up her job. Now she just had to decide what to do with the rest of her life.

During my interview with Barbara, I commented that she appeared to be a risk taker. I based my observation on the fact that she had done things like teaching in South Korea and Mexico and selling her home while unsure where she would live. Barbara stopped for a moment and corrected me: "Bill, you are saying risk and I am really thinking more about adventure. I always believe that if I try something and it does not work, I can change some things and make it work—that's part of what makes it an adventure. Risk sounds to me like stepping out of a plane without knowing how to use the parachute strapped to my back. Adventure is about what I will gain, and risk is more about what I may lose. I have been wrong with some decisions but I never end up losing something I could not afford."

Barbara's response indicated to me that she is essentially an optimist, someone who sees the good in every situation and adjusts to what is not so good. Dr. Martin Seligman, in his book *Learned Optimism*, defines optimists as those who "tend to believe defeat is just a temporary setback, that its causes are confined to this one case. . . . Confronted by a bad situation, they perceive it as a challenge and try harder."[9]

Facing her new situation of retirement and mild loneliness, Barbara met the challenge by seeking out a friend she had known for many years through work. Lois Sullivan had retired from another big city public school system a few years before Barbara. But Lois had not stopped working. Her approach to her new adulthood was to pursue temporary jobs. She had always enjoyed working and knew she could not be without some structure in her life. She and Barbara had not seen each other until Barbara retired. When they got together, the creative sparks flew. Barbara told me that Lois became a mentor on how to enjoy life after teaching, which, in their case, means finding odd jobs to do together in order to explore the world and meet new people. Both of them have reasonable retirement finances, so neither needs the money they earn at these jobs to live on. Together they do what they call their "larks, barks, sparks, and marks."

Barbara explains:

> The "larks," these are odd jobs—temporary jobs that Lois usually finds through the newspaper or on the Internet. I think of odd jobs as social extensions because through them I always meet other retired people who are doing the same things. One lark we did was working as movie extras.

---

9 Martin Seligman, Ph.D., *Learned Optimism* (New York: Free Press, 1998), p. 5.

Another was working at a convention center. I was also registered with a temporary service. So there is quite an array of experiences we have had and people we have met.

The "barks" are the periodic work we do with Holland America, helping out with embarkations and debarkations. We greet the passengers as they leave the ship and give them ideas of what to do in our city, and we then greet them when they return. We hear great stories about what fun they had and we learn more about our town.

That was actually our first job. It was this job that helped us both to get over our teaching careers very quickly. The first day that we worked there, I almost had tears in my eyes because 2,500 people had just said thank you to me. And Lois said the same thing happened to her. In our career in public service, neither of us had ever heard a thank you. So that was fulfilling for us.

"Sparks" is our shorthand for our stocks and bonds investing. It is a takeoff of the S&P Index, SParks. We both got very interested in managing money because we now had this extra money from our cruise ship work and we wanted to have fun with it. We decided to learn how to invest. Neither of us knew a stock from a bond before we took a trading stocks program. Now we love it. We are not stupid women; we knew that we could do this. We also knew that we would only use new money and never touch our retirement monies, and that we would carefully invest this new money in businesses that we knew something about. So we took our cruise ship earnings, and we bought a cruise line stock. More than half the fun for us is researching and talking about the stocks. It's going very well. Our portfolio is up by about 18 or 19 percent.

And then we come to our "Marks." We learned from a person working at the cruise line that retired teachers were in demand to proctor various standardized tests. There was a guy down there who said, "I know you were teachers; this might interest you." It seemed like a perfect match, but not so. We could easily do the work but it felt just like work. No adventure, no challenge, no fun. We were not working for the money; we were working for the enjoyment and experience. The job just did not fit our needs.

There was, however, a good outcome: through the proctoring supervisor, we met some other great retired people. Every summer the proctoring supervisor hosts a great party for the proctors. At the party, I said to some of the other proctoring team members, "I know why I did what I did. I have met some great people proctoring." So the "marks" turned into an enjoyable social network of people whom Lois and I are still in contact with. The group is always telling each other about people who are doing interesting things, so you feed off each other. We meet people whom we not only might enjoy and get to know, but they're also doing other things that we wouldn't have thought of doing. It's about putting yourself out there and creating space and seeing what fills in.[10]

In turn, Lois Sullivan told me her thoughts about the odd jobs that Barbara and she have had and what they have meant to her. She calls them their "silly jobs."

The first silly job was with the Holland America cruise line. That was last summer. I found this job in the newspaper's classified section. I just saw it. I am a scourer of the newspapers. The guy who interviewed me said, "Okay, I'm looking at your resume and you are more than qualified. I have to ask you one question, do you need ten bucks an hour, or do you want ten bucks an hour?" I said, "Neither. I don't really care about the money; I need something that's fun." He said, "You're hired."

The reason I call them "silly jobs" is because of how silly Barbara and I can get. The first day of the cruise line job, Barbara picked me up. It was quite a warm day in early May, but I had a raincoat on. I got in the car, and Barbara had a raincoat on as well. We were both covering up our uniform, our very red vest, navy blue pants and white shirt, with a little printed scarf at the neck. It was tasteful, but we were a little embarrassed, probably because the last time we wore uniforms was when we were in Girl Scouts. I got in the car and we both began laughing, and we laughed all the way to the cruise ship.

The job for movie extras also came out of the newspaper. I saw a tiny ad for extras needed for a Duane Johnson (the Rock) movie, The Game Plan. *Barbara and I went, and it was one of the absolute craziest days of my life. I really enjoyed it, and we were paid quite handsomely. I had never done anything like that, never. We had to wear very fancy clothes. The scene we were in was to look like fancy people at a fundraiser at a ballet. Very classy. It's a Disney movie, so they had wonderful food—breakfast and lunch and dinner for us. A little bit of Hollywood.*[11]

10 Personal interview, July 11, 2007.
11 Personal interview, July 11, 2007.

Barbara and Lois both know that they each have a friend they can count on to explore the world. Their friendship continues with laughter and discovery. An important factor in their friendship is that they each know the other is not dependent on them for living a good life. Barbara travels locally, nationally, and often internationally. Lois enjoys her time with her husband. When they do get together, they pick up where they left off, having fun.

As I was nearing the end of my interview with Lois, I told her that she and Barbara reminded me of Lucy Ricardo and Ethel Mertz heading off to try some crazy scheme. Lucy would say to Ethel, "Ooooh, look what I found in the newspaper; we can be in the movies. Let's go, Ethel." Lois's response was to laugh and agree.

Barbara and Lois are prime examples of what like-minded friends can make happen for themselves. I expect that most of us do not quite have that Lucy and Ethel approach to friendship and adventure. But that doesn't mean we can't make new friends beyond work. A master social network builder, Irv Kooris, tells us how he builds and manages his group of friends.[12]

FIRST MAKE A FRIEND, THEN BUILD A FRIENDSHIP

Irv Kooris, a close friend of mine, has many other friends. Ask anyone who knows him and they will tell you he is a great friend. When I asked him how he does it, he could not immediately answer my question. It is not something he thinks about consciously when he's meeting people; it comes to him naturally. But he thought it through and talked with me about what he does.

Meeting People

Irv finds that the best way to meet people is to put himself in situations where there are people who have a common interest. He enjoys cycling and sailing; he is a corporate executive in Atlanta and has an interest in the business community; and he and his family are active members in their congregation. So he may take part in an organized bike riding event, attend community business meetings, or participate in activities sponsored by his congregation. This involvement

---

12 Personal interview, August 9, 2007.

puts him in the company of people who share at least one of his interests.

Once at the event, he relaxes and listens to the people he is with. He is not looking for people who may be interested in *him*, but, rather, those whom *he* finds interesting—those he is drawn to. He makes simple comments on what he has heard a person say and shares his thoughts. For example, he might say to Jack, a new neighbor, "I just heard that you have a daughter living in Vancouver. I have been to Vancouver. Where does she live and what do you enjoy doing when you visit?" Irv sees this as the beginning of sharing their stories. He begins his story in a mild manner—"I have been to the Vancouver area"—and then quickly provides an opportunity for the other person to tell his story: "What do you like to do when you visit your daughter?"

Jack may pick up on Irv's comments or he may not. He may go on to describe his enjoyment in spending time with his daughter and two grandchildren, then add that he enjoys the skiing and biking in the area. The reference to family and the biking engages Irv's interest further, and off they go into a conversation. One of Irv's talents is that he can find something interesting in what most people say. If Jack does not respond to his initial overtures, Irv may try again or he may move on.

At this point, some people might feel rejected. You may have screwed up your courage to talk and then receive little or no response. You may experience the lack of response as a negative thought about you. Irv is not predisposed to feeling rejection. When he is in a group of people, he is always "fishing." He would consider a lack of response from Jack simply to be a natural part of fishing. If you fish for an hour and land only one fish, does that mean that the other fish have rejected you? Or does it mean that fishing has successfully provided you with a fish? "I always think that there may a person in this crowd who I will find interesting," says Irv.

Exploring Common Interests

Irv may meet people he enjoys and others who are not to his liking. If Jack does respond to his overtures, Irv can decide to continue talking with Jack or to let the conversation go. What influences his decision?

Exploring common interests is important to Irv. When Irv does find a potentially interesting person, he listens more than he talks, asks questions, and looks for more commonalities. Does Jack reciprocate and ask Irv about his family and his interest in cycling, or does he continue to talk without knowing or asking much about him? If Jack likes talking more than he does listening and learning, Irv might politely walk away. It is important to Irv to be with people who are as interested in him as he is in them. But an equally important factor is shared values. Jack may love his daughter and her family but has disowned his son because he refused to go into Jack's business. Is this a person Irv wants to spend time with?

Exploring Compatibility

Irv and Jack have made a connection, but is friendship in the cards?

"This may sound simplistic," says Irv, "but if you and the other person are interested in similar things, like cycling, you can suggest, 'Why don't we go for a ride together?' And it just continues to build from there. We get to know more about each other as we ride and talk. We can learn if we enjoy each other's company."

Building a Friendship

Assuming that Irv and Jack have found their times together enjoyable, they cross the boundary from being acquaintances to considering themselves friends. From here they may go on to become good friends, having lunch together every so often or meeting for dinner with their wives, or they may remain as they are, friends who are happy to see each other occasionally at events.

The Responsibilities of Being a Good Friend

Friendship between two people implies that there are occasional meetings, planned or unplanned, and that there is a certain expectation of a willingness to help each other out in times of need. This level of friendship can be active or go dormant until a reason to connect appears.

Being a good friend implies a larger commitment of time and energy.

"I sometimes find it challenging to maintain friendships," says Irv. "They require a certain amount of effort and attention. On a night when I am tired, I might have agreed to have dinner with a friend and when the time comes I really don't feel like going out, but if I decide to go I know I am going to feel connected when I get there. So sometimes there's a challenge in terms of spending my time with growing friendships while also keeping time for people I have known for years who are very close friends in my life."

THE BENEFIT OF FRIENDS

I asked Irv to tell me why he enjoys having friends. He told me that it is good to know that people like him and enjoy spending time with him. He feels that they validate him as a good and interesting person. Friends also provide a sense of security—a certainty that they will be there if they are needed—just as he will be there for them in their times of need. "Friends provide me with energy to get out and do things and to try new things," says Irv. "They add excitement to life, and they teach new ideas. They help me to feel connected to the world and to recognize my place in it. I get renewed by friendships."

One way of realizing the benefit of friends is to look at how people are affected by *not* having many friends. Irv has a professional background in human behavior, from which he shared these thoughts:

I believe—and I know that research shows this to be true—that people without social networks do not manage stress as well as people who have a good social network do. They are not as resilient; they're not as physically healthy. It doesn't mean that if you have a social network you're not going to have cardiac disease, you're not going to have cancer, but you're going to be healthier in general. Social networks do affect how susceptible you may be to a disease. I also think that when you have a social network, you're able to turn to your friends in times of difficulty, and they help you get back on your feet. And when you have a joyful event, a birth of a grandchild, a wedding, a celebration of a birthday, an achievement at work, it's nice to have a few people to share the joy with. It multiplies joy and success. For those without friends, if they're on their own, they have no one to celebrate with or to depend upon.

How Good Are Your Social Skills?

Paul Horn (www.paulhorn.com) is a communication and leadership skills consultant, as well as a professional actor. He often leads social networking courses for people who want to improve their social networking skills. As Paul told me, "Basically, they want to meet more people and make more friends." At the beginning of his course he asks the participants to complete a 20-question "social aptitude" self-assessment to provide them with an understanding of their social strengths and weaknesses. Paul has offered this tool to you. It is in Appendix 4. It takes five to ten minutes to complete.

This assessment has not been put through a statistical analysis to prove its validity. Rather, it has "face validity"; it makes sense when you look at it. Use it for a general appreciation of your social aptitude.

IF MAKING FRIENDS IS NOT YOUR STYLE

Janet and Herb Hardbrod raised their family, and both had successful careers when they lived in New Jersey. They eventually moved south and now live in Florida. They happily enjoy the life that some people fear and others envy. They live in an active community of seniors. Friends were important to them in New Jersey and are just as important in their new home. They identified an interesting difference between socializing when they were working and socializing as new adults.

> HERB: *In New Jersey, when everybody was working, all the socialization had to take place after working hours and on the weekend, so that the amount of time for socializing was much less than we have here in Florida. Here, everybody is retired and you can socialize 24 hours a day, seven days a week. But, as is the case everywhere, there are different types of people. There are some people that basically sit in their house and look at the four walls and listen to their arteries harden, and then there are people that get out and do things. Now, Janet and I were always doers. Even when we were working full time, we were both very active in our Temple, we were both officers of the Temple, we both served on the board of directors. I was President of the Temple and the Men's Club.*
>
> JANET: *I was always an officer of the Temple and the Sisterhood.*
>
> HERB: *And when we moved to Florida, there's really been very little difference because of the types of personalities we have. We were active right away, meeting people and making new friends and getting active in different clubs and community activities and so forth. We now have great friends here, and we get to spend more time with them than we could with friends up north.*[13]

---

13 Personal interview, June 18, 2007.

In keeping with Janet and Herb's nature, they continued with their socializing as they had in New Jersey and have expanded it. If you are yet to retire and are not a natural socializer, you may want to test the social waters before you retire. Choose one time-limited activity, club, project, or group to join for which you have minimal expectations, such as "I will not hate this activity." You can probably succeed at attaining this goal. Now, build on this first success, take it slowly, and learn what you enjoy. If you do this while you are still working, you can reduce the concerns you may have about how you will make friends. If you have already moved beyond work, you can also begin slowly and build some successes for yourself. Let's hope that you don't "basically sit in your house and look at the four walls and listen to your arteries harden."

Barbara, Lois, and Irv, along with Janet and Herb, are natural social network builders (NSNBs). They think about making friends and they see it as work worth doing. I must confess that I am not a natural at building social networks. I have a good number of "business" friends and a few close friends. My circle of friends has not really grown in years, except when my wife introduces me to people she knows.

If you are like me, you may wonder if you can really pull off expanding your social network. I believe that when faced with loneliness, most people can—even I. This would be the time to begin putting yourself in situations where you might meet people, the way NSNBs do.

However, if putting yourself out there is beyond you, there is an alternative. Find someone you know who is an NSNB and hang around with that person. If he or she is a close or good friend, you could tell your friend that you want to expand your social network and ask for help. My experience is that NSNBs are happy to help out.

Of course, the question is how do you identify an NSBN? When I co-authored a book with Margaret Butteriss called *Corporate MVPs* (Wiley, 2004), we conducted qualitative research to learn what made the most valuable people (MVPs) in businesses so good. We talked with top executives and the people they identified as MVPs, across many types of businesses and non-profit organizations. We identified seven traits common to MVPs. After the book was published, I conducted quantitative research that identified an additional six traits common to MVPs. Six of the 13 traits also apply to NSNBs. I have listed these traits below, along with descriptions. The descriptions of these traits may help you to identify NSNBs who could be of help to you and may also provide you with ideas on how to improve your own socializing.

Common Traits of MVPs and NSNBs

Most Valuable People (MVPs) and Natural Social Network Builders (NSNBs) Are:

Socially Skilled
- Comfortable working with others
- Attractive to other interesting people
- Great listeners
- Good at describing their thoughts to others in ways that are easily understood
- Open when they talk and get others to talk openly
- Respectful of differences among people
- Empathetic and insightful
- Regularly reach out to others
- Modest
- Members that improve groups and bring others into groups

Assertive
- Advocates for their beliefs, values, needs, and expectations
- Confident, self-assured
- Decisive
- Good at easing the social interaction for other people
- Comfortable talking with people from diverse backgrounds
- Cordial and gracious
- Sociable
- Friendly
- Appreciative of others

Extroverted
- Positive
- Outgoing
- Enthusiastic
- Action-oriented
- Resilient
- Ambitious
- Bold
- Unreserved
- Willing to take risks (adventuresome)
- Passionate
- Competitive

Skilled Communicators
- Good at listening and understanding
- Understandable
- Articulate
- Open and honest
- Understanding of human behavior
- Positive and optimistic
- Agreeable and congenial

Principled
- Respected and admired
- Ethical and consistent
- Responsible while sharing credit easily
- Rarely impulsive; they think things through
- Seen by others as having integrity
- Successful in any area they choose
- Conscientious
- Trustworthy
- Open to questions and ideas

Explorers
- Curious
- Open to new thinking
- Questioning
- Eager to learn
- Lacking pretense
- Future-oriented
- Innovative
- Impatient

MOVING BEYOND WORK

My clients who are moving into retirement often say to me, "All my friends are at work. How will I make friends outside of work?" This comment comes much more frequently from my male clients than from women.

These career-focused men, and many women too, have spent most of their adult lives at work, with occasional social evenings spent with their families. They haven't had the time or inclination to establish friendships outside of work and family, and so their social network has been centered on their work. They know that it will be difficult to maintain their work friendships when they are outside of the work setting—and they are right. If they are lucky, they may have one or two friends with whom they maintain a good friendship. But the opportunities to connect informally with new people outside the workplace do not readily appear, and many people often do not know how to make the opportunities happen. For men, playing sports is a possible avenue for making new friends, as is getting to know the husbands of their wife's friends. The truth is that career-focused people, no matter what their gender, are often worried about finding friendships and do not know how to become more comfortable in the unstructured role of a friend.

Pete, a client who was very focused on his career, was almost as focused on his weekly tennis games with seven other men. He enjoyed tennis greatly. Two years ago, Pete began having joint problems that were just bad enough for him to have to give up tennis. His wife told me that not long after he stopped playing tennis, he became "edgy and grouchy at home." She worried that he might be depressed except that he seemed fine when he was at work. She was also tired of his misery. During our discussion, Pete said that although he missed the tennis, he missed the guys more. This revelation surprised him. The men had rarely had contact with each other outside of the tennis games, and he assumed that that was the way friendships worked—very task-focused. Being a "man of action," he called the man he enjoyed being with the most and learned that he and another ex–tennis partner had had to stop tennis as well. They were thinking about playing poker once a week and of calling him to see if he wanted to play as well. Pete joined them and is no longer edgy and grouchy at home, making his wife very happy.

Many very talented men are poor social networkers, relying on the woman in their life to manage the social parts of their world. While this statement is a broad generalization, it is often accurate.

I have found that the best way for these men and women to build a non-work social network is to look at *what worked for them at work and replicate a similar situation outside of work.* I ask them to think about what it was, or is, about work that makes it a comfortable place to meet people and to make friends. Typically, the response I get is that they share common interests and goals with their colleagues—the interests and goals that made each of them gravitate to their particular place of work or profession in the first place. The common interests are also structured around roles that define a person's place at work. Formal contact with others occurs at meetings, on projects, and at places defined by work. They also have informal contact within the structured setting, for instance, "Charlotte, do you want to grab some lunch?" "Frank, did your son get that job he was after?"

If the social structure of employment has worked well in the past, it is likely it will work in the future. I ask clients who are having trouble making friends to look for a setting that will attract people with interests similar to their own; a setting that provides a structured set of roles and has a role for them that they will be comfortable taking on; a setting that has work and projects that could use their skills; and a setting that offers an opportunity for informal contact.

Whether it is a for-profit or non-profit business or other community organization, a structured work-like setting can provide a good transition from nine to five at the office to a career beyond work. Consider a charity, your local hospital, local government, and social service agencies; your golf, tennis, boating, hunting, shooting, or quilting club; or your dance, meditation, yoga, writing, or cooking class. No one says that you must volunteer; like Barbara Perry and Lois Sullivan, you can also try new jobs. Try things that you think you might enjoy but did not have time for when you were career-focused. I know of a number of executives who left the corporate world and are now doing things like running their town's Little League or working at a retail plant nursery. One is now working for a longtime client who is located near his home. This is about finding comfortable ways to put yourself into situations so that you can meet people, just like Barbara and Lois do. Once you create these opportunities to meet people, you can use Irv Kooris's approach to building friendships.

Ann Caldwell was about to become a woman beyond work. Ann was three months from retirement when I spoke with her. Her career included management and executive positions at Harvard and Brown universities, Wheaton College, and Boston's Museum of Fine Arts. When we spoke she was the president of the MGH Institute of Health Professions; an academic affiliate of Massachusetts General Hospital. She held that position for more than 10 years, and at the request of the institute's board of trustees continued in it longer than she had planned. Ann talked about what she believes makes for a successful retirement.

I was always interested in how people aged and retired. And so I have a number of different retired people whom I admire and who are my models. Most of them are people who have remained intellectually vibrant in one way or another, whether they play Scrabble, read voraciously, or in some way continue other intellectual pursuits. I have great admiration for my father-in-law, who turns 95 next week, partly because he's planned his life very thoughtfully and carefully for himself and his family as he's aged and pretty much stayed in control of his life. He was a CEO and he kept that role to become CEO of his retirement. He's done a pretty admirable job of that because he's always anticipated things before he had to do them. He was ready do the next thing and he did it. He does not suffer from looking backward, only what challenges and opportunities lie ahead.

I have one very good friend who is on my board now and she has been on many other corporate boards as well. She's now 75, so she's off most corporate boards. When she first retired she expected that she would "find one more big thing to do." She never expected to do what she is doing now. I can't tell you how much time she spends with her grandchildren and how happy she seems to be. She is still on many non-profit boards, but smaller things now. I think that she has found her next big thing, and it is not what she thought it would be. I have lots of ideas as to what I will do, and I am excited to find out what I actually do.

I know that many of us do not find this post-work approach to friend-ship easy—just thinking about it makes our discomfort about the idea evident. I can only suggest that you give it a try and keep your expecta-tions moderate. Meeting one person whom you enjoy is more likely than finding an intact social network that will adopt you.

THE INTERNET SOCIAL NETWORK

The Internet has added a dimension to our society that could hardly have been imagined in the mid-1990s. Over the past decade, the Internet has grown from a university researcher's tool to a major cultural agent of change. Almost every aspect of society has adapted to the Internet. In the previous chapter, I listed eight medical trends that are either occurring or will occur within the next 20 years. At least five of these innovations involve the Internet. The definition of social networks is expanding to include contact and connections via the Internet. E-mail has replaced a great deal of phone contact while also increasing the overall amount of contact. I can now send my brother, who lives more than a day's drive away, a thought or story as it comes to mind at 11:30 at night. I no longer have to wait until the morning to call him and most likely forget what I was thinking. Some of the thoughts, maybe jokes, are so incidental that I probably would not have called him about them anyway. This rise in informal contact makes us both feel closer than when we relied on calling two or three times a month.

Many people wonder how Internet social networking will play out. Will it tear apart the fabric of society by having people holed up in front of their glowing computer screens, hardly ever interacting face to face? Will this lack of contact reduce the caring and empathy that grow with direct contact? It may.

But it may also create a new channel for people to connect with friends. Internet social networks can add to the tried and true phone calls (which have really only been widely available since the mid-1940s), as well as family gatherings, work, paper mail, the local gathering place, and the many other ways we connect. People who are not computer or Internet savvy can take courses in how to navigate through the technology. (Taking a course on using the Internet can itself become an opportunity for meeting people.)

We also see special interest groups gathering on the Internet. People like my aunt Adele regularly visit websites dedicated to macular degeneration. Bob Hardy, my 88-year-old father-in-law and a retired airline pilot, regularly visits aviation websites and shares pictures and stories with old friends who are scattered around the world. Without the Internet, he would have few resources, apart from a few aviation magazines, to remain current or to stay in touch with pilot friends.

The "traditions" of the Internet are just beginning to firm up. People have experimented with chat rooms, personal websites, and now blogs and other social networking businesses such as facebook.com, which describes itself as "a social utility that connects you with the people around you," or eharmony.com, which provides matchmaking services. Although I cannot endorse a particular site, aarp.com and eons.com are geared for people aged 55 and over. All these sites are active as of summer 2007 but, as is true with the Internet as a whole, that may have changed by the time you read this.

The Internet is filled with interesting people, as well as scammers, thieves, and other criminals. It is a new and powerful place, with etiquette, rules, and laws forming as abusers make it clear where the problems lie. (As I mentioned in Chapter 5, identity theft is a real concern that can now be insured against, just like a hurricane.)

I have talked with many new adults who have created informal social networks (actual informal face-to-face talking) to explore the Internet. During their gatherings, they talk about what they have discovered, what to stay away from, and what to enjoy. It reminds me of distant memories of early television when neighbors would talk about the new programs and share ideas on how to jiggle the antennas to improve the reception. Today, the talk is about new websites and higher speed connections.

The Internet is an incredible social resource that can be used by those who enjoy the experience. The caveat once again is to keep your eyes wide open as you grow along with the Internet.

ISOLATED AND IN PAIN

> *"If the phone doesn't ring, it's me."*
> —Jimmy Buffett

Isolation and loneliness constitute a significant medical condition that can aggravate, or even cause, serious illness. Robert D. Putnam, professor of public policy at Harvard University, has written about the decline in America's social structures and the rise in social disconnection. He tells us that "social connectedness matters to our lives in the most profound way" and that research shows that it "is one of the most powerful determinants of our well-being."[14]

> *Most intriguingly, social capital [social networks and the associated norms of reciprocity] might actually serve as a physiological triggering mechanism, stimulating people's immune systems to fight disease and buffer stress. Research now underway suggests that social isolation has measurable biochemical effects on the body. Animals who have been isolated develop more extensive atherosclerosis (hardening of the arteries) than less isolated animals, and among both animals and humans loneliness appears to decrease the immune response and increase blood pressure.[15]*

Isolation is more than just not being invited to the party. It is more like not knowing about any parties at all. I have great respect for individual preferences. I know people who prefer to live what most of us would consider an isolated life. They draw energy and good feeling from such things as intellectual pursuits, woodworking, reading, crafts, and other similar individual activities. This does not mean that they are in jeopardy.

---

14 Robert D. Putnam, *Bowling Alone* (New York: Simon & Schuster, 2000), p. 326.
15 Putnam, *Bowling Alone*, p. 327.

Isolation is not the problem; the problem is unwanted isolation, which causes loneliness. The problems arise for the people who want more interaction with people and are unable to find it.

I could cite dozens of other experts who report that social isolation can cause significant medical problems. This link brings social isolation into the realm of your physical well-being, and it should therefore be addressed with your health care professional.

For some, social interaction can be uncomfortable, even painful. One reason for this may be that the person is depressed and does not know it. It is very hard to take positive action on your own behalf when you are depressed. Professionals who can help you with your isolation are widely available through most health care systems and community and religious organizations.

If you cannot improve your isolated world using the ideas of the NSNBs, talk to a trusted advisor and get help. It is not just good for your outlook—it is also important for your health. You cannot enjoy solid financial and physical assets without your social and personal assets also working on your behalf.

SUMMARY

In this chapter we looked at

- The role of your social domain. A supportive and enjoyable social network builds resilience, both physical and emotional. It is an important part of healthy living. Social support correlates with a healthy and long life. The pleasure derived from the good times of life is increased when shared with family and friends. The pain during difficult times is cushioned by the support they provide. A good social network allows you both the company of others and the solitude you want.

- What a social network is. A social network is made up of a range of relationships from acquaintances, to friends you see periodically, to family and friends who you are in contact with on a regular basis. Each can offer their own measure of connection, comfort, and enjoyment.

- Making friends and building friendships. Many people are concerned about their abilities to make new friends. Meeting people, making a friend and building a relationship come naturally to some people and can be learned by others.

CHAPTER SEVEN

THE PERSONAL DOMAIN

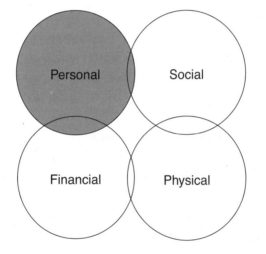

"There's only one corner of the universe you can be certain of improving, and that's your own self."
—Aldous Huxley

Most people have set views on what it means to "know yourself." In the 1940s people focused more on "family, God, and country" and less on themselves. By the late 1960s the focus was on questioning everything, including family, God, and country. We began to view our world from our personal perspective, not from that of the establishment.

During our formative years we saw psychology moving out of the shadows of managing mental illness to the light of self-knowledge, and sometimes beyond into the overblown realm of "pop" psychology. When we talk about family values and personal freedoms, we are echoing the ideas that began with the 1960s' idea of "finding yourself." Remember when the Beatles traveled to India where they embraced "Eastern" ideas? They exposed millions of us to a very different understanding of who we are in the world. Whether you liked this new thinking or not, you decided what this new thinking meant to you. You may have embraced it, ignored it, or were repulsed by it, but you did make a decision about what was right for "me." Do you recall the "me generation"?

Some people think that a self-orientation feeds today's rampant self-aggrandizing and selfish society. Others consider a lack of self-awareness the main reason that people are easily led into the chase for external status symbols—cars, gadgets, fancier homes, and spoiled children—to indicate happiness and fulfillment.

What I can say is that the idea of who you are, what it means to be you, and how happy and satisfied you are, are the most personal truths you hold. I will not, and cannot, try to change your ideas of who you are. I will attempt to share with you the benefits of knowing, questioning, and improving your self.

Your *self* is the most personal domain, the one that ultimately determines the value of the financial, physical, and social domains. Later in this chapter I present the power derived from self-awareness—your knowledge of yourself. While many people believe that self-awareness is a healthy and good idea, I see it as the differentiator between being good, even very good, and being great. In our book, *Corporate MVPs* (Wiley, 2004), my co-author, Margaret Butteriss, and I found that the most valuable people really knew what was important to them and what was happening in their world. The greater the self-awareness the better the decisions, and better decisions result in more success.

THE UNIQUENESS OF SELF

"The whole is more than the sum of its parts."
—Aristotle

The financial, physical, and social domains are more easily understood than is the personal domain. Do you have enough money; are you healthy; do you have satisfying relationships with your family, friend, and community?

These questions are more easily knowable than the questions that are asked of the personal domain. Are you happy; what do want in life; does your world work? There are few objective measures that can be applied. This is where we enter the murky waters of how you feel about things and what you believe. One person may have prostate cancer and feel blessed that the doctors were able to contain it and manage the related effects while another person may have shoulder problems and feel miserable because his golf score has gone up by ten strokes. These perceptions, how you understand your feelings, is based in large part on your personality.

Two and a half years ago, my nephew Eric and his wife, Melissa, had triplets. These three little ones are similar in so many ways, yet each has his or her own personality. Jack loves trucks, Eve loves bunnies, and Charlotte is drawn to books. What makes each one unique when they are physically so similar? They each have a self.

Your self is much like a cake, made up of many parts, including (in the case of the cake) flour, sugar, milk, eggs, flavorings, and other ingredients. But we all know that a cake is much more than just the sum of its ingredients; when baked with skill, a cake is delicious. The ingredients may be constant, but it is the baker who makes the cake. To understand your self, you need to know about the many "ingredients" from which you are made. Once you know yourself, you can blend your personal, social, physical, and financial domains into an integrated whole that is greater than the sum of its parts.

HOW WOULD YOU DESCRIBE YOUR SELF?

"When a person can no longer laugh at himself,
it is time for others to laugh at him."
—Thomas Szasz, psychiatrist and author

There is a popular exercise on many Internet sites that asks you to "describe yourself in five words." Here are some examples of people's responses:
- Spiritual, caring, energetic, curious, fun
- Ugly, unfriendly, miserable, loud, smart
- Caring, introverted, creative, polite, analytic

- Solid, creative, thoughtful, curious, bold
- Happy, compassionate, friendly, spiritual, independent
- Wife, grandma, organized, smart, friendly
- Independent, strong, adventurous, young, powerful
- Six feet three inches tall
- Handsome, tall, dark, successful, liar
- Clever, sentimental, curious, vivacious, lovable
- Happy, funny, reliable, creative, sensual
- Honest, irritating, annoying, faithful, overweight
- Stormy, mighty, scholar, disturbed, contained
- Taller than most my age

I think that this five-word exercise is popular because it asks people to think about themselves, and people like to think about themselves. Are the five-word descriptions accurate? It's hard to say; much of it depends on the person's ability to take a step back and look at him or her self from a new vantage point—to gain perspective.

There are thousands of ways to describe your personal side. I see the personal domain as containing two main components: personality and character. Personality describes how you behave in this world; *what others see* you doing, while character describes why you do what you do: *how your internal beliefs and values* determine how you behave. Others learn about you based on what they see you doing. They may see a gregarious person who is unreliable or a quiet person who honors commitments. Personality and character work together to make your experience in the world comfortable and understandable or uncomfortable and confusing. They also provide information to others that determines their experience of you.

PERSONALITY

We know others by what they say and do. Emma Soames, granddaughter of Winston Churchill, recalled one of Churchill's many famous quotes: "I like pigs. Dogs look up to you, cats look down on you, but pigs treat you as an equal."[1] What can we learn about Churchill from

---

1 Hon. Emma Soames, "Chartwell Childhood." Accessed from http://www.winstonchurchill.org/i4a/pages/index.cfm?pageid=414 on August 9, 2007.

this statement? He likes pigs, that is obvious, and he likes them better than dogs, and much better than cats. Even with his reputation as "the great man," he maintains a measure of humility by appreciating the pig's view of us as equals. He has a sense of humor. He may be using pigs, dogs, and cats as a metaphor for people he knows: he likes people who view others as equals, has feelings for those who feel lesser than others, and disdains those who assume they are better. Or maybe he just likes pigs.

Psychology has worked for over 100 years to define and refine our understanding of personality. We continue to improve our descriptions of personality, expanding the number of working definitions. I will focus on a personality theory called the "Big Five," which I think best communicates a working understanding of what makes up who you are. This theory gets its name because it uses five broad dimensions of personality: Extroversion, Agreeableness, Conscientiousness, Neuroticism (Emotional Stability), and Openness/Intellect.[2] Each of the five dimensions is divided into "low" and "high" categories with adjectives listed under each heading that would describe a person who rates "high" or "low" in each dimension of personality.

Lawrence Pervin and Oliver John in their *Handbook of Personality*[3] provide an understandable and therefore useful description of the traits related to each of the Big Five's dimensions. They provide words that describe a person who would be low or high in each dimension.

The following table by Pervin and John was developed to help mental health professionals describe the personalities of patients in a more consistent and detailed manner than through general statements such as "He's depressed" or "She's happy." I have included it here to help you understand the traits that go into making up a person's personality. Look at each of the five dimensions and circle the traits that you think describe you. This can provide you with a general description of your personality. How would you describe your personality based on the traits you circled?

---

2 Lawrence A. Pervin and Oliver P. John, *Handbook of Personality: Theory and Research*, 2nd Edition (New York: Guilford Press, 1999), p. 113.
3 Pervin and John, p. 113.

Extroversion		Agreeableness		Conscientiousness		Neuroticism		Openness / Intellect	
High	Low	High	Low	High	Low	High	Low	High	Low
Talkative	Quiet	Sympathetic	Fault-finding	Organized	Careless	Tense	Stable	Wide interests	Commonplace
Assertive	Reserved	Kind	Cold	Thorough	Disorderly	Anxious	Calm	Imaginative	Narrow interests
Active	Shy	Appreciative	Unfriendly	Planful	Frivolous	Nervous	Contented	Intelligent	Simple
Energetic	Withdrawn	Soft-hearted	Quarrelsome	Efficient	Irresponsible	Moody	Unemotional	Original	Shallow
Outgoing	Retiring	Warm	Hard-hearted	Responsible	Slipshod	Worrying		Insightful	Unintelligent
Outspoken		Generous	Unkind	Dependable	Undependable	Touchy		Curious	
Dominant		Trusting	Cruel	Conscientious	Forgetful	Fearful		Sophisticated	
Forceful		Helpful	Stern	Precise		High-strung		Artistic	
Enthusiastic		Forgiving	Thankless	Practical		Self-pitying		Clever	
Show-off		Pleasant	Stingy	Deliberate		Temperamental		Inventive	
Sociable		Good natured		Painstaking		Unstable		Sharp-witted	
Spunky		Friendly		Cautious		Self-punishing		Ingenious	
Adventurous		Cooperative				Despondent		Witty	
Noisy		Gentle				Emotional		Resourceful	
Bossy		Unselfish						Wise	
		Praising						Logical	
		Sensitive						Civilized	
								Foresighted	
								Polished	
								Dignified	

Pervin and John, *Handbook of Personality*, p. 113.

Two Notes on the Big 5 Personality Dimensions

The Other Side of Neuroticism
Neuroticism is a charged word that carries many meanings with it. In this context, think of it as describing a person who is overly sensitive, anxious, or obsessive. Also, note that low neuroticism equates with emotional stability, while high neuroticism equates with high levels of sensitivity to problems, anxiety, and worry.

Your Use of this Information
The use of the information from the Pervin and John table is intended to help you to understand some of the components of a personality. It is not intended to provide you with an accurate description of your personality. If you want to deepen your understanding of your personality or if you are concerned about aspects of your personality, I urge you to talk to a close friend or trusted advisor. You can also go to the American Psychological Association's website (www.apa. org) and click on "Find a Psychologist" to find association members in your area (Canadian members are included).

Your personality is like your face; it is how others initially see you. You may be engaging or shy, cheerful or somber, calm or tense. You may know wealthy and healthy people who have many friends but are either unhappy or are disliked. You probably also know people who have varying degrees of financial security and health but seem to enjoy their life and their friends. The saying usually goes "If you don't have your health, you have nothing." I would amend it to "If you don't enjoy life, you have nothing." What you have is what living day to day gives you. It is what you make of what you have that creates your life. Personality helps to sculpt a good life.

Phil and Lou: Two Very Different Personalities

I was once asked to work with two business partners, Phil and Lou, who were at great odds with each other. During discussions with each alone and with them together, I began to see that Phil was a fairly straightforward person who focused on the work to be done and perceived his world fairly accurately. He was trusting and good-natured, yet calm, organized, insightful, quiet, and reserved. He seemed to be a trustworthy, nice guy who had a talent for his successful business. He was also passive and shied away from conflict. This often allowed Lou to ignore Phil's ideas and concerns.

On the other hand, Lou could not really see any problem with his relationship with Phil except that Phil was not as adventurous and resourceful as Lou was. Lou saw himself as very intelligent, imaginative, sophisticated, and sharp-witted. He loved to talk and socialize, acknowledging that he often dominated business meetings. This domination was part of the problem that Phil had with Lou. Lou defended his behavior as "stepping into the breach when Phil was too quiet." Lou knew that he was the reason for their business success and wished Phil would stop complaining: "We could be 10 times as busy if Phil would let me call all the shots." Lou was a sociable but careless person who blamed others for problems and took credit for success. Lou seemed to me to be a creative tornado who taxed others and ignored any damage he did. Lou thrived on conflict.

Here were two smart men who had very incompatible personalities that caused them to see the world very differently. I spoke with a number of the business's key employees and two clients who saw the differences between the two. The employees described Phil as thoughtful, experienced, trustworthy, and smart, while acknowledging that he was passive and "a little boring." They all told me that Lou was not boring but dynamic, sometimes too outspoken and difficult to work for since he was constantly coming up with "new and better" ways to do things that already worked well. One employee told me that he thought of Lou as cruel after he harshly fired two good people. Both customers told me that they kept doing business with the company "in spite of Lou" and because of their "respect for and trust with Phil."

Much work was done to find ways to accommodate these differences but none truly worked. Lou had "had it" and Phil agreed. Phil now understood that his personality clashed with Lou's and would continue to do so. He and his wife had decided to accept a proposal that Lou had put on the table a year prior. He would buy Lou out of the "boring part of the business," and Lou could take the exciting and growing part for himself.

After Lou left, he took off like a rocket and then exploded like a firecracker. He found that most of his friends in the industry did not seem to understand the value of his creative new ideas and they preferred not to do business with him.

Now on his own, Phil began visiting all their major clients and received a warm welcome from each one. He was often asked, "Why did you put up with that guy for so long?" Now that the customers were in touch with Phil, a person they could trust, they shifted more business to Phil's company. The business quickly but thoughtfully grew, and the *more business Phil did with the clients, the more business he got. Phil's calm and steady approach served his industry and his employees well.*

Phil had a personality that drew others in and made him appreciate what he had. Lou's personality pushed others away and made him constantly seek what he did not yet have.

CHARACTER: PERSONALITY WRIT LARGE

"Character cannot be developed in ease and quiet. Only through experience of trial and suffering can the soul be strengthened, vision cleared, ambition inspired, and success achieved."
—Helen Keller (1880–1968)

If you take your personality and add to it your experience and knowledge, your beliefs (what you consider right and wrong) and your values (what you consider good and bad), you have the makings of your character.

Imagine two people, Alice and Mary, who are moderately extroverted, agreeable, and emotionally stable, and who are also very conscientious but not generally open to new ideas. From this description of their personalities, you might expect each to be a likeable and good person.

Now add this information: Alice believes that it is okay to do whatever she wants as long as she does not get caught, and that the only thing of importance is how much money she has. Mary believes that society has valuable rules that the community has agreed upon and that keep us all safe; therefore, she is free to pursue her life within the norms of society. In addition, Mary considers helping those in need an important part of her responsibilities.

One day, Alice and Mary each found $100 in an envelope marked with the name of a community charity. I will leave it to you to decide what each woman did with the money she found.

As you can see from this case, Alice and Mary have similar personalities, but different beliefs and values. Together, they describe their character. Your character incorporates your beliefs and values with your personality to describe more than what you like and dislike: it describes *who you are* as a person.

In their remarkable and comprehensive book *Character Strengths and Virtues: A Handbook and Classification*,[4] Christopher Peterson and Martin Seligman classify character strengths. Here is a summary of their character classification:

1. **Wisdom and Knowledge**—cognitive strengths that entail the acquisition and use of knowledge.
2. **Courage**—emotional strengths that involve the exercise of will to accomplish goals in the face of opposition, external or internal
3. **Humanity**—interpersonal strengths that involve tending and befriending others
4. **Justice**—civic strengths that underlie healthy community life
5. **Temperance**—strengths that protect against excess
6. **Transcendence**—strengths that forge connections to the larger universe and provide meaning.[5]

These six character strengths take our personality and tie it to our social context. In this context, we are not just individuals; we are part of the larger family of people. This context takes us out of ourselves and makes us part of the world. Together, personality and character describe the whole person that we are.

If we think about character in terms consistent with the Big Five personality factors (Extroversion, Agreeableness, Conscientiousness, Neuroticism [Emotional Stability], and Openness/Intellect), we can understand the personality traits underlying a person's character. To add another layer of complexity, every culture has its own definition of what makes up a strong or a weak character. Most cultures describe a person of strong character as a person who does the right thing when nobody is watching. Of course, each culture maintains the privilege of deciding what the "right thing" is to be.

The quality of a new adult's life begins with the right ingredients: well-managed financial, physical, and social domains. It is then up to our

---

4 Christopher Peterson and Martin Seligman, *Character Strengths and Virtues: A Handbook and Classification* (Oxford, England: Oxford University Press, 2004).
5 Peterson and Seligman, *Character Strengths and Virtues*, pp. 29–30.

personality and character to take these parts and create the whole new adult life. The better you know your personality, your self, the better you can use the ingredients you have.

Must you know your self to live a rewarding life as a new adult? No, but knowing your self provides you with much more control over your life and increases your resilience, your ability to manage what will come. Self-awareness is the tool we use to know and understand ourselves.

THE POWER OF SELF-AWARENESS

"Knowing others is intelligence; knowing yourself is true wisdom.
Mastering others is strength; mastering yourself is true power."
—Lao Tzu, Chinese philosopher, 6th century B.C.

Lao Tzu was not the only philosopher to have equated self-awareness with wisdom and power—the Greeks did as well.

I have a distinct memory from when I was in Grade 6. We were learning about the Greeks and their terrific myths. My friends and I were quite interested in Hercules, Ulysses, Pericles, and the pantheon of gods. I suppose this was our version of today's Harry Potter: heroes battling the Gorgons and Cyclops; Ulysses, lashed to the mast of his ship, enduring the songs of the sexy sirens who sang sailors to their deaths. Pretty engaging stuff.

Our studies then turned to the Greek philosophers. While monsters, raging seas, battles, and heroics made sense to me, the philosophy left me cold. I do remember that the teacher made a big deal of the Oracles of Delphi and of the motto carved into the entrance of the temple of Apollo at Delphi, "Know Thyself." She seemed to be enthralled with that statement, and I had no idea why. After all, I knew myself: I liked baseball, peanut butter, my family, and television. What more did I need to know? Little did I know that this simple statement would underpin my future career in psychology.

For thousands of years, philosophers have worked to understand what makes us human. It appears that our "mind" is what differentiates us from a rock or dog and even each other. For the purposes of this book,

I will say that your mind is defined by your personality and your character. To know your own mind is to know your personality and character. The more you know your own mind, the more control you have of your world, and the more you feel in control of your world, the more powerful you feel. By "powerful," I'm not talking about having power over other people, but having power in yourself—increasing your knowledge of what works for you and using this to your advantage.

Tiger Woods is one of today's most powerful athletes. He is renowned for his ability to focus and control his emotions during very demanding competitive play. He rarely cracks at the end of a golf tournament, while others seem to fall away. An article in the *Wall Street Journal* described Woods's use of what works for him to his advantage. He has created a "play" routine that builds on his strengths.

> *You can see Mr. Woods settle into his preferred mental state on the practice range. He arrives there about 50 minutes before each round and begins by working his way through his bag, usually hitting only three or four balls per club. Frequently, however, he pauses for a full minute or two, sometimes longer, and just stands there looking around and chatting easily with his caddie, Steve Williams. On the putting green, as his tee time approaches, he wanders off by himself and rolls two balls back and forth, walking between the putts with extreme, exaggerated slowness.*
>
> *There's a tendency, under pressure, for time and motion to speed up. Clearly, Mr. Woods wants none of that.[6]*

Tiger Woods and many other accomplished people regularly translate their self-awareness into knowledge, and then into power. They know how to prepare themselves for what they will do, and they then do it. Their power is to stay focused, often by blocking out interference from the world that might distract them.

I see Nelson Mandela as an example of a person who has used his incredible personal power to take his experiences, including 27 years of imprisonment, to change his country, and hopefully the world.

Self-awareness is much more than a nice idea; it is the root of personal power. Keep this in mind:

---

6 John Paul Newport, "Why Tiger is Different. Watching Woods up close reveals his unusual approach; inside his mental game," (*Wall Street Journal*, September 22, 2007), p. W3.

- The more *raw emotions* that intrude on your thoughts, the more distracted you become and the lower the likelihood you will perform well.
- The more *examined emotions* you include in your thoughts, the greater your focus and the greater the likelihood you will perform well.

The simple fact is that we all have emotions; you cannot choose not to have them. You can choose how to use them.

Another form of "power" derived from self-awareness and knowledge is your ability to bounce back from a setback. Self-awareness (knowing your personality and character) can increase this ability by building resilience. The more you know, the more ideas and choices you can create. The more choices you have, the more resilient you are because you are better able to manage the roadblocks of life. You can realistically and accurately identify problems and avoid or fix them.

The Path from Self-Awareness to Personal Power

Many people live happy lives with little self-awareness. They do not know why their world works, but they are happy that it does. Their world works, so why interfere? The problem arises when something happens: a trauma occurs that changes their world. The trauma can disorient them, and they find it very difficult to adapt to the new situation. They find it hard to interact in their world when it does not work well for them anymore. They may withdraw or become fearful or bitter.

SELF-AWARENESS AND THE CHANGING WORLD

New adults are entering the time beyond work when most reliable components of their world are changing and they must adapt to these changes. Health issues, financial realities, and loss of close friends and family can cause dramatic change. This can be very disorienting. A measure of self-awareness allows new adults to bend and adapt, to be flexible. They can make their new world work for them. The great thing about moving beyond work is that you really do get to control what you want to do and how you want to do it.

Yet many people feel *a loss of control* as they move beyond work. They may feel adrift with no job to structure their days or to provide income, extra health insurance, or opportunities for socializing. They may also fear aging as a progressive loss of control and growth of dependency. How you manage these legitimate (but often exaggerated) fears definitely affects the quality of your life.

To understand just how much these fears can affect a person, consider the idea that many new adults embrace what they once found insufferable. So much of the career adult's decisions and time commitments were given over to the family, community, work schedules, demanding people, and career success that they felt out of control, burdened, and exhausted. Just as new adulthood provides the opportunity to gain control over one's life by returning the ability to make decisions, many people see that they will miss the structure of the career adult's life. Fear of the new adult future has the power to change what was once a burden into a fond and security-filled past. Yet returning to the past is not a productive way to create a satisfying future.

When John Kimpel moved beyond his job as a senior lawyer in a large global firm, he found some unexpected challenges.

I think what was most surprising was the degree to which my self-image was related to my work. It seems obvious now but I didn't understand why I had been feeling displaced, untethered. I had a very full schedule when I was working and everything was automatic. I would wake up in the morning, get dressed, and go to work. I would work all day; it was routine. Then I would come home, have a drink with my wife, eat dinner, read, watch a game, sleep, and begin again the next morning. I am not saying that I was not having a good time and a great life, but that was the routine. Habit can be a wonderful thing.

The routine was almost like a narcotic in the sense that I was not even aware of how little thought it required; when I took that routine away I had to learn more about who I am—simple things like what I like and what I don't like. After years of work routine, even the small-est thing became a decision. What would I do for lunch? I suddenly had to ask myself what to do. You learn about yourself pretty quickly when everything is a decision. Routine used to mask all those decisions. When I was working, I ate most of my lunches at my desk; there was no thought involved.

It also surprised me that I felt the loss of my corporate status. I had thought I was lower key and less concerned about the image I projected. Little things, like not having a business card, would remind me that I was on my own. I found that I needed to create my own new image. It's funny: there is still a little bit of discomfort when I meet someone and they ask, "So what do you do?"

One day I was at my computer and I wanted to get some informa-tion, so I did what I had always done: I clicked on a bookmarked page that I would always use on my company's internal website. "ACCESS DENIED" popped up instead of the web page. I thought, "Of course, I know that." But that stark statement went past what I knew to what I felt. I was locked out of the place that was almost like home.[7]

Sometimes you don't truly know something until you feel it. John's self-awareness allowed him to recognize that he initially felt uncer-tain of his place in the world and that he felt a disconnection from his comfortable routine. By looking at what was happening, he could understand it. Once he understood the problem, he could begin to fix it. He set up a new daily routine that is working well. He is also find-ing new ways to define himself so that he can be happy with what he is doing. John took self-awareness and has created wisdom for himself. He has applied this wisdom and has created personal power over life's uncertainties. He and his wife have built their new adulthood as they want it to be.

Those lacking self-awareness often rely on luck to create their new world from their old. Reliance on luck is not a position of power. Don Shula, the great coach of the Miami Dolphins, relied heavily on luck: "Sure, luck means a lot in football. Not having a good quarterback is bad luck."

---

7 Personal interview, September 1, 2007.

INCREASE YOUR LUCK

"A wise man will make more opportunities than he finds."
—Sir Francis Bacon

What is luck? My work with clients and my research with MVPs has helped me to understand the nature of luck in life. Aside from happenstance, like the chance of winning the lottery (which is a statistical probability more than luck), most luck is actually made. What appears to be luck is really a person's ability to notice an opportunity that others do not. So the first part of luck is opportunity. In addition, the person who identifies the opportunity is prepared to capitalize on it. This is the second part of luck, preparation. Put opportunity together with preparation, and you become a lucky person.

As you can see, a significant part of preparing yourself to make use of opportunities is self-awareness.

My brother Steve plays a much better game of golf than I do (witnessed by his 10 handicap as opposed to my 25). Let's say we both hit our tee shots into the same sand trap. Steve enters the trap and sees an opportunity to hit a sand shot to the left side of the green and have the ball roll toward the hole to leave him with an easy putt. He sets himself up for the shot, takes his time, and hits a great shot that does what he had hoped. I, on the other hand, am upset with myself that I hit into the sand trap, so I lunge into the trap and swing away. The ball clears the trap and sails past the green to the right, setting up another difficult shot: bad luck. Steve relied on his confidence in his sand shots, which is based upon hours of practice, and on his ability to forget about the bad shot that put him there and then to look past the sand shot to what opportunities lay before him. He was prepared and he saw the opportunity. What a lucky shot he had.

My brother illustrates an important point: the more you prepare, the more opportunities you can see and the more you will be able to capitalize on them. People can build their own luck.

Why don't I practice more to improve my game? Because of my personality; I am not that disciplined and I do not like to practice. I know that about myself and I am fine with it. By the way, I am a better cook than Steve.

I am not breaking new ground here. In an 1854 lecture at the University of Lille in France, scientist Louis Pasteur spoke about his ability to notice things that others miss and the role of chance. He said: "In the fields of observation, chance favors only the prepared mind." Similarly, self-awareness is the mechanism that alerts you to a potential opportunity. This feeling is then translated into thought, which you then use to make decisions that will enhance your life because they are based on who you are and what is important to you. Those with little self-awareness are more likely to miss opportunities and to have less knowledge on which to base their decisions, reducing the likelihood that the decisions will support who they are and what is important to them.

Prepare your mind by combining your self-awareness (your constantly refreshed understanding of your self) with constant learning. This will highlight opportunities as you create them.

What do self-awareness and luck mean to you? Many new adults believe that aging reduces opportunities and therefore constrains their choices and their lives. If you believe this, you are likely to stop looking for opportunities to live life as you want. As with so many things in life, the less you look the less you see. People who believe that many opportunities do exist as we age understand that there are fewer opportunities than we might have pursued when we were 40 or 50 but that there are also many opportunities for us as new adults that we could not have imagined, or taken advantage of, when we were younger. And it is in the nature of our generation to create new ideas and opportunities as we continue to grow. Look and you will see; learn and you will live.

A DOSE OF REALISM

"It is unwise to be too sure of one's own wisdom. It is healthy to be reminded that the strongest might weaken and the wisest might err."
—Mahatma Gandhi

Self-awareness has a bad name among many people. It conjures up pictures of worriers second-guessing their thoughts and decisions. It is often linked with depressed people who so over-evaluate their actions that they cannot get things done. In his book *Authentic Happiness*, Martin Seligman cites research that supports the importance of both positive emotions and what Seligman calls "depressive realism."

> *Depressed people are accurate judges of how much skill they have, whereas happy people think they are much more skillful than others judge them to be. Happy people remember more good events than actually happened, and they forget more bad events. Depressed people, in contrast, are accurate about both. Happy people are lopsided in their beliefs about success and failure.*[8]

I am not advocating that you try to become depressed to improve your self-knowledge. Personally, I will take being happy and slightly self-deluded to being depressed with a more accurate view of things. But I do wonder what it is about depression and its potential for realism that can help a person to manage his or her world. According to Seligman, "Less happy people [people edging toward depressive thinking] are more skeptical"[9] than happy people. Some skepticism provides an entryway for doubt and critical thinking, which is part of what makes smart people smart.

Smart *and* happy people can do something that smart but less happy people have a difficult time doing, which is to "readily switch tactics and adopt a skeptical and analytical frame of mind."[10] Smart and happy people have a full complement of tools to use as they live life, while depressed people can become mired in skepticism and self-doubt.

Are you happy, less happy, or depressed? This is a question that only self-awareness can accurately answer. A lack of self-awareness reduces your ability to *consciously* use your analytical abilities to incorporate your emotions in your decisions. *The less aware you are of your emotions, the more likely you are to be run by your emotions.* Sound strange? If you cannot consciously incorporate your emotions into your critical thinking, then you will *always make emotional decisions*, and you will not know that you are doing it. Emotions are strong determinants of behavior. If you do not know that you have an emotional response to a situation, you will not know how your thinking is being influenced by

---

8 Martin E.P. Seligman, *Authentic Happiness* (New York: Free Press, 2002), p. 37.
9 Seligman, *Authentic Happiness*, p. 38.
10 Seligman, *Authentic Happiness*, p. 38.

your emotions; therefore, you will unknowingly use your emotions to decide your actions. Whether you are aware or not aware, your emotions always influence your view of the world and the decisions you make.

I know a man I'll call Mike, who was paralyzed by his emotions. One Sunday, a family wedding was to be held that evening and Mike truly wanted to attend it. His problem was that he had a major report to present the next morning to the head of his company, who was known for his sometimes blistering appraisals of reports he did not like. Mike was meticulously prepared for his report, but he was also understandably anxious, so he felt compelled to stay home and review his presentation.

He did not realize until later just how anxious he was about this presentation. By Sunday afternoon, his back had begun to stiffen up as it had never stiffened before. As the evening approached, his back pain worsened, but he decided to attend the wedding. He had a good time, despite his pain and having to forgo dancing.

On his way home he realized that he had not given much thought to the next day's presentation; the wedding had been an enjoyable distraction. When he arrived home he was again thinking about the next morning. As he got into bed his back completely stiffened again and he could not move at all. Any movement was excruciating. His wife called their doctor, who phoned in a prescription for a painkiller and a muscle relaxant. Needless to say, Mike could not make the 8 a.m. meeting to present his report. His boss presented it, and it was well received by the head of the company.

Mike's anxiety, much of which he was not aware of, made his decisions for him. His was able to push the anxiety out of his mind so that he could attend the wedding, but when he returned home it flooded back and disabled him enough that he could not present the report. Mike believed he had no choice but to do what he wanted to do, not do the presentation.

People who lack self-awareness can be not only manipulated by their feelings, but also more easily manipulated by others. Sam was one of my clients who was, and is, very successful. He was part of the senior executive team at a global financial company. He came to see me because he had a tendency to be disruptive during meetings.

I attended several of the meetings to observe what happened. Sam was attempting to get some of his plans approved by the team, but when he broached the topics, several of his colleagues would bring up contentious points that would inevitably get Sam off the topic and fail to make the case for his initiatives. I could see that it was at the point when he probably would have had agreement from the rest of the team that he would lose his train of thought and go off topic. What was happening was that Sam was being manipulated by three team members who did not support his ideas. These individuals would link Sam's ideas to a topic that, according to Sam, would raise his "blood pressure to the point of exploding." It was as if Sam had a red button attached to his forehead that people could push and watch him explode. He was unaware of his own emotions, while others were keenly aware of them.

Sam and I talked, and he gained an awareness of what was happening. At the next meeting, his colleagues tried to push the exploding button again, but to no avail. Sam took a breath and told them they were off topic, and he continued with his point. He eventually did get his initiatives approved.

You may recall the 2006 World Cup soccer final, when emotion trumped good sense for Zinedine Zidane:

Insult Behind Zidane's Head-Butt Revealed

MILAN, Italy, Aug 18, 2007—Italy defender Marco Materazzi finally disclosed what he said to Zinedine Zidane in the World Cup final that provoked the French star to retaliate with a head-butt.

"I prefer the whore that is your sister," Materazzi wrote in his yet-to-be-released autobiography, according to Italian news reports Saturday....

Zidane head-butted Materazzi in the chest with 10 minutes left in last year's final. He was sent off for violent conduct, ending his stellar career with a red card. Italy went on to win the game in a penalty-kick shootout after the score was 1–1 after extra time.

Materazzi, who received a two-game ban for incitement, has since apologized to Zidane. France coach Raymond Domenech this month lauded Materazzi's strategy for getting Zidane out of the game.

"I say 'bravo' to him," the coach said.[11]

---

11 © 2007 The Associated Press. All rights reserved. Updated: 3:36 p.m. ET August 18, 2007.

It is understandable that emotions run rampant in the highly charged atmosphere of a World Cup soccer match. Still, it would be unusual for a rude comment to have as much impact as Materazzi's did. But Materazzi knew Zidane's personality and he used his knowledge to win the World Cup. For his part, Zidane demonstrated how emotions can force poor decisions and actions; the best way to control emotions is to know them. When you know your emotions, you change them into thoughts, and thoughts are manageable. Thought tempers emotions, and emotions inform thought, as illustrated here:

Thoughtful versus Emotional Decisions

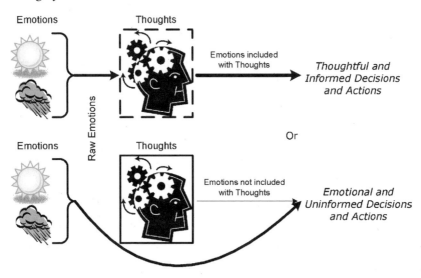

When you include your raw emotions with your thoughts you are generating insight. Insight focuses and improves your perception of your world. This opens the intuitive and creative channel of information that many people miss.

Think of your emotions as the atmosphere in which you live your life. One day you may feel sunny and bright, while another day you may feel overcast and threatening. In effect, you carry your own weather system around with you. If you ignore it, you may very well get rained on or burned. The point of building self-awareness is to add your atmospheric data to your rational thinking and improve your decisions.

KNOW THYSELF

"Do not look back in anger, or forward in fear,
but around in awareness."
—James Thurber

There are many, many ways to learn about your self. We can't cover them all in this chapter. The simple way to build self-awareness is to use introspection or self-reflection. Looking inward has been going on for a long time. It is said that Plato saw introspection as a key to learning, describing it as calmly and patiently reviewing our own thoughts, and then thoroughly examining what we see. Deep introspection and therefore high levels of self-awareness are obtained through meditation and prayer. Using these approaches requires dedication and often belief.

Reflection: Pause for Thought

A simpler, and very effective, type of introspection is something most of us use all the time: we pause for thought or we reflect. If you are driving and come to a four-way-stop intersection, you stop the car and think about which other cars have the right of way. Simple concept. If, however, another car approaches the stop sign and the driver is heavily engaged in a telephone call, he or she may pause but be thinking only of the phone conversation, and charge through the intersection without even noticing any other cars.

By stopping, you allow yourself time to consider your thoughts and emotions and then to reflect on their meaning for you.

Below are three graphics that detail three typical styles to managing our interaction with the world. Here is the key that explains what is meant by each shape:

Three Tools Used to Manage Our Experiences as We Interact with Our World

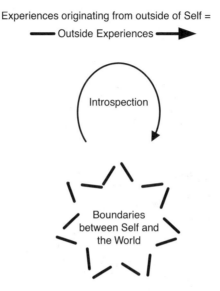

The first is the **Very Open** style. This approach leaves a person's self open to the world, allowing unfettered access to ideas and information. Little introspection takes place because the very open person is ruled by what he or she last heard. Very open people are easily manipulated and can feel out of control in a changing world.

How Very Open People Use the Tools to Manage Their Experiences as They Interact with Their World

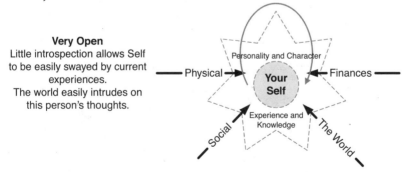

The next style is the **Open** style, which sets up some boundaries against full exposure to the effects of the world. This allows the self to maintain its integrity while having access to new ideas. The boundaries are porous, creating points of exchange between the person and their world. In the Open style, introspection is a valuable tool for assessing and managing the benefits and conflicts that occur in the person's world. Open people make the most of their world and are able to adapt and grow as their world changes.

How Open People Use the Tools to Manage Their Experiences as They Interact with Their World

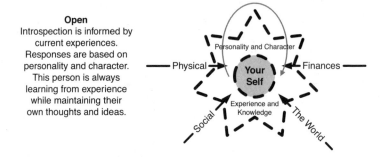

Open
Introspection is informed by current experiences. Responses are based on personality and character. This person is always learning from experience while maintaining their own thoughts and ideas.

The third style, the **Closed** style, walls the self off from information and ideas originating outside of the Closed person's insular world. Only prescreened information and ideas that support the self's current view are allowed in. Introspection is used as the way to assess worldly information and ideas to ensure their consistency with those firmly held. The Closed person lives in a tiny world and has great difficulty adapting to change.

How Closed People Use the Tools to Manage Their Experiences as They Interact with Their World

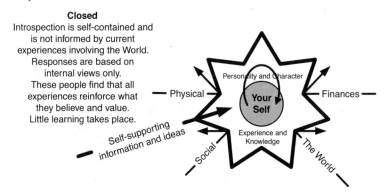

Closed
Introspection is self-contained and is not informed by current experiences involving the World. Responses are based on internal views only. These people find that all experiences reinforce what they believe and value. Little learning takes place.

People who maintain an Open style are most adaptable and realistic. They are able to make their world work for them. They know themselves. They accomplish this by *pausing for thought*, considering what they want, what they believe and value, and what the world has for them. This pausing, introspection, allows valuable new information to be added to current information, which these people then use to modify or confirm their understanding of their world. They consider this up-to-date information in light of their personality and character so they can determine what they should do. The decisions they make are therefore more informed and are usually more likely to produce the desired results than the decisions made by the Very Open or the Closed person. The Open person is, in effect, acting from self-awareness.

In practice, you do not need to remember this chain of ideas. It is simply what happens when you maintain an Open style. All you really need to do is purposely take the time to pause for thought; the rest will follow.

Over time you learn *what motivates you*, what you need and desire, and what creates positive feelings—enjoyment, love, desire, warmth, satisfaction, fulfillment, and happiness. You also learn *what stalls you*, and what creates the negative feelings—misery, dislike, hate, lack of desire, coldness, dissatisfaction, lack of fulfillment, and unhappiness.

When you pause for thought, you "know thyself" more. The better you know yourself, the better you can manage your world. As Tiger Woods and Nelson Mandela so eloquently demonstrate, self-knowledge is powerful.

SELF-KNOWLEDGE AND THE NEW ADULT

You may recall this chart from Chapter 2:

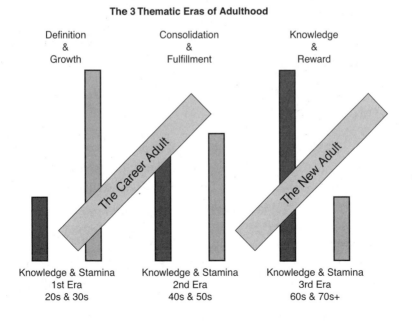

The 3 Thematic Eras of Adulthood

The new adulthood—the Third Era—is the time of our greatest knowledge, including our own self-knowledge, which we build over the years using self-awareness. If we have maintained some self-awareness throughout our adult years, we have not only experienced life but also learned from our experiences. Every time we learn from experience we slightly, or greatly, alter our understanding of the world and our place in it.

I greatly dislike licorice. One of the ways I could describe myself is to say, "Bill hates licorice." My wife, on the other hand, enjoys licorice. I love her despite this major flaw. So my position on licorice is a truth for me. A related truth is that I do not like fennel, a licorice-flavored vegetable that I do not believe I have ever knowingly eaten. About a month ago, my wife brought home a new item from our local grocer, a Spanish crispy flatbread with caramelized sugar on top. We both loved it. It had an interesting but unfamiliar flavor that neither of us could identify. It also had black specks sprinkled throughout the bread. We read the ingredients, and one of them was fennel seed! I could not believe it; I was eating and enjoying something that had a subtle licorice flavor. At this point, I could either maintain my long-held licorice truth or I could accept that I had learned that I might actually like fennel, that cousin of the black candy.

This was not a life-changing event, but I do now sometimes order restaurant dishes that include some fennel. I have learned something about myself, and my behavior is beginning to change as a result. Knowing yourself is more than just your likes and dislikes; it is also about your willingness to learn new things and incorporate them into your world.

BEING MORTAL

> "The young man who has not wept is a savage,
> and the old man who will not laugh is a fool."
> —George Santayana, early 20th-century Spanish–American
> philosopher, poet, and novelist

No matter how aware or unaware you are, there is a major fact that we must incorporate that until now was a distant and unpleasant thought. We are mortal. Many of us reach our new adulthood without having truly faced mortality, although war, accidents, illness, and the loss of loved ones can, through experience, force an early awareness of the fragility of life. But as we enter our new adult years, the fragility of life begins to feel more real and more personal.

Some people attempt to deal with it by denying their mortality. Doctors often have a problem with patients who are recovering from major surgery and try to quickly prove that they are as vital and strong as ever. A client who had recently suffered a heart attack told me, "Once they let me out of the hospital I had to play tennis as quickly as possible. It was more than just proving I could play as well as I could before; it was proving to myself that the uncomfortable and unknown feeling of being near death did not stay with me. I had to shake the feeling that I would die." Within two weeks he was back in the hospital after fainting on the tennis court. He was fortunate that he suffered no major damage, and his doctor told him so in no uncertain terms. He took this idea to heart and began thinking of himself as fortunate. To this day he believes that he is very lucky to have survived his heart attack and to live at a time when medicine can actively treat his ongoing heart disease. Two to three times per week he reminds himself of this thinking before his first tennis serve.

It happens to us all; we are touched by an incident that brings us face to face with the reality of mortality. How do we deal with our own mortality?

I have been noticing in the obituaries that more people my age or younger are dying. Some of them I even knew. This was not the case 20 or even 10 years ago. A growing reality for me, and for all new adults, is that aging eventually ends in demise.

During my interview with Dan Cashman, the Sunday morning basketball player in his early 60s whom you met in Chapter 6, I asked him, "What's it like to be mortal?" His response was direct and honest: "It scares the shit out of me."

Mortality is a difficult reality for new adults. Coming to grips with the reality of our future death becomes a major task. I'm not suggesting that we should spend all our time focused on our mortality: preoccupation with death diminishes the enjoyment of the present, an unnecessary waste of time when we value time more than we did before. As you know, scarcity increases value. However, we do need to face the fact of our mortality.

Accepting our future mortality, as opposed to worrying about it, builds gratitude for what we have, and therefore we enjoy it more. Gratitude is a powerful force against the aches of future mortality.

The best of us are grateful for what we have, and we manage without what we do not have. Spirituality is a strong asset when trying to understand what mortality means and how to live with it.

THE POWER OF OUR SPIRITUAL MIND

Spirituality is a big concept that deals with the big questions. Who am I? Why am I here? What have I accomplished? What is the best way to live? What is the meaning of life? What is meaningful in my life? These are the questions that come to the fore as a new adult. We now have the time to pause and think about life and to reset our life's goals. Your personal belief of who, what, and why you are who you are leads to these spiritual questions. Many new adults explore this part of their personal domain and many do not. The benefits of at least understanding this part of your self will become clear as we proceed.

At this point, some readers may be balking at the word *spiritual*. They are not religious and don't believe in a higher power. But I believe that everyone has a spiritual understanding of his or her world. Let me explain what I mean by *spiritual*.

You can have a spiritual understanding either as part of your religious beliefs or without having religious beliefs. On the other hand, it is difficult to be religious without having a spiritual core that is shared with other members of your religion. Religion is a sub-set of spirituality.

In 2006, a study was published in the journal *Rehabilitation Psychology* on how people living with a major disability employ their spirituality to manage their quality of life. All the study subjects had endured a major injury to their spinal cord, leaving them permanently disabled to one degree or another. All of them had to come to grips with their loss and then redefine what was meaningful to them. In setting up the study, the authors first had to define spirituality and then measure its effect on their subjects' perceived quality of life. They found that their subjects described two variations of spirituality:

> *The first, religious spirituality, can be defined as a relationship with God or a higher power and typically is observed among individuals attending*

*organized religious services with a community of other people. The other
type, existential spirituality, is not directly related to a specific place of
worship or set of widely accepted ideals. Instead, it refers to a worldview
or perspective in which individuals seek purpose in their life and come to
understand their life as having ultimate meaning and value.*[12]

(The word *existential* may conjure up some dense philosophical theory
held by radical fringes of society. Think of it here as simply a way that
someone understands what it means to them to exist, to live, and to
experience life.)

The authors of the study found that 98 percent of the subjects reported having a spiritual belief system. They found that of the 98 percent, 16 percent were classified as high in their degree of spirituality, 83
percent were classified as moderate, and 1 percent were classified as low.
The authors also reported that no matter what type of spiritual concepts
were held, the greater a subject's spiritual core, the stronger their sense
of well-being. If you compared a study subject who has a high degree of
spirituality with another who has a low degree of spirituality, the person
with the high degree of spirituality would report greater meaning in, and
satisfaction with, life.

Interestingly, 33 percent of the subjects' spirituality was classified
as religious and another 33 percent was classified as existential. What
about the other 32 percent? They fell in between the two categories and
were put into a *nonspecific spirituality* category, indicating no clear pref-
erence for a particular type of spiritual understanding. Yet almost 100
percent of the subjects classified themselves as spiritual. I know many
people who are not highly religious or existential who could fall into the
nonspecific classification. I would not, however, describe their spiritual
core as nonspecific. I do see that they have a personal blend of spirituality
that pulls from both religious and existential thinking and traditions. I
would classify them as "blended."

Here is a graphic view of how the study authors define existential
and religious spiritual understandings.

---

12 Elizabeth N. Matheis, David S. Tulsky, and Robert J. Matheis, "The Relation Between Spirituality and Quality of Life Among Individuals with Spinal Cord Injury," *Rehabilitation Psychology*
August 2006, Vol. 51(3), pp. 265–271.

The Range of Personal Spirituality

Existential	Nonspecific (Blended)	Religious
A worldview or perspective in which individuals seek purpose in their life and come to understand their life as having ultimate meaning and value.		A relationship with God or a higher power and typically is observed among individuals attending organized religious services with a community of other people.

Source of existential and religious definitions from Matheis, Tulsky, and Matheis, "The Relation Between Spirituality and Quality of Life Among Individuals with Spinal Cord Injury."

This is one small study among thousands that can provide fodder for almost any position you want to take on spirituality. But I think that it documents what most of us see as obvious: almost all people have spiritual beliefs that help them understand and live in their world, and their approaches to spirituality are as diverse as they are.

We can learn from the many people, like the spinal-cord-injury patients, who use their spiritual perspective to improve their quality of life. This spiritual perspective can be used to build your spiritual identity. Here is a good definition of spiritual identity: "A persistent sense of self that addresses ultimate questions about the nature, purpose, and meaning of life, resulting in behaviors that are consonant with the individual's core values."[13]

Knowing your spiritual identity can help you to answer the often difficult question "Who am I?" As you move beyond work, your world changes in many ways, but having a spiritual identity can provide you with the continuity to know who you are, even in unfamiliar and strange circumstances. A spiritual identity represents your personality and character and uses your self-awareness to help you understand, to make sense of, your world.

In 1942, Viktor Frankl was a 37-year-old Austrian psychiatrist when he and his family, and many others, were rounded up and shipped off to concentration camps. Remarkably, Frankl had a life-changing experience in the camps, caring for and treating the psychiatric conditions of many of the prisoners. As Frankl writes:

---

13 Chris Kiesling, Gwendolyn T. Sorell, Marilyn J. Montgomery, and Ronald K. Colwell, "Identity and Spirituality: A Psychological Exploration of the Sense of Spiritual Self," *Developmental Psychology*, November 2006, Vol. 42(6), pp. 1269–1277.

If a prisoner felt that he could no longer endure the realities of camp life, he
found a way out in his mental life—an invaluable opportunity to dwell in
the spiritual domain, the one that the SS were unable to destroy. Spiritual
life strengthened the prisoner, helped him adapt, and thereby improved
his chances of survival.[14]

Frankl was the sole survivor of his imprisoned family. After he was liberated in 1945, he went on to have a remarkable career, in which he shared his knowledge that even the most degrading, dehumanizing, and violent experiences can produce meaning if the person will search for it. He lived to the age of 92 and died in 1997.

If you search for meaning or even if you do not, your experiences are understood within the context of your view of who you are and why you are here. It is up to you to determine how valuable it is for you to understand your spiritual core. By all standard measures, I am not a very spiritual person. I do not pray or preach, I do not belong to any organized religious congregation or follow any religious traditions. Yet I am comfortable with who I am. I know that if you asked people who know me, they would tell you that I am a good and trustworthy person. It is from family and friends that I derive my strength and my views of what is important in my life. This works for me. What works for you?

THE ROLE OF RELIGIOUS TRADITIONS

Having just explained my existential spiritual nature, I want to say that I envy my religious friends. Much of my envy comes from their congregating with many like-minded people and the friendships that grow from this religious base.

Studies of people more religiously oriented than I am have shown that "religious commitment is positively associated with greater overall well-being and quality of life. This was determined by measuring life satisfaction, positive affect, hope and optimism."[15] This study also found that those with a religious commitment had lower rates of suicide and of alcohol and drug abuse. Importantly, the authors, Erin Moss and Keith Dobson, reported that "spiritual well-being was negatively correlated with

---

14 Viktor E. Frankl, *Man's Search for Meaning* (Boston: Beacon Press, 2006), p. 123.
15 Erin L. Moss and Keith S. Dobson, "Psychology, Spirituality, and End-of-life Care: An Ethical Integration?" *Canadian Psychology/Psychologie Canadienne*, November 2006, Vol. 47(4), p. 283.

end of life despair."[16] In other words, spiritual well-being improved people's understanding and acceptance of their own mortality. I spoke with the Right Reverend R. Stewart Wood, Jr., bishop of the Episcopal Diocese of Michigan. Bishop Wood, who invites people to call him Stew, talked with me about his church's ideas about and approaches to mortality.

I asked him about his experience with people considering their mortality. His answer surprised me: "I've got to be honest with you. I can't recall anyone that I've known or worked with as a parish priest who was at all anxious about their mortality. Of course, I have been with many church members who had a major illness or injury and had to deal with their imminent death."

Stew helped me to understand that over time, participation in the church and in its traditions provides members with a larger perspective—the idea that their life is tied to many others, and that with the support of others they can manage what will come. There is continuity to life that is comforting.

He also emphasized the importance of active participation in the congregation. Supporting others who are grieving a loss reduces discomfort with a death and demystifies it as well.

Funerals themselves are changing. At least as an Episcopalian, I can say that the services are now more marked by folks sharing memories. It's not just a clergyman standing up and providing some sort of sermon about our understanding of life and death, but opportunities for folks who were really touched by the deceased to share how that person affected their life, changed their life, enriched their life. These are very positive experiences that enable loved ones to both share their grief and to appreciate just how their loved ones affected so many others, perhaps in ways that have never been talked about openly. And so their whole sense of entering into the grief process as folks who are being accompanied by others who are in grief, I think that's a very helpful thing.

It helps the most intimate grieving members to know that their loved one was cherished by others who are sharing in that grief. And I think it helps the community itself to talk about what they're experiencing, what the loss of that person means to the community. I don't know that it speeds

---

16 Moss and Dobson, p. 288.

up the grief, but it certainly keeps it from being bottled up, which is very,
very helpful. And so I think it's a healthy process.

Also, it helps members of the congregation to understand that whether
it happens sooner or later, [they're] not going to be alone. And [their] con-
cern about leaving [their] family behind, while still a concern, is mitigated
somewhat by the knowledge that they will not be alone either.[17]

The company where my wife used to work had an unwritten tradition
that colleagues would attend the wake or funeral of a fellow worker's family member. It was an acknowledgement that the fellow worker was cared
about and respected as a person. My wife and her colleagues attended
many services, of many religious and existential traditions, for people
they had never met. When my wife's mother, Ann, died, her funeral was
attended by many of my wife's colleagues, and it felt very caring.

Buddhism, originally an Eastern religious tradition, is making in-
roads into the United States and Canada. It is estimated that there are
now more than 1.5 million practicing Buddhists in the United States
alone.[18] During his years at the University of Virginia, Jeffery Hopkins, a
professor in the department of religious studies, taught a course in Buddhism. He has also written more than 30 books and translations from the
Tibetan Buddhist works and served for 10 years as the interpreter for the
Dalai Lama. In 2003, he translated into English the Dalai Lama's book
Mind of Clear Light: Advice on Living Well and Dying Consciously.[19]

Buddhists believe that by accepting that every life has an endpoint
and by meditating (focused and peaceful thought) on it, you improve
both your comfort with and understanding of your end. This acceptance
prepares you for that point in time when you die and, in Buddhist tradition, can be born again.

Dr. Hopkins pointed out that awareness of your mortality heightens
your experience of the present. Understanding that each day your time
is limited makes it more valuable, and wasting time becomes uncomfortable. This awareness then acts as motivation to use time well. The
awareness of death builds awareness generally so that you become more

---

17 Personal interview, August 15, 2007.
18 Accessed from http://www.religionlink.org/tip_060123.php on January 23, 2006.
19 His Holiness the Dalai Lama, translated by Jeffrey Hopkins, Ph.D., *Mind of Clear Light: Advice on Living Well and Dying Consciously* (New York: Atria Books, 2003).

aware of your living, whether it's how you spend your money, how you spend your time, or what you do that you consider meaningful.

I asked Dr. Hopkins, "What if you realize that you have wasted a great deal of time throughout life? How would you improve using the Buddhist understanding?" This was his reply:

Intentionally focus on what you have done and contemplate what actually does bring happiness. Focus on the fact that happiness, generally speaking, has something to do with relationships with other people, and that what we're seeking, as the Dalai Lama often says, which sounds horribly simple minded, is that "we want smiles from other people." If we want smiles from other people, the best way to get them is to be nice to them. That calls for a change of attitude in all situations, not just ones that seem as if they could be favorable in the future, but even ones that are unfavorable now. Instead of exploding and getting angry at either minor or major events, think about whether such explosions are going to be helpful at all. Probably, with thought, you will decide that those explosions are not going to be helpful. If something has already happened that's really unfavorable, it's not going to help in the least to explode and get angry.

Take someone who tends to be volatile and finds that their volatility creates problems. They could reflect on whether their volatility in the past has made them happier or not. It helps to think about examples from their life. They were in a restaurant and the food was brought out cold. Did it help to explode at the waiter? Did the explosion heat up the food? No. And, as importantly, it made the whole evening more miserable. Alternatively, if you thought, "This sort of thing happens," and took it with a smile, that smile would probably help you a lot more, and if you did say something to the waiter, the waiter would be more apt to do something nice for you, like bring you a new plate of hot food. But even if the waiter didn't, you at least wouldn't have made yourself more miserable.

Buddhism promotes realism, sometimes stark realism. It may be counterintuitive, to look at how bad something could be or is likely to be, so that you can appreciate how good it is. For me, the core of Buddhism, which to some people appears to be horribly negative, is that by looking the negative in the face you're seeing what positive you can do in the midst of all that. It's really heartwarming and encouraging; it develops courage. Courage is actually looking at your fears.

How, then, do Buddhists understand being mortal? The consistent message from Buddhism is to live your life today with joy, to love your people, to focus on what you want to accomplish and to do what you can to stay healthy. When your time comes, you will feel completeness and love.

Buddhism, which has experienced a great deal of interest and growth in the West recently, is one of many Eastern practices that encourage self-knowledge.

Other religions offer other, but similar, views of the end of life. Rabbi Harold Kushner is well known to many people because of his book *When Bad Things Happen to Good People.*[20] He has also written other books, including *When All You've Ever Wanted Isn't Enough*. In this book is a chapter called "Why I am Not Afraid to Die."[21]

I was not afraid of dying because I felt satisfied with what I had done with my life. I had a sense that I had not wasted it, that I had lived with integrity, had done my best, and had an impact on people which would outlast me. . . .

Virtually the only people I have known who were afraid of dying were people who thought that they had wasted their lives. They would pray that if God would only give them another few years, they would use them more wisely than they had used all the years up until then.

Rabbi Kushner's message is in line both with Dr. Hopkins's Buddhist message of living life today with joy and accomplishment, and with Bishop Wood's emphasis on the continuity of life.

Continue on, if you are living an accomplished life today. Begin today, if you do not feel that you have accomplished what you want in life. While you live, you have time to create accomplishment. Live life today as if you know that you will die. Do not become the dying person praying for more time so that they can use it more wisely. It is much better to use your time wisely today.

---

20 Rabbi Harold Kushner, *When Bad Things Happen to Good People* (New York: Anchor, 2004).
21 Rabbi Harold Kushner, *When All You've Ever Wanted Isn't Enough* (New York: Fireside, 1986), pp. 155–156.

TODAY'S UNIQUE OPPORTUNITY

You have lived for almost 40 years or more as an adult. As you transition into your new adulthood you have an opportunity that has not existed since your early 20s. You have the opportunity to choose who you want to be and how you want to live, and this opportunity is backed by your years of hard-won knowledge of what works and does not work for you.

Of course, we bring along many important aspects of life that we want to continue, we still have responsibilities that limit our complete free choice, and we have financial, physical, and social restrictions that we must consider. Nonetheless, if you have been able to move beyond work, you have more control over how to live your life than you have ever had as an adult. You are also better equipped to consider your future than you have ever been, and you now have the opportunity to try out your decisions.

I have provided you with many ideas and tools to use as a new adult. If life has not been satisfying, you can use these ideas and tools to pinpoint the areas that you could improve and do just that. We all have parts of our life that could be improved and when we approach these areas through our personal domain, we lead with our knowledge of who we are and what we want. This is the best set of criteria on which to base your decisions for your future.

IT'S ALL IN YOUR ATTITUDE

"An optimist stays up to see the New Year in. A pessimist waits to make sure the old one leaves."
—Bill Vaughan, American columnist and author

I have provided you with a good deal of information about your personal domain. To sum it up in one sentence, your personal domain is all about you, how you see your self, how you feel about your self, and what you believe you should be doing. You can have a million dollars and feel rich, or you can have a million and feel poor. If a million dollars was more than you ever expected to have at retirement, you will feel rich. If you expected that you would have five million dollars, then you feel poor. It is always amazing how facts have so little influence on attitude. Your attitude can be managed by being self-aware and by recognizing and appreciating what you have, while discounting what you do not have. You can't always change your circumstances, but you can change your attitude about your circumstances.

Your attitude also influences your experience. Aging has its great, good, and difficult aspects. Focus on the difficulties, and difficulties are what you will find. Focus on the great, and you may become deluded, since it is not all great. Focus on the good and be aware of the great and the difficult, and you will be more likely than others to age well.

Jack Kasten, deputy director of the Harvard University Health Services, has had a distinguished career in public health and health care administration. Although Jack, at 80 years old, enjoys sitting on his dock, reading in the sun and watching the boats glide across the water of Lake Winnipesauke in New Hampshire, he is most often found at his office at Harvard University by 7 a.m. He is there between 20 and 30 hours each week.

Although Jack now has no direct authority, he reports to the director and is highly valued for his knowledge, experience, expertise, and engaging and creative mind. When something needs to be done, Jack is often consulted.

Why, at this age, does he do this? "Because it's fun." When I asked him if he thought that his age is a detriment in any way, he replied:

> I really don't. I don't think I'm thought of as 80 by other people. They generally seem surprised when they find out, if they find out. I don't think that chronological age means anything. The only thing is that I try to do as much as I can to push things off to other people, because I don't know how long I'm going to be around.

Jack's colleagues see him as a valuable consultant and coach and they often ask for his input on a variety of topics. He told me that it is gratifying to know that there are "people floating around who are getting exposed to my philosophy about the delivery of medical care. So you could say I'm getting paid for my hobby."

Jack has a great attitude, but most of us would probably give up such an accomplished position by age 80—especially if we were dealing with the other challenges that Jack is. His wife is not well, and Jack had to be hospitalized at age 79 after being hit by a car while out walking. As if that's not enough, he has just completed chemotherapy for prostate cancer. He faces up to these physical problems and does what he can to manage them. Yet Jack's life does not revolve around illness and accidents. He is too busy spending good times with his wife and enjoying his hobby. Jack is aging well.

Each of the four domains plays an important role in aging well as we live as a new adult. Recall that these are the financial, physical, social, and personal domains. The important role of the personal domain as the keeper of your perceptions of your world, and most importantly, your attitude about yourself, raises its profile and modifies our picture of the domain relations from this:

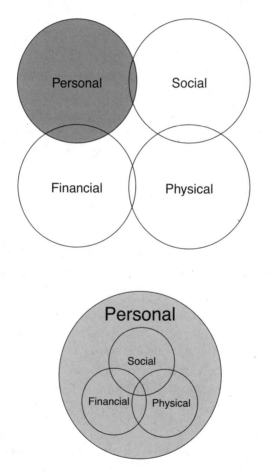

to this:

Now that you are familiar with life's four domains, we can look at how to live a successful life beyond work as a new-era adult who is aging well.

SUMMARY

In this chapter we looked at

- What sets us apart from other people. Our personal domain defines who we are and how others know us.

- The Big Five dimensions that make up a personality—Extroversion, Agreeableness, Conscientiousness, Neuroticism (Emotional Stability), and Openness/Intellect—and how these dimensions can describe each of us.

- What makes up a person's "character." Character incorporates a person's beliefs and values with their personality to describe more than what the person likes and dislikes: it describes *who they are* as a person.

- The power of self-awareness, how knowing what is going on inside our minds helps us to understand and manage what is going on in the world outside.

- How self-knowledge improves our ability to take advantage of what new adulthood has to offer.

- The role of our spiritual nature as we move beyond work.

- The powerful impact of our attitude on our quality of life.

CHAPTER EIGHT

REAPING THE REWARDS

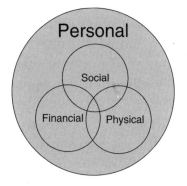

"Don't part with your illusions. When they are gone you may still exist, but you have ceased to live."
—Mark Twain

If you want a gold watch when you retire, buy it yourself. This is but one reality of how expectations of retirement have changed during our generation. What has also changed are our expectations for our personal retirement. Past generations had no idea what it meant not to work. Our parents and grandparents were retirement pioneers, expanding the concept of retirement from the wealthy to the masses.

Over the years many of us have grown into adults who are very different from our parents. This is not an indication of disrespect for them, rather the result of growing up in our unique times. As we look toward retirement, I think that we are becoming more like our parents than many of us may think. We want what our parents and all people, no matter where or when they lived, have each wanted: we want to live the best life possible, given who we are and what we have.

Now is the time to take what you have read in the previous chapters of this book and create the best possible life you can, given who you are and what you have.

LIFE BEYOND WORK: FAMILIAR TERRITORY

In the previous seven chapters we have looked at how living the life of a new adult is conceptually different from the life of career adults in their 20s through 50s. Rest assured that it is different and it is often much better. But in truth, life as a new adult is more familiar than foreign. You will still wake up in the morning and see yourself in the bathroom mirror, have breakfast, and live your daily life. What is different is that life may now include many things that you did not have the time to do when you were still working. You may find that the amount of free time you have weighs heavily when you do not know how to make use of it.

The simple fact is that whether you're working or have moved beyond work, you are still the same person. Moving beyond work provides the opportunity to change and improve, but it does not force you to change, and it does not guarantee the result of that change.

There is continuity to life that we often overlook. Our 20s introduce us to life as an adult and prepare us for our 30s; our 30s build our adult life and position us for achievement; our 40s take advantage of the past to attain our goals and/or to reassess, adjust, or change them; our 50s are the time when we either fulfill our goals or come to peace with them or regret what we have not done.

Our 60s and beyond is a continuation of what has come before except with more choices on how to live life. Think of life as a speeding train. It rumbles and rattles along the tracks, sometimes too fast and other times too slow. You may feel great about the ride, or you may grumble about the direction, but the train does not care: it just keeps rolling along. And you would not want it to stop. You have two choices with this train of life. Get aboard and make the ride as good as it can be, or stay in the station and watch it speed by. If you don't climb aboard, you have no chance of going anywhere; you just watch life speed by. If you hop on, you can live life, just as you have before. You can also take advantage of new opportunities and move past what is out of date. Retirement does not mean stepping off the train. It means continuing to live in new ways.

INCREASING OPPORTUNITIES

I was a child when my grandfather, Abe Shectman, gave up his dry cleaning business. It was the late 1950s, and I was about eight years old. He and my grandmother, Bertha, had immigrated from Russia in about 1915. I remember him as a strong man and a loving grandfather—he was great. Looking back, I have always assumed that he enjoyed retirement as much as I enjoyed having him around more. This was not the case.

I recently asked my uncle Sid, my grandfather's surviving son, about my grandfather's retirement. It seems that my grandfather missed working, which included a cross-town commute early in the morning to get to his small dry-cleaning shop. He also missed delivering clothes to his customers after a long day of work. He missed the people he had grown to know over more than 30 years of working in the same shop.

When he retired, he closed up his shop and sat at home, which was what retired people did in the late 1950s. My grandmother, a seamstress in my grandfather's shop, brought her work home with her. Her loyal customers made the cross-town trip to her. She, of course, also ran the house, and Abe was driving her crazy. I learned that he became pretty lethargic and depressed. He had nothing meaningful to do with his time and his life. He began to fade away. He had no choices. He wanted to work but his shop was gone. His sons, my two uncles, had a furniture store, and they began bringing him in to the store. He worked there for the next five years until he died at home one evening after a family dinner. This wasn't a bad way to complete his life. There were few opportunities for a retired person to pursue back then. He and my grandmother were lucky that their sons could provide an opportunity for him to get back to work.

Compare Abe to Uncle Sid. Sid retired from the furniture business in the 1980s, and he and my aunt Adele are still exploring life's opportunities and enjoying themselves after more than 20 years of retirement.

It should come as no surprise that today's new adults have more opportunities available to them than any previous generation in their 60s and 70s. If our generation has been consistent about anything, it has been in our demand to think what we want to think and do what we want to do. We consider any limitation on choice an infringement of our rights. The fact that we each see different opportunities that we want to pursue is what makes me different from you and you different from your best friend. It also makes us different from 40- or 50-year-olds.

NEW ADULTHOOD'S OPPORTUNITIES WITHIN THE FOUR DOMAINS

Now that you are familiar with life's four domains, we can look at how to live a good life beyond work as a new adult. Here are the components of a good life:

The Components of a Good Life

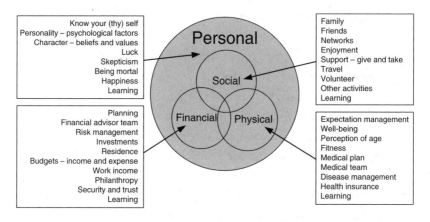

You may look at this picture and wonder why disease management, budgets, or mortality would be listed with the components of a good life. These less-than-pleasant realties are included because they are part of life, just like the pleasant realities. When you are traveling through life, you have to manage the bad to enjoy the good.

The Big Picture

Look at the picture above and you will see what goes into a good life as a new adult. What you may not see is the result of what the whole picture conveys. We can become so caught up in living our lives that we miss the point of our lives. The picture above shows you the trees that make up the forest. But by focusing only on the pieces, you may miss the whole—the point of life.

To illustrate: You may assemble all the ingredients and cook some good food. But unless you are a professional chef, the creation of the food is not the point or the purpose of the cooking. The purpose is the eating of the meal. The purpose can include your enjoyment of cooking, feeding loved ones, satisfying your own hunger, or using the food to enliven a party. It is *why* you cook the food that matters more than *what* you cook. And, yes, the food must taste good for this whole to work.

Nancy Hobson, a nurse and executive director of Westminster Palms, an active living community in Saint Petersburg, told me her observations of how retirement has changed for older new adults: "They want more than just a place in the sun. They come in saying, 'Okay, I've given up the career that has given me the financial foundation to do what I want to do; I don't want to just do nothing and enjoy myself personally; I still need something meaningful. So what will that meaningful piece be for me?'" Nancy sees this recognition of the importance of a life that is meaningful as new and central to a successful retirement.

If you asked me, "What is the key to a good life after retirement?" I could point to the picture above and show you what goes into a successful retirement, but I would also remind you that the first key to living a good life as a new adult is to know what is meaningful—to see the big picture in all its complexity and build your life around it.

ARE YOU LIVING THE GOOD LIFE?

The only useful definition of the good life is the one that you define for yourself. Life is good when it feels good to you, whether that involves working, hitting a golf ball, helping others, or playing with the grandkids.

Like many of us, Bob Ruscitto has worked for more than 40 years and he is now looking forward to the next 40 or so years. Bob has been the vice president of electric delivery for a large utility. He was responsible for safely getting electricity into people's homes. He has also been an energy consultant and now works with an organization that develops safety standards for an industry that has high-risk jobs.

Bob has a good pension and generally feels secure with his finances. Physically he is healthy and actively cares for himself. Bob's hard assets are in good shape. As he contemplates moving beyond work, he sees that he is entering some uncharted social and personal territory.

Here are Bob's thoughts about retirement:

I think my knee-jerk reaction, as I think about retirement, is that it's almost like going out to pasture, where things come to an abrupt halt. . . . *I think the reality of it is I am not ready to do that. I just don't see the pasture as an option for me. . . .*

I need to be busy. At a minimum, I'd need a several-year transition, I think. It is going to take me time to begin slowing down. Yes, that would be quite an adjustment for me.

I don't like the idea of not working seven days a week. I expect that I will find plenty to do; I will have to because I'm not one to sit still for very long. The closest I come is reading the Sunday New York Times. *But even then I am "working on" the paper.*

Then, of course, I visit my parents. They are in their 90s and doing pretty well. Some people feel burdened by elderly parents, but I feel honored. I can give them back a little of what they gave me.

I have a list of what I want to do. It's not a five-day work-week list; it covers much more than that. My parents are on my list, as are my grandkids. Retiring does not mean I will give up my list.

When I leave work I have a lot of things already on my list. I have a small business working with athletes to improve their performance. I got into this about five years ago and I get pretty good results. Also, I want to rehab another house. The worse the shape, the better. . . .

I expect that I will keep the basic work structure I have now. Up and out early, breakfast at Dunkin Donuts, and then working through my list. I have more than enough on my list for the next five years. Something's got to fill that gap and it's not going to be golf.

One of the things that does bother me as I get older—it feels like I am losing my social clout. If I am at a meeting it sometimes seems that the people under 40 look right through me, like I am transparent. I even notice it at family gatherings to some extent. The 35-year-olds are dominating the conversation now. It is that generation's time to be the focus of attention. Of course, I have no trouble making myself known.[1]

Bob has a pretty good idea of how he feels about his life. To provide you with a general idea of how you feel about your life, you have to step back, way back, to see the big picture. The questions in the quiz below are gathered from each of life's four domains described in chapters 4 through 7. This quiz should help you to find out how close you are to living the good life and identify areas you may want to improve.

---

1 Personal interview, November 26, 2007.

Quiz: How Confident Are You in Each of Life's Four Domains?

This quiz is designed to give you an idea of how you are doing with the components of each Life Domain. This is not an in-depth assessment of yourself, and your scores can change as you proceed with your life. In fact, I hope that you do change some things for the better.

Read each question and decide which score best indicates your answer. Place your score in the Score column to the right. Add up your score for each domain and enter it in the domain's **sub-total** box. When you're finished, add the four domain subtotals together and enter the score in the **Total each of the 4 sub-totals** box.

Base your answers on what is true for you. Rely on your perceptions; there is no right or wrong answer.

How well does each item describe you?
1 = Not at all, **2** = To a Small Extent, **3** = To a Moderate Extent, **4** = Well, **5** = Extremely Well

	Financial	Score
1	I have a financial plan that I have confidence in.	
2	I have a qualified person that I trust to talk about or to manage my finances.	
3	I am confident that my insurance plans are up to date.	
4	I am pleased with the performance of my investments.	
5	I have enough money to live a secure life.	
6	I am reasonably debt free.	
7	I am happy with my income-producing work or I am happy with not having income-producing work.	
8	I am comfortable with the way I use my money.	
9	I feel that my retirement (beyond work) income will support how I want to live.	
10	I try to learn new things about how to best use my finances.	
	Range = 10 to 50 **Financial sub-total**	
	Physical	
11	I am doing a good job of managing my health.	
12	I feel good about my health.	
13	I keep myself fit.	
14	Others tell me that I seem fit.	
15	Within the past year I have talked with my doctor about how to manage my health based on my health status.	
16	I feel confident with my medical team.	

(continued)

17	I feel confident that I can manage illness.
18	I feel free of major health problems.
19	I believe that I have access to good health care that I can afford.
20	To maintain my health I try to learn more about how to maintain and improve my health.
Range = 10 to 50	**Physical sub-total**

Social

21	I have the relationships I want with my family members.
22	I feel that I have enough friends.
23	I am comfortable meeting new people.
24	I have mutually supportive relationships with friends.
25	I travel as much as I want.
26	I volunteer as much as I want.
27	I feel that I enjoy myself enough.
28	I feel loved or appreciated.
29	I love or appreciate others.
30	I look for new ways to enjoy my social life.
Range = 10 to 50	**Social sub-total**

Personal

31	I know what is important to me to have a good life.
32	I feel good about how I live my life.
33	I am proud of my personal beliefs and values.
34	I see myself as generally fortunate.
35	I often question my own assumptions.
36	I trust the ideas of others while also thinking for myself.
37	I do not spend a lot of time worrying about my mortality.
38	I would describe myself as generally happy.
39	I am pleased with my life.
40	To improve my life I try to learn more about myself.
Range = 10 to 50	**Personal sub-total**
Total Range = 40 to 200	**Total each of the 4 sub-totals**

How to Understand Your Scores:
Domain Scores
Each life domain's sub-total score indicates your confidence in that domain. If you scored:

42 to **50** your confidence in the domain is **strong**.

34 to **41** your confidence in the domain is **good**.

26 to **33** your confidence in the domain is **acceptable** but could be improved.

25 or less your confidence in the domain is **problematic** and should be attended to as described in the chapter on that domain. (The life domain chapters are Financial, Chapter 4; Physical, Chapter 5; Social, Chapter 6; and Personal, Chapter 7.)

Total Score

A score of **170 or higher** indicates **strong** confidence in your life beyond work.

A score of **155 to 169** indicates a **good** level of confidence in your life beyond work. You may want to pinpoint areas with scores below 3 and determine if you want to make improvements.

A score of **140 to 154** indicates an **acceptable** level of confidence in your life beyond work. Look at which scores are 3 or below and consider making improvements in these areas.

A score of **90** to **139** indicates a **problematic** level of confidence in your life beyond work. You should consider this a wake-up call to improve your life domains. Look at which scores are below 3 and determine how to best make improvements in these areas.

A score of **89 or less** indicates a **significant** lack of confidence in your life beyond work. Please do not take this score lightly. Talk with a physician, counselor or clergy about your situation and how you can improve it.

Hopefully, your score indicates that you have confidence in your life beyond work. If your scores are below 90, I urge you to take action to create a more satisfying life for yourself.

Note: A much more detailed assessment tool that estimates your readiness to move beyond work is available at www.beyondwork.net.

WHAT REALLY HAPPENS BEYOND WORK?

What happens during that great time span after you've capped your career and begin to live life as a new adult? I asked this question of many of the people I interviewed.

When I talked to Mary Carey, she had recently retired as the academic dean of the MGH Institute of Health Professions in Boston. She is a colleague and friend of Ann Caldwell, who recently retired as the institute's president and was introduced in Chapter 6. As part of her career, Mary lived in many parts of the country. This included Kansas City, where she now lives.

Kansas City is where I started my professional career, and I have lots of friends here, including one very good friend whom I have known since graduate school. I looked at other very nice places to live but Kansas City is the best for me. I heard Garrison Keillor say that the city has more fountains than any city except Rome and more boulevards than any city except Paris. So it's a really pretty city.

It probably took me a couple of years to decide that this was what I really wanted to do. My friend and I found a great piece of land that abuts the Nelson Atkins Museum in the city. We built a comfortable house on the land. The patio looks out on the lawn of the Nelson, which must have 10 or 12 Henry Moore sculptures.

Mary told me that her life has always been filled with interesting challenges and she expects that to continue.

I don't think of myself as a risk taker. But you know the challenge has always been very exciting. I didn't think about building a house as being a risk but many people have said, "Oh, I'd never do that." So I think I'm more of a risk taker than I would identify myself. What I do know is that I am always looking for what is both challenging and fun.

This is a new life for me and I am definitely enjoying it. I now see that transitioning from my full-time career to my new life goes in stages. The first stage, and the first year, I think will really be settling into this new house, reacquainting with friends, nothing extraordinary. I mean, it takes a tremendous amount of time to put together a new home, to plant and do the yard, and get things in place. . . .

I love getting up and having coffee on the porch or the patio and reading the morning paper. And I never did that. I'm a morning person, so I got up, and I went into the office. And the first couple of hours were often very productive doing the kinds of things that I needed to do without much interruption. That was part of it. And I enjoyed it. Now my time is my own.

I can walk to the Country Club plaza when I want. I've been walking my new neighborhood and the museum grounds.

I'm going to Shakespeare in the Park next week. I went to the Starlight Theatre here. I have season's tickets to the Unicorn Theatre. I'm planning lunches and dinners with friends, having people over, even if the place isn't ready. I also think in the next few years, travel. I have these voids in the country where I've never been, and I have other places that I'd like to go. I've never been to the state of Washington.

I'm also going to learn to cook. Although I'm a dietitian, I haven't experimented much with food. Now I find that I just enjoy trying new things.

What remains constant for me is the importance of challenge that provides me with an opportunity to learn. I find that my curiosity is expanding. And if I don't like what I try, I can try something else.

Mary provided me with a description of the first stage of becoming a new adult. I describe it as the "orientation" stage. Using the descriptions of how the people I interviewed use their time, I found seven identifiable stages that carry people through their new adulthood. These stages give a general framework for you to consider as you move beyond work. I also divide new adulthood into three "ages":

1. Making the Move
2. Enjoying the Life
3. Appreciating the Life

The example below is of a 60-year-old person leaving his or her career-focused work life behind. You can adjust the age to fit your situation.

Seven Stages of New Adult Development

Pre-New-Adulthood Transition: Approximately three to five years before leaving work, accomplished people begin seriously planning for their post-career years. This is often initiated as financial planning becomes a priority.

The ages listed on this chart are based on a person of 60 moving beyond work. The timeframes included with each stage indicate the approximate duration of that stage. Your stages may begin at a younger or older age, and each stage's duration may vary but the progression will be the same.

Age I. Making the Move—2 to 12 years

Age

60   **Stage 1**
Orientation: Get used to a new schedule and disrupted life. Years of expectation meet reality, for good and for bad. (6 to 18 months)

(continued)

61	**Stage 2**
	Transitioning: Settle into the mindset of a new adult. Experiment and explore; expect missteps and surprises. Test the new adulthood's new realities and find what works for you. (3 to 24 months)
63	**Stage 3**
	Setting Up Shop: Living your life as a new adult. (1 to 6 years)
70	**Stage 4**
	Taking Stock: Review your satisfaction with life as a new adult. What are your new realities? Continue, experiment, plan, or change? (1 to 2 years)

Age II. Enjoying the Life—4 to 8 years

71	**Stage 5**
	Living Life: Incorporate the new realities of being a more experienced new adult into your new adulthood. (1 to 2 years)
79	**Stage 6**
	Balance and Fulfill: Create a stable and fulfilling way of life that accommodates changes in your circumstances. (3 to 6 years)

Age III. Appreciating the Life—3- to 5-year Increments

85+	**Stage 7**
	Appreciate, Enjoy, and Manage: Repeat stages 5 and 6 every 2 to 3 years to respond well to new realities.

Life beyond work is not one long period—20 or 30 years of routine. When we were in our 20s, 30s, 40s, and 50s, we would tend to plan our lives in five- to ten-year blocks:

- "When the kids enter school."
- "My plan is to stay in this job for three years and then be promoted to vice president."
- "After a few years I will decide what to do next."

Timeframes for new adults are shorter than in their earlier lives. The people I spoke with had some general plans but mostly talked of the next "couple of years" or "for the next six months." The more recent their retirement, the shorter their timeframes. This produces two benefits:

1. Decisions about the next year are not as momentous as they would be if you were planning for the next 10 years.
2. You have the time to explore many options. That is how Mary described her next few years.

What these stages clearly show, and what I hope you have learned in this book, is that retirement is not one long stretch of continual decline.

As has been the case in our lives to date, retirement is made up of many experiences from which we continue to grow and find new meaning in life. It is also the time to appreciate what we have had and still have.

Remember that life beyond work is filled with a continuing array of choices; more choices than we had during our career and family focused years. In our 40s and 50s we would never have planned for 20 or 30 years at a time. So why would we think in a block of 20 or 30 years about our retirement? Would you have expected to be in the same job for 30 years? Most members of our generation have not thought that way. You may have changed jobs—sometimes even careers—looking for new opportunities, trying to improve your situation or your salary, trying new challenges, and adjusting to changing life circumstances. It's the same when you move beyond work. The decision you make about life after work, about the day after you stop working, is no more irrevocable than the decision you made when taking your first job.

The big difference in retirement is that the five- or ten-year planning horizons we used as career adults reduce to one to four years. Once you set your financial, physical, social, and personal base you are free to choose what works best for you. You make the best choices you can make today to move you in the direction you want to go while also creating as little risk as possible. You have been doing that all your life and you will continue to do so.

It is the nature of all feelings that they are elusive and fleeting. Enjoy the happy moments as you have them, and then enjoy remembering them. At the same time, cultivate inside yourself an enduring sense of well-being and sustained happiness, sprung from gratitude that will see you through all of the ups and downs of your new adulthood.

It is now time to translate satisfaction with our life's four domains into what most of us understand to be the reward for 40 or so years of hard work: that reward is happiness.

HAPPINESS: THE MEASURE OF LIFE BEYOND WORK

Happiness: Enjoy it when you have it … for it is sure to slip away. This is my own opinion, and it is also supported by a great deal of research. Happiness is an experience, not an asset that you can lock up in a safe. Happiness comes, and we enjoy it; it goes, and we can remember it. It is fortunate that happiness does come and go. For one thing, constant happiness ruins a good thing. You may have heard the tale that new workers in a candy factory are urged to eat as much as they want because the managers have learned that people quickly tire of too much candy. I cannot attest to the truth of this tale, but it does illustrate a point that I believe we all know. Too much of a good thing can ruin that good thing. Similarly, too much happiness reduces our enjoyment of it.

Arnie, an avid sailor, retired from work three years ago with the plan that he and his wife, Betty, would live on their sailboat year round. They would spend summers in the north and winters in the south. They had dreamed of this life on the water for years. Paradise. But about two and a half years after putting their plan into action, Arnie and Betty bought a condo in Toronto, near where their daughter and grandchildren live.

What happened to their dream of paradise? They told me that they had had a fabulous time on the boat for the first 18 months. They did it all, and then realized that they had done it all. After about two years the thrill was gone. They had lived the happy life they envisioned, but it soon became routine. Happiness had become routine.

While Arnie and Betty were living on the boat, their daughter and her husband had twin girls. Arnie and Betty found themselves aching to see more of them. So they bought the condo near the kids. But they did not sell the boat. They keep it down south and live on it for three months during the winter. "What do you think, are we crazy?" Betty asked me. "We love being on the boat and being out of the cold. But we also love being grandparents and parents. We had the best of the boating world; now we have the best of both worlds. You don't know how good you have it until you try something different and learn that the new arrangement is even better."

Who enjoys a good bottle of wine more? The person who loves wine and has great wine every evening, or the person who loves wine and has it once or twice a week? Over time, the every-evening great wine becomes expected and routine. While still delicious, it is no longer special. The every-so-often great wine remains a treat to be savored and brings a smile. Random happiness has a more powerful impact than does constant happiness. Eventually, the every-night great wine loses its impact and it takes an exceptional wine to bump up the person's happiness.

The situations I have described above illustrate the most common way we use the word *happiness*, a feeling of joyfulness, pleasure, or elation that comes in response to external events in our life. As the external events change, so does our emotional response, our level of happiness. The happiest people are not constantly happy. They recognize their happiness as it comes, and they savor it. They also manage the disappointments and pain that we all experience at times by knowing that happiness will come again. They use their self-awareness to know when they are happy and when they are not.

You might say that this kind of happiness describes a short-term feeling or experience. But there is a longer-term experience of happiness that has a very different meaning, one that is very important to the new adult.

THE OPPOSITE OF HAPPY

From the illustrations above, it would seem clear that the opposite of "happy" would be either "sad" or "unhappy." But this is not the type of happiness I am thinking about when I think of new adults being happy. While I hope that we each feel joy and pleasure in our lives, I am thinking of a more sustained happiness. In the book *How We Choose to Be Happy*, authors Rick Foster and Greg Hicks define happiness this way:

> *True happiness is a profound, enduring feeling of contentment, capability and centeredness. It's a rich sense of well-being that comes from knowing you can deal productively and creatively with all that life offers—both the good and the bad. It's knowing your internal self and responding to your real needs, rather than the demands of others. And it's a deep sense of engagement—living in the moment and enjoying life's bounty.[2]*

This definition of happiness correlates well with the core messages of this book. The authors go on to say:

> *Truly happy people are certainly not in denial. In fact, they allow themselves to feel life deeply. They experience elation and great joy, sadness and hurt. They are not buoyant every minute of the day. They see happiness as a long-term emotional state. On balance, they stay elevated, content and moving ahead with the positive parts of their lives.*

---

2 Rick Foster and Greg Hicks, *How We Choose to Be Happy* (New York: Perigee Books, 2000), p. 4.

Actually, happiness doesn't come from any specific personal circum-stance [financial, physical, social, or personal]. We discovered extremely happy people everywhere we went. They are ordinary people who live lives very much like our own. They endure the same daily disappointments and frustrations as the rest of us. And they don't lead lives free of pain.[3]

Happy people "stay elevated, content and moving ahead." If this is the case, then it follows that people who are not happy are sinking, discon-tent, and stuck. What can cause such a situation? Worry can, and does, degrade happiness. I see worry as the opposite of happiness.

Edward Hallowell, a nationally known psychiatrist, author, and speaker, has written a book titled, simply, *Worry*. In the book, Hallowell explains worry this way:

The uniquely human process called worrying depends upon having a brain that can reason, remember, reflect, feel, and imagine. Only humans have a brain big enough to do all this simultaneously and do it well. Worry is what humans do with a simple fear once it reaches the cerebral cortex. They make it complex.[4]

We make life complex, and we create the little nooks and crannies where worry can take root and grow. Life is not simple, but it is not as complex as worriers fear it is. If you can manage life's four domains, you can be happy with life.

Dr. Hallowell provides a "Basic Equation of Worry": Increased Vulnerability + Decreased Power = Increased Worry.[5]

This equation makes sense. The more vulnerable you feel and the less power you have to do something about the vulnerability, the more wor-ried you become about what might happen to you. For example, if you are not confident in how your retirement funds are invested and you do not know how to improve your comfort with your investments, it would follow that your worry about your finances would increase.

Dr. Hallowell's equation can be reversed to find ways to decrease worry. If you can decrease your vulnerability while increasing your

---

3 Foster and Hicks, *How We Choose to Be Happy*, p. 5.
4 Edward M. Hallowell, *Worry* (New York: Ballantine Books, 1997), p. 9.
5 Hallowell, *Worry*, p. 44.

power, you should be able to decrease your worry. And if we think of worry as the opposite of happiness, then decreased worry will increase your happiness.

You can decrease vulnerability by increasing your luck. In Chapter 7, I described luck as the marriage of preparation and opportunity. I told you about my brother's luck when hitting a difficult golf shot—luck being the result of his preparation during practice and his focus on his next opportunity, while letting go of his recent bad shot. The more you prepare, the more opportunities you will see and the better you can capitalize on them. New adults can prepare by actively managing their financial, physical, social, and personal domains. These are the domains that contain your vulnerabilities. The better prepared you are, the less vulnerable you will be.

You can increase your power by taking control of difficult situations; you can do this by seeing them as solvable problems. Problem solving begins with identifying problems at the earliest possible stage. As we saw in Chapter 7, self-awareness gives you an early start on both identifying and solving problems. It also helps you identify your areas of choice and responsibility.

By reducing your worry—that is, by increasing both your luck and your self-awareness—you provide yourself with the first steps to being happy.

If you feel chronically or deeply worried, I strongly recommend that you read Dr. Hallowell's book *Worry* and talk with a trusted advisor. Worry can be managed.

THE BENEFITS OF BEING HAPPY

In 2005, three researchers—Sonja Lyubomirsky, Kenneth Sheldon, and David Schkade—published an article that provides both a comprehensive review of happiness research and results from a study they conducted.[6] Here are some of the tangible benefits the study found that happy people enjoy:

- Social rewards such as a higher odds of marriage and lower odds of divorce
- More friends

---

6 S. Lyubomirsky, K. Sheldon, and D. Schkade, 2005, "Pursuing Happiness: The Architecture of Sustainable Change," *Review of General Psychology*, Vol. 9(2), pp. 111–31.

- Stronger social support
- Richer social interactions
- Superior work outcomes due in part to greater creativity, increased productivity, higher quality of work and higher income, and more activity, energy, and flow
  - Greater self-control and self-regulatory and coping abilities
  - A bolstered immune system
  - Living a longer life[7]

This list of benefits raises the question: Do we garner these benefits because we are happy, or are we happy because we have these benefits? This chicken-and-egg question is best answered by *yes* in both cases. The happier you are, the more likely you are to find the benefits listed, and the more benefits you have, the happier you are likely to be. Each supports the other. Your best bet to entering this upward cycle is to find ways to increase your happiness with your current situation. When you feel and are seen as happy, you will begin experiencing the benefits.

There's no doubt about the benefits of being happy. But how do you get there?

BUILDING HAPPINESS

Lyubomirsky, Sheldon, and Schkade describe three components to happiness:

1. **The genetic set point** (inherited genes that partially determine happiness): It is not known if this set point can be changed in significant ways, leaving us with little control over this component of our happiness.
2. **A person's circumstances:** We can make our own circumstances and sometimes circumstances happen, leaving us with some control over our happiness.
3. **A person's activities:** We intentionally choose what we do and how we live our lives, providing the most control of our happiness.[8]

The authors report that these three components directly influence happiness to varying degrees. The genetic set point determines 50 percent of a person's happiness. It is no surprise that people with a high set

7 Lyubomirsky et al., "Pursuing Happiness," p. 112.
8 Lyubomirsky et al., "Pursuing Happiness," pp. 114–16.

point feel happiness more easily than others. I expect that you know someone who could be hit in the face with a pie and enjoy the custard filling. Others may win the lottery and bemoan the fact it wasn't more. A 50 percent influence on happiness is a strong indicator of the power of our natural tendencies. It also leads to the question: Can we do anything to improve our happiness given that the set point is unlikely to change?

Remember, our genetic set point influences only 50 percent of our happiness. The other 50 percent influence rests with our circumstances and our activities—the other two components listed above. Of these two components, it may seem clear that it is our circumstances that have the second greatest impact on happiness. This turns out to be wrong. Circumstances can include being caught in a rain storm, spending time at a boring party, or buying a sack of oranges only to find when you get home that you got lemons. Do you get into a funk or do you make lemonade? The researchers found that circumstances had a small influence on a person's happiness. The greater influence on happiness stems from a person's activities—specifically, the authors propose, *intentional* activities. The key is the word *intentional*. An "intentional" act is one in which a person makes a thoughtful decision to do something, to act. If you do something because you are forced to do it, or because it is habit, it is not intentional. These forced acts, like paying taxes, generally do not increase happiness. A habitual act is by definition a routine act that is done without thought. It is those activities that we choose to do, of our own free will and choice, that offer the best potential route to higher and sustainable levels of happiness.

So, to return to my previous question: given that half the influence on our happiness is from our genetic set point, is there anything we can do to improve our happiness? What we have is a glass half full/glass half empty situation. How do you see it? Is the 50 percent influence from managing your circumstances and choosing your activities enough for you to improve your happiness, or is the set point's 50 percent enough to deter you?

If you see the glass as half full, that is, if you are willing to actively manage your happiness levels, you should know that the intentional acts that the authors cite as most reinforcing happiness and well-being are thoughtful *self-reflection, forgiveness,* and *gratitude*.

Self-Reflection

Self-reflection is the calm and often lengthy consideration of who we are, who we have been in the past and our ideas for who we want to be in the future. With more time to think in our new adulthood, we naturally become more reflective than we were in our busy younger years. Reflection is taking the time to look at how we have lived our life and how we want to continue to live our life. It is a time when we can appreciate what we have and feel grateful for it. This reflection, the result of which is often thought of as wisdom, fuels our development as a new adult.

Forgiveness

Forgiveness is equally important as self-reflection. We often tend to blame not only our circumstances but other people for the things that aren't going right in our lives. It is important to realize that we can't change the way others behave. We can only change our reactions to them. We can accept the people in our lives for who they are, with all their foibles and imperfections. We can forgive them when we perceive they have "wronged" us. If you hold on to anger, bitterness, or resentment toward some people, you are the only one affected. The other person can choose to ignore you and leave you with your anger. You forgive people less for what it may do to the person who has wronged you and more to unburden yourself from the heaviness of your anger. Some anger is so deep that you cannot let it go, but it is worth trying, for your own good.

It is equally important to forgive ourselves. I have found that forgiveness of self works especially well for driven and aggressive people. You often hear others telling these people, "Cut yourself some slack." The basic message in that familiar line is "Appreciate what you have done well and don't ruin it by always thinking what still needs to be done." Chapter 5 has a section called "Improve Your Health by Managing Your Expectations," which explores ways to manage what you expect of yourself while continuing to be focused and determined. People who fear failure and cannot forgive themselves may have unrealistic expectations of what can be done. Many people use failure as information on what to do next time to succeed and it is often creating a more attainable description of what success will be. Dan Cashman and his friends continue to play intense basketball, but they know better than to get on the court with 40-year-old players.

Gratitude: Reinforcing Happiness

The best way to notice your current happiness level is to recall what you are grateful for. As the authors of the "Pursuing Happiness" study point out, gratitude strongly reinforces happiness.

What specifically does gratitude do? The study's authors explain it this way:

> Gratitude promotes the savoring of positive life experiences and situations so that maximum satisfaction and enjoyment are distilled from one's circumstances. . . . This practice may directly counteract the effects of hedonic adaptation (rapidly and inevitably adapting to good things by taking them for granted) by helping people extract as much appreciation from the good things in their lives as possible. In addition, the ability to appreciate their life circumstances may also be an adaptive coping strategy by which people positively reinterpret stressful or negative life experiences, bolster coping resources, and strengthen social relationships. Finally, the practice of gratitude appears to be incompatible with negative emotions and thus may reduce feelings of envy, anger, or greed.[9]

Of particular interest to new adults is that the study's authors also reported the following:

> Recent findings indicate that older people tend to be somewhat happier than younger people. Specifically, research work has shown that older persons report higher life satisfaction and lower negative affect [emotions]. Additional research suggests that older people learn to structure their lives and pursue particular goals that maximize positive emotions, which is consistent with the proposal that people can learn to sustainably increase their well-being. Age-related increases in well-being are in part mediated by volitional changes, including older people's ability to select more enjoyable and self-appropriate goals.[10]

I believe that gratitude opens the road for another very important feeling: hope. When you appreciate the good that has happened in your life, even if it does not outweigh the bad, it supports your belief that good things

---

9 Lyubomirsky et al., "Pursuing Happiness," p. 121.
10 Lyubomirsky et al., "Pursuing Happiness," p. 114.

may happen again, even during bad times. Hope derived from gratitude buoys the spirit.

Count Your Blessings

*"When I started counting my blessings,
my whole life turned around."*
—Willie Nelson

What does this all mean? First, it means that new adults are better equipped to actively increase their happiness than those who are younger than us. In addition, people can increase their happiness by intentionally acting in ways that have been shown to increase happiness in the short term, and possibly in the long term. These would include reminding yourself of what you have to be grateful for, practicing forgiveness, acting kindly toward others, and engaging in self-reflection. These sound like the basic tenets of most religions and many self-help books. Why do so many say the same thing in many different ways? The answer is simple: Because it works.

I believe that there is a way to actually increase the positive effect of gratitude. I have no research to back up my opinion except to say that it is based on my experience with accomplished and happy people such as Edith Hardy.

Edith Hardy is one of the happiest 87-year-olds I know. Widowed, she lives a full life that includes her daughter and her family, church, and her many friends. She is always telling people what a wonderful life she has, even though they know that her life is not easy, that she has difficulty hearing and walking, and that finances are always tight. She is always giving, in many ways. One of her regular acts of giving is her weekly visit to her town's nursing home, where she plays the piano and leads the people in song. She has done this for years and she has told me that she gets much more than she gives. I recently learned that she has been working, even staying up until after 11 p.m., to learn new songs for her "gig." She says it is time to "shake things up a bit" and update her performance.

Follow Edith's lead: begin with gratitude, appreciating what you have, then give some of it away.

BEYOND THIS BOOK

"And in the end it's not the years in your life that count.
It is the life in your years."
—Abraham Lincoln

It is my hope that in reading this book you have found some ideas, thoughts, and challenges that will aid you as you continue with your life.

In chapters 1 and 2, we looked at how our shared and individual experiences have sculpted our lives. Chapters 3 and 4 presented our changing priorities and life as a new adult. Chapters 5 through 7 described life's four domains and looked at how they work together to structure our lives. Finally, this chapter has asked you to look at how your life is working and how happy you are.

If your attitude is that aging consists of inevitable decline, then that is what it will probably be for you. I believe that this book has demonstrated that this does not have to be the case. As I have said, aging has its great, good, and difficult aspects. Focus on the difficulties and that is what you will find. Focus on the great and you may become deluded, for it is not all great. Focus on the good, and be aware of the great and the difficult, and you will age well.

If you take only one thing away from this book, I hope it is the idea that life after work can be a rich, demanding, enjoyable, and manageable time. You can look honestly and clearly at your life and use your abilities to make it what you want. The accomplished people I interviewed have demonstrated that this is the best way for new adults to live. When you can secure your financial and physical well-being, you can enjoy your world of family, friends, and of yourself. Please, enjoy your life.

> Assess your confidence in the four domains described in this book at www.beyondwork.net.

TYPICAL BUDGET CATEGORIES

Budget based on a 60-year-old single man earning $75,000 per year.

Monthly Income			
Income—Work	$6,250		
Investments	$0		
Extra income	$0		
Total monthly income	$6,250		
Monthly Cost		**Monthly Cost**	
Housing		**Personal Care**	
Mortgage or rent	$1,000	Medical	$50
Second mortgage or rent	$0	Hair/nails	$25
Phone	$50	Clothing	$25
Electricity	$75	Dry cleaning	$25
Gas	$0	Health club/ Activities	$30
Water and sewer	$20	Organization dues or fees	$0
Cable	$50	Other	$0
Waste removal	$0		
Maintenance or repairs	$50	**Pets**	$0
Supplies	$50		
Other		**Entertainment**	
		Video/DVD	$20
Transportation		CDs	$0
Vehicle 1 payment	$0	Movies	$10
Bus/taxi fare	$0	Concerts	$0
Insurance	$50	Sporting events	$50

Licensing	$5	Live theater	$0
Fuel	$1,200	Other	
Maintenance	$25		
Other		**Loans**	
		Personal	$0
Insurance		Student	$0
Home	$50	Credit card	$100
Dental and Supplementary Health	$150	Credit card	$0
Life	$25	Other	$0
Other	$0		
		Taxes	
Food		Federal	$1,500
Groceries	$250	State/Provincial	$30
Dining out	$50	Municipal	$0
Other		Other	$0
Children		**Savings or Investments**	
Medical	$0	Retirement account	$700
Clothing	$0	Investment account	$0
School tuition	$0	College	$0
School supplies	$0	Other	$0
Organization dues or fees	$0		
Lunch money	$0	**Gifts and Donations**	
Child care	$0	Charity 1	$20
Toys/games	$0	Charity 2	$0
Other	$0		
		Total Monthly Costs	**$5,685**

Total Monthly Income	$6,250
Total Monthly Costs	($5,685)
Balance	$565

Source: This budget is a composite of several budget templates available as part of Microsoft Excel.

CHECKLIST FOR INTERVIEWING A FINANCIAL PLANNER

Provided by the Financial Planning Association and the Certified Financial Planner Board of Standards, Inc.

(www.fpanet.org/public/tools/tenquestionschecklist.cfm)

Planner Name:
Company:
Address:
Phone:
Date of interview:

Do you have experience in providing advice on the topics below? If yes, indicate the number of years.

- Retirement planning
- Investment planning
- Tax planning
- Estate planning

- Insurance planning
- Comprehensive planning
- Education planning
- Business planning
- Other

What are your areas of specialization?

What qualifies you in this field?

How long have you been offering financial planning advice to clients?
- Less than one year
- One to four years
- Five to 10 years
- More than 10 years

How many clients do you currently have?
- Fewer than 10 clients
- 10 to 39 clients
- 40 to 79 clients
- 80+ clients

Briefly describe your work history.

What are your educational qualifications?

Give area(s) of study.
- Certificate
- Undergraduate degree
- Advanced degree
- Other

What financial planning designation(s) or certification(s) do you hold?

What financial planning continuing education requirements do you fulfill?
_____ hours every _____ year.

What licenses do you hold?
- Insurance
- Securities
- CPA
- J.D.
- Other

Are you personally licensed or registered as an Investment Advisor with the:
- State(s) / province(s)?
- Federal government?

If yes, will you tell me when you are acting as a sales agent of the brokerage firm and when you are acting as an investment advisor?

If not, why not?

Is your firm licensed or registered as an Investment Advisor with the:
- State(s) / province(s)?
- Federal government?

If not, why not?

Will you provide me with a written disclosure detailing any disciplinary history for you or your firm?

If not, why not?

What services do you offer?

Describe your approach to financial planning.

Who will work with me?
- Planner
- Associate(s)
- Other

Will the same individual(s) review my financial situation?
- Yes
- No

If not, who will?

How often?

What type of clients do you serve?

Do you have a minimum net worth or income requirement for your clients?

What kind of services can I expect?

How are you paid for your services?
- Fee
- Commission
- Fee and commission
- Salary
- Other

What do you typically charge?
a. **Fee:**
Hourly rate $ _____
Flat fee (range) $ _____ to $ _____
Percentage of assets under management: _____ percent

b. **Commission:**
What is the approximate percentage of the investment or premium you receive on:
stocks and bonds _____ ; mutual funds _____; annuities _____ ; insurance products _____; other _____

Do you have a business affiliation with any company whose products or services you are recommending?

- Yes
- No

Explain:

Is any of your compensation based on selling products?

- Yes
- No

Explain:

Do professionals and sales agents to whom you may refer me send business, fees, or any other benefits to you?

- Yes
- No

Explain:

Is the account that you are offering an "advisory account," or is it a "brokerage account," exempt from investment advisor registration?

If it's a brokerage account, are you required under law to act as a fiduciary by always placing my interests first?

Regarding any brokerage account that I may open, what are the potential conflicts of interest that you have when recommending certain products for sale to me, and how will you disclose these to me prior to purchase, including any special cash payments or incentives that you receive?

Are you an owner of, or connected with, any other company whose services or products I will use?

- Yes
- No

Explain:

Do you provide a written client engagement agreement?
- Yes
- No

If not, why not?

How might you address my particular needs?

How often will my plan be updated?

Are you affiliated with any professional associations?

TEN QUESTIONS TO ASK TO FIND THE BEST DOCTOR FOR YOU

1. How did you locate this doctor?
   a) Did a trusted friend or advisor refer you?
   b) Did you participate in the choice of this doctor?

2. What is the doctor's training? Where did he or she train? (It is best to find a doctor who is a family medicine specialist, an internist, or who has a specialty in geriatric medicine. An extra measure of credentialing is to learn if the doctor is "board certified.")

3. Does the doctor specialize in mature adult patients?

4. Is the doctor a solo practitioner or part of a group practice? How available will the doctor be? What arrangements are there for coverage when your doctor is not available? Does the doctor work with a physician's assistant? (Having assistants can be very good, since these professionals, working in conjunction with your doctor, can provide additional personal care and can spend more time with you.)

5. Is the doctor affiliated with a hospital(s) in your area that you respect?

6. How old is the doctor? (It may be nice to have a competent doctor of your age, but that will mean that he or she is also considering retirement. If that occurs, you may have to find another doctor in five or

ten years. It may be wise to find an experienced doctor who is 20 years younger than you.)

7. Is the doctor's office convenient for you to get to when you feel ill?

8. Are the office hours convenient and how much ahead of time do you need to schedule a routine appointment?

9. Are you comfortable with the doctor?
   a) Does he or she include you in your exams and your diagnosis by asking for your thoughts and ideas?
   b) Does the doctor listen to what you have to say?
   c) Do you respect this person?
   d) Do you know how much this doctor's care will cost you?

HOW GOOD ARE YOU AT BEING SOCIAL?

There are Cave Dwellers and there are Cave Networkers: Which one are you?

Paul Horn is a professional actor and a communications and leadership skills consultant who often works with people who want to improve their social and business networking skills. As Paul told me, "It's all about giving my clients a new attitude, awareness and approach to stepping outside their comfort zone—or 'cave' as I like to call it. Whatever the participant's goals—purely social, business-related or a mix of the two—these workshops build confidence through new self-awareness and by introducing some practical steps they can take, whatever their current comfort level."

Typically, as an opening exercise, Paul asks the participants to complete a 20-question "Networking Aptitude" self-assessment to provide them with an understanding of their social strengths and weaknesses. With his permission, he and I have adapted it for your use to focus on social networking.

Please note: This assessment has not been put through a statistical analysis to prove its validity. Rather, it has "face validity"; it makes sense when you look at it. Use it for a general appreciation of your social and networking aptitude.

THE PAUL HORN SOCIAL NETWORKING SELF-ASSESSMENT

How often are these statements true for you? Check the box that best describes how often the statements are true for you. Choose these as *honestly* as possible to determine your Social Networking Aptitude.	Hardly ever	Sometimes	Almost always
1. If I am walking and see a group of people trying to figure out a map, I'll ask them if I can help.			
2. When I sit down at a table of strangers at a party or event, I introduce myself to everyone.			
3. I invite friends and acquaintances to activities I think they may enjoy.			
4. When someone I know joins my circle of conversation, I introduce that person to others.			
5. I am comfortable offering a handshake to men and women when meeting them for the first time.			
6. I keep an eye out for articles that might interest a friend or colleague, and if I see something, I'll send them a copy or tell them about it.			
7. I send a thank-you note within a few days after a friend or acquaintance does something nice for me.			
8. While waiting in a long line, I am comfortable striking up conversations with strangers.			
9. I know and use the names of friends, acquaintances, and others with whom I often interact.			
10. I remember people's names after I've been introduced.			
11. If I notice someone I admire standing alone at a party or event, I will introduce myself and strike up a conversation.			

12. I have a 10- to 30-second "elevator speech" I can use when I meet someone that sums up what I want people to know about me.			
13. I do regular volunteer or pro-bono work for a charity or non-profit organization.			
14. I return all phone calls within 24 hours.			
15. I can comfortably enter or exit a group conversation with people I've just met.			
16. If I learn that a friend of a friend is moving to my area, I'll offer to help them out.			
17. If I notice that a new family has moved in across the street, I'll make a point of introducing myself.			
18. When I talk with someone I ask more about them than talk about myself.			
19. I am on a committee of at least one community project, club, team, congregation, or other social group.			
20. I initiate group activities with friends and acquaintances.			
Total			

ARE YOU A KEEPING YOURSELF ISOLATED, OR ARE YOU A SOCIAL NETWORKER?

Calculate Your Social Aptitude:

Total by Column   **Multiply Each Row by:**

Number of <u>Hardly ever</u> answers: _____ $\times 1 =$

Number of <u>Sometimes</u> answers: _____ $\times 3 =$

Number of <u>Almost always</u> answers: _____ $\times 5 =$

Total Score

ARE YOU A CAVE DWELLER OR A CAVE NETWORKER?

Paul Horn sees that people today share a good deal with our cave-dwelling ancestors. Have you evolved?

Social Profile: Interpreting Your Score Profile

<u>Less than 25 points</u>: You are a *Cave Dweller*. You are keeping yourself isolated. You should get out more.

<u>Between 25 and 50 points</u>: You are a *Cave Guard*. You wait for others to come to you. You are on the lookout for approaching people but may be wary of engaging with them.

<u>Between 50 and 75 points</u>: You are a *Cave Scout*, curious about others, and ready to approach them when you feel it's safe, but reluctant to visit other caves or to deepen friendships.

<u>Between 75 and 100 points</u>: You are a *Cave Networker*, comfortable seeking connections and visiting other caves; you are also eager to invite new acquaintances into your circle of friends.

If you want to improve your social networking, you can focus on upgrading your status one level. If you are a Cave Guard you can aim to become a Cave Scout. To do this you can look at the 20 items and choose two or three that you will do more often. For example, if you answered "Hardly ever" to item 20 (I initiate group activities with friends and acquaintances) you may decide to plan one activity that includes three or four others. Make the arrangements to get the tickets for a ballgame or a play; scout out a new restaurant and ask the others to join you for dinner; ask a friend or acquaintance to play tennis or go shopping with you. Do this once and then do it again. This will improve your social networking score, and more importantly, your social life.

Source: Paul Horn, Copyright 2007   www.paulhorn.com

INDEX

Note: *Italicized* numerals indicate charts and illustrations; *italicized* numerals followed by *n* indicate footnotes.

ABOUT THE AUTHOR

William Roiter, Ed.D.

Like most career-focused people, Dr. Bill Roiter had not really thought much about retirement until something happened: many of his clients began to ask him his ideas on the subject. Over the past 30 years Bill, a psychologist, has used his knowledge of human behavior to consult to organizations and to coach their executives. Many of the people he has known and worked with over the years are retiring or are contemplating it. Many have asked him what they should know and think about as they move beyond their work-focused lives. Then, four years ago, Bill's wife retired from her corporate job and focused Bill's attention on the personal, as well as the professional, aspects of this dynamic part of life. This book is the result of Bill's work with these accomplished people.

Bill maintains his own executive coaching practice in the Boston area. In 2004, he coauthored a book with Margaret Butteriss that identified and described *Corporate MVPs* (Wiley, 2004). He has also owned and sold two businesses, been a vice-president for sales and marketing of a publicly traded company, and helped found a venture capital–backed electronic communications company. For the past 12 years, Bill has focused his work on coaching executives as they transition to their next challenge.

Bill's professional training includes a bachelor's, master's, and doctoral degree from Boston University and post-doctoral training and teaching at Harvard University. He also teaches executive coaching to professionals looking to develop this expertise.